I0061610

Making the Cut?

Low-Income Countries and the Global Clothing Value Chain in a Post-Quota and Post-Crisis World

Cornelia Staritz

THE WORLD BANK
Washington, D.C.

ISBN: 978-0-8213-8636-1
eISBN: 978-0-8213-8642-2
DOI: 10.1596/978-0-8213-8636-1

Library of Congress Cataloging-in-Publication Data

Staritz, Cornelia.
 Making the cut? : low-income countries and the global clothing value chain in a post-quota and post-crisis world / Cornelia Staritz.
    p. cm.
  ISBN 978-0-8213-8636-1 — ISBN 978-0-8213-8642-2
 1. Clothing trade--Developing countries--Case studies. 2. Exports--Developing countries--Case studies. 3. Global Financial Crisis, 2008-2009. I. Title.
  HD9940.D462S73 2011
  338.8'87870091724--dc22   2010043472

Contents

Figures

Boxes

Acknowledgments

This study was prepared by Cornelia Staritz (Junior Professional Officer, International Trade Department, World Bank). Many thanks to representatives of buyers in the United States, the European Union, and South Africa and to representatives of clothing firms, industry associations, research institutes, and other institutions in Kenya, South Africa, Lesotho, Swaziland, Mauritius, Cambodia, and Bangladesh, who took time to discuss dynamics and challenges in the clothing sector in the post-quota and post-crisis world. Without their time and valuable insights this study would not have been possible. Many thanks also to Thomas Farole, Ian Gillson, Paul Brenton, Mona Haddad, Gary Gereffi, Ganesh Rasagan, Smita Kuriakose, Zeinab Partow, William Milberg, Gladys Lopez, Jose Cuesta, Patrick Conway, and Leonhard Plank for comments on an earlier draft of this study, as well as to Mike Morris for support and discussions on the research on Sub-Saharan Africa, to Diepak Elmer, Md. Abul Basher, and Sanjay Kathuria for support and comments on the chapter on Bangladesh, and to Stephane Guimbert, Huot Chea, and Julian Latimer Clarke for support and comments on the chapter on Cambodia. Melissa Mahoney provided excellent research support for the trade data analysis; Thomas Frank excellent editing; and Stacey Chow excellent publishing support. Finally, thanks to the governments of Finland, Norway, Sweden, and the United Kingdom, which supported this study through the Multidonor Trust Fund for Trade and Development. The study was carried out under the overall supervision of Mona Haddad (Sector Manager, PRMTR). Peer reviewers were Zeinab Partow (AFTP1), Ganesh Rasagan (AFTFP/PSD), and Gary Gereffi (Duke University).

Executive Summary

The clothing sector has traditionally been a gateway to export diversification and industrial development for low-income countries (LICs) but recent developments may condition this role. In most developed and middle-income countries, the clothing sector was central in the industrialization process. Given its low entry barriers (low fixed costs and relatively simple technology) and its labor-intensive nature, the sector absorbed large numbers of unskilled, mostly female, workers, and provided upgrading opportunities into higher value-added activities within and across sectors. Recently, however, the environment for global clothing trade has changed significantly, driven by the rise of organizational buyers and their global sourcing strategies, the phase-out of the Multi-Fibre Arrangement (MFA) at the end of 2004, and the global economic crisis in 2008–09. These changes may condition the role of the clothing sector in today's LICs with regard to export diversification and industrial development.

Recent developments have led to global consolidation whereby leading clothing supplier countries and firms have strengthened their position. In the context of the MFA phase-out and the global economic crisis, low-cost clothing exporter countries such as China, Bangladesh, India, and Vietnam have increased their market share in the main import markets of the United States and the European Union (EU). This has happened primarily at the expense of regional supplier countries, including Mexico and Central American and Caribbean suppliers to the United States as well as North African and Central and Eastern European suppliers to the EU, Sub-Saharan Africa (SSA) clothing suppliers, and smaller LICs in different regions. At the firm level the increasing adoption of supply chain rationalization strategies by global buyers has benefited larger and more capable suppliers to the detriment of smaller and marginal suppliers in all countries.

Global consolidation has increased entry barriers at the country and firm level, which challenges LIC suppliers. The MFA phase-out led to increasing entry barriers at the country level as quotas no longer secure market access for LICs. At the firm level, global buyers' supply chain rationalization strategies have resulted in increased entry barriers as more capabilities and higher standards are expected from suppliers. Thus, firms are only able to enter supply chains of global buyers if they can offer high manufacturing capabilities, including low costs, high quality, short lead times, production flexibility, and labor compliance. In addition, buyers increasingly demand nonmanufacturing capabilities, including input sourcing on suppliers' accounts, product development and design, inventory management, logistics, and communications. These capabilities require financial and human resources at the firm level as well as reliable and low-cost infrastructure and backbone services, education and training facilities, and access to finance at the country level. For LICs these new developments are challenging as low labor costs and preferential market access are not enough to be competitive in today's clothing sector.

On the positive side, suppliers able to provide broader capabilities have developed strategic relationships with global buyers. Strategic relationships with core suppliers have become key in buyers' sourcing strategies. This trend has been accelerated in the context of the MFA phase-out and the global economic crisis as buyers have confined relationships to their most capable suppliers. These suppliers face further learning and up-grading opportunities—at least up to a certain level where upgrading does not encroach on buyers' core competencies. Some first-tier suppliers and intermediaries, in particular transnational producers and global trading houses, have captured high value-added activities and control far-flung sourcing networks. This may even signal a shift in the governance structure of global clothing value chains that may limit the power of global buyers.

Marginal and new suppliers are still able to enter global clothing value chains through intermediaries but face limited upgrading opportunities. The persistence of intermediaries implies that in spite of global buyers' supply chain rationalization strategies, there remains a role for second-tier suppliers, which are integrated into global clothing value chains via intermediaries. In particular, in triangular manufacturing networks of transnational producers, entry barriers are substantially lower and suppliers that only offer basic manufacturing functions may enter. However, upgrading opportunities are also limited by the intermediaries' control over key decisions and functions. A main motivation for intermediaries to source from LICs has been preferential market access (and before 2005, MFA quota hopping), and the competitiveness of certain LICs, in particular in SSA, has heavily depended on these preferences.

Many LICs are integrated into global clothing value chains via foreign direct invest-ment (FDI) and triangular manufacturing networks of transnational producers where entry is easy but upgrading is limited. LICs (for instance SSA countries and Cambodia) are integrated into global clothing value chains via FDI and triangular manufacturing networks of transnational producers. These producers are mainly based in Taiwan, China; Hong Kong SAR, China; and the Republic of Korea; but also in Singapore, Malaysia, China, and India. On the one hand, this type of integration has promoted access to global sourcing and merchandising networks and, hence, facilitated entry to export clothing. On the other hand, it has limited upgrading possibilities as critical decision-making and certain higher-value functions are confined to the headquarters of transnational produc-ers. Headquarters are generally in charge of input sourcing, product development and design, logistics, merchandising, and marketing, and have direct relationships with buy-ers. Transnational producers are able to leverage the capabilities of their headquarters and global sourcing networks for value-adding activities, which sets limits for capacity building, investment, and upgrading in lower-tier supplier firms.

Many LICs face challenges in how to use FDI and triangular manufacturing net-works as a basis for upgrading and building locally embedded clothing industries. FDI has been central in the development of export clothing sectors in LICs. However, inte-gration via triangular manufacturing networks in particular has locked LIC suppliers into second-tier positions and has resulted in limited development of local skills, linkag-es, and spillovers. Building a locally embedded clothing sector is a precondition for sus-tainable upgrading, but local involvement is largely absent in many LICs today (such as SSA countries or Cambodia). Other developing countries, for instance Bangladesh and Mauritius, have been successful in developing locally embedded industries. The timing of integration, local skills and entrepreneurship, the structure of local business systems, as well as government policies have played central roles in raising local involvement. In the 1970s and 1980s entry barriers in the clothing sector were lower and local firms were able to start exporting on a small scale. Moreover, market access was guaranteed by MFA quotas. However, increasing entry barriers have raised the bar for local firms in

LICs such as Cambodia or SSA countries where the export clothing sector only started on a larger scale in the late 1990s and early 2000s. In contrast to Mauritius, which had an entrepreneurial tradition, Bangladesh had no relevant entrepreneurial tradition. But government support was crucial in both countries. In SSA LICs and in Cambodia there are limited entrepreneurial traditions and policies to support local skills, linkages and spillovers, as well as locally owned firms.

Changes in global supply and demand structures have increased competition between LIC exporters but also offer new opportunities in fast-growing emerging markets. The second half of the twentieth century was characterized by a rising demand for clothing and the replacement of developed countries' domestic production by imports from developing countries. Today, however, demand has stagnated and import penetration levels are close to 100 percent in most developed countries. Thus, the growth of clothing exports from a few developing countries largely comes at the expense of clothing producers in other developing countries. The heightened competition between developing countries has been reinforced by overcapacity in the global clothing industry since the MFA phase-out and has been accelerated by the global economic crisis. However, changes in demand structures post-crisis may lead to new opportunities. While import demand for clothing in the Unites States, the EU, and Japan might stagnate, demand will increase in fast-growing emerging markets.

The clothing sector still provides opportunities for export diversification and industrial development, but proactive policies will be needed to increase the competitiveness and local embedding of LIC clothing exporters. Entry into and upgrading in global clothing value chains have become more difficult for LICs in the post-quota and post-crisis world. Besides country differences, there are common internal challenges faced by LIC clothing exporters, which have to be addressed to increase competitiveness and to secure a sustainable impact of clothing exports on export diversification, industrial development, and economic growth. Main policy recommendations for LIC governments, industry associations and clothing firms can be summarized as follows and are discussed in more detail below:

1. Improve productivity, skills, and capabilities within firms and develop from cut-make-trim (CMT) to full package suppliers.
2. Increase backward linkages and reduce lead times.
3. Improve physical and bureaucratic infrastructure.
4. Improve labor and environmental compliance.
5. Diversify end markets to fast-growing emerging markets.
6. Increase regional integration.
7. Build locally embedded clothing industries.

First, increasing productivity and upgrading production capabilities as well as skills is crucial for LIC clothing exporters in the context of supply chain rationalization strategies. Buyers increasingly demand advanced manufacturing capabilities including low costs, high quality, short lead times, production flexibility, and labor compliance, as well as a broader range of capabilities such as input sourcing on suppliers' accounts, product development and design, inventory management, logistics, and communications. In this context, suppliers have to move away from CMT and develop full package capabilities. Firms will play a central role in this upgrading effort but a government-supported 'upgrading fund' could help by offering low-cost funds for investments in new machinery, technology, and skills. Education and training of production workers, and of supervisory and management staff in particular, will be central to overcome skill deficits that hinder productivity improvements and upgrading.

Second, lead times have significantly increased in importance in buyers' sourcing decisions and this development has been accelerated in the post-quota and post-crisis world. The largest lead time reduction would occur through backward linkages into textiles. Hence, a favorable environment for textile investment should be ensured, including the provision of long-term loans for textile investments, the attraction of FDI or joint ventures in the textile sector, and greater emphasis on skill development in areas relevant for textile production. Increasing local textile supply is however challenging and there are complementary policies to reduce lead times, including improvements in decision-making processes, production structures, and supply chain management at the firm level; improvements in trade facilitation; increasing the capacity of the dyeing and finishing industry to be able to dye and finish fabric quickly and close to the production of clothing; establishing central bonded warehouses to be able to stock up inputs that manufacturers can purchase directly as export orders are received; and increasing regional sourcing.

Third, improvements in physical and bureaucratic infrastructure are crucial for competitiveness in the post-quota and post-crisis world as exporters are faced with higher demands from buyers. Infrastructure and regulatory weaknesses that limit access to and raise costs of backbone services have to be addressed urgently by LIC clothing exporters, particularly in the areas of transport, logistics, customs facilities, energy, water, and waste treatment. If these challenges are not addressed it will become increasingly difficult for LIC clothing exporters to compete in the global clothing value chain. In addition, access to low-cost finance is central when firms develop from CMT to free on board (FOB) and full package suppliers, because they will need to finance inputs and production and offer credit lines to buyers. A stable exchange rate also constitutes a crucial macroeconomic requirement for export competitiveness.

Fourth, labor and environmental compliance has become central in sourcing policies of global buyers and often constitutes a precondition to enter sourcing networks. LICs could approach labor compliance proactively and promote themselves as 'countries of choice' for global buyers. Departments of labor in LICs often have limited resources to implement and enforce labor compliance. Nevertheless, as in Cambodia's Better Factories Program, LIC governments and industry associations could only provide export licenses to firms that are part of industry-wide compliance and monitoring programs. Additionally, governments could work together with the International Labour Organization (ILO) and the International Finance Corporation (IFC) in their newly established Better Work program. Recently, pressures from buyers have also increased in the area of environmental compliance, which will be mandatory to compete in the future.

Fifth, end-market diversification is crucial as LIC clothing exports are concentrated in few end markets and clothing import structures will change post-crisis. Besides general problems and risks associated with end-market concentration, recent developments reinforce diversification: (i) demand for clothing in the major import markets of the EU and the United States may remain at a lower level post-crisis; (ii) clothing demand in fast-growing emerging markets, in particular China, India, the Middle East, Turkey, the

Russian Federation, Mexico, Brazil, and Argentina will increase; and (iii) regional and domestic end markets have gained in importance in LICs' clothing sales in the context of the global economic crisis. Hence, it will be central for LICs to diversify export markets and refocus on fast-growing emerging, regional, and (if relevant) domestic markets. It will be important to understand these new markets and the sourcing policies of buyers selling in these markets. Negotiating favorable market access in the context of bilateral or regional trade agreements has to be complemented by marketing, promotional, and networking initiatives.

Sixth, regional integration is crucial for improving the competitiveness of LIC clothing producers in the post-quota and post-crisis world. Regional integration could play a central role in reducing lead times and costs, capturing more value added in the region and diversifying end markets. Different complementary advantages in regions could be leveraged and economies of scale, vertical integration, and horizontal specialization could be promoted. The most important challenge to intraregional trade and investment are intraregional trade barriers as tariff and non-tariff barriers on clothing and textile products have remained high in many developing countries. Improvements in intraregional transport, logistics, and customs facilities are also central to reduce costs and lead times of regional trade. Moreover, intraregional trade must be actively promoted by facilitating partnerships between textile mills, clothing factories, and regional buyers.

Seventh, building locally embedded clothing industries is crucial for upgrading and for using the sector as a basis for export diversification and industrial development. FDI has been central in the development of export clothing sectors in most late-industrializing countries, but eventually local involvement, skills, linkages, and spillovers have increased. Such developments are largely absent in many LICs today (such as SSA countries or Cambodia), which limits upgrading possibilities and undermines the sustainability of the sector. Other developing countries (for instance Bangladesh and Mauritius) have been successful in developing locally embedded industries. Besides the timing of integration, local skills and entrepreneurship, the structure of local business systems, and government policies are central to explain different developments in LICs. There are no straightforward policy recommendations for developing local entrepreneurship. However, certain policies are at least preconditions for local entrepreneurial activities: (i) access to low-cost and long-term finance as well as to insurance facilities to leverage certain risks; (ii) access to education and specific training in areas such as management, merchandising and sales, and technical and design/fashion skills; (iii) support in establishing relationships with foreign investors, buyers, and input suppliers; (iv) access to at least the same (or higher) incentives for local and foreign investment with regard to duty free imports, providing infrastructure, fees for public services, access to land and factory shells, and tax holidays; and (v) incentives to hire locals at the management level.

Acronyms and Abbreviations

ACP	African, Caribbean, and Pacific countries
ACE	ASEAN Competitiveness Enhancement Project
ACTIF	African Cotton and Textile Industries Federation
AFTA	ASEAN Free Trade Area
AFTEX	ASEAN Federation of Textile Industries
AGOA	African Growth and Opportunity Act
ASEAN	Association of Southeast Asian Nations
ATC	Agreement on Textile and Clothing
BGMEA	Bangladesh Garment Manufacturers and Exporters Association
BIFT	Bangladesh Institute of Fashion and Technology
BIMSTEC	Bay of Bengal Initiative for Multi-Sectoral Economic Cooperation
BKMEA	Bangladesh Knitwear Manufacturers and Exporters Associations
BTMA	Bangladesh Textile Mill Association
CASDEC	Cambodia Skills Development Center
CBW	central bonded warehouse
CEE	Central and Eastern Europe
CEPT	Common Effective Preferential Tariff
CGTC	Cambodia Garment Training Center
CMT	cut-make-trim
CoC	Codes of Conduct
CSR	corporate social responsibility
DCC	Duty Credit Certificate
EAC	East African Community
EBA	Everything but Arms Initiative
EDI	electronic data interchange
EPA	Economic Partnership Agreement
EPZ	export processing zone
FBO	free on board
FDI	foreign direct investment
FIAS	Foreign Investment Advisory Service
FTU	Free Trade Union
GATT	General Agreement on Tariffs and Trade
GIPC	Garment Industry Productivity Center
GMAC	Garment Manufacturing Association in Cambodia
GMROI	gross margin return on inventory investment
GSP	Generalized System of Preferences
HHI	Herfindahl-Hirschman Index
IFC	International Finance Corporation
ILO	International Labour Organization

ITGLWF	International Textile, Garment, and Leatherworkers Federation
L/C	letter of credit
LDC	least developed country
LIC	low-income country
LNDC	Lesotho National Development Corporation
MFA	Multi-Fibre Arrangement
NAMA	Non-Agricultural Market Access
NGO	nongovernmental organization
NIE	newly industrialized economy
ODM	original design manufacturer
OEM	original equipment manufacturer
PIP	Productivity Improvement Program
R&D	research and development
ROO	rules of origin
SAARC	South Asian Association for Regional Cooperation
SACU	Southern African Customs Union
SADC	Southern African Development Community
SAFTA	South Asian Free Trade Area
SAPTA	South Asian Preferential Trading Agreement
SAR	special administrative region
SIPA	Swaziland Investment Promotion Agency
SSA	Sub-Saharan Africa
STEA	Swaziland Textile Export Association
STEP	Skills and Training Enhancement Project
TUDS	technology upgradation fund scheme
TCF	Third Country Fabric
T&C	textile and clothing
TNC	transnational corporation
VAP	Vientiane Action Program
WTO	World Trade Organization

CHAPTER 1

Introduction

Export diversification into higher value-added products and away from primary commodities remains a major development objective for low-income countries (LICs). The clothing sector has traditionally been a gateway to export diversification for LICs and is generally regarded as a first step for developing countries embarking on an export-oriented industrialization process. In most developed countries of today and newly industrialized economies (NIEs) the clothing (and textile) sector was central in the industrialization process (Dickerson 1999). Historically, this was the case in the United Kingdom; the Unites States; Germany; Japan; and in the NIEs of Hong Kong SAR, China; Taiwan, China; and the Republic of Korea. More recent cases are Malaysia, Thailand, Indonesia, Sri Lanka, China, Vietnam, Bangladesh, Cambodia, and Mauritius. Given its low entry barriers (low fixed costs and relatively simple technology) and its labor-intensive nature, the clothing sector absorbed large numbers of unskilled, mostly female, workers and provided upgrading opportunities into higher value-added activities within and across sectors.

Recently, however, the environment for global clothing trade has changed significantly, which may condition the role of the sector in promoting export diversification and industrial development in LICs today. The main drivers of change have been (i) changes in the strategies of lead firms, in particular the rise of organizational buyers and their global sourcing policies; (ii) changes in the regulatory system, in particular the phaseout of the Multi-Fibre Arrangement (MFA), which provided access for many LICs to the markets of developed countries, under the World Trade Organization (WTO) Agreement on Textile and Clothing (ATC); and (iii) the global economic crisis and the related downturn in global demand for clothing exports.

In the context of these changes, this study analyzes how the clothing sector can still provide a gateway to export diversification and industrial development for LICs today. Specifically, the study has three objectives. First, the study assesses main developments in the global clothing sector associated with the MFA phaseout, the global economic crisis, and global buyers and their sourcing strategies. Second, the study analyzes challenges that LICs are facing in the post-quota and post-crisis environment in entering global clothing value chains and upgrading within those chains. Third, the study identifies policy recommendations to increase the competitiveness of clothing producers and to further their integration into and improve their positions within global clothing value chains.

The methodology of the study involves trade data analysis as well as fieldwork, including semi-structured interviews with buyers and with a variety of representatives of firms and institutions in five LICs in Sub-Saharan Africa (SSA), Southeast Asia, and South Asia. Interviews with large global buyers in the United States and the EU[1] (in

June, July, and September 2009) and with regional buyers in South Africa[2] (in September 2009) were conducted with emphasis on their sourcing patterns and strategies. In the five case study countries, including Kenya, Lesotho, and Swaziland (in August and September 2009)[3] as well as Cambodia and Bangladesh (in January 2010), interviews with clothing firms, relevant institutional actors and sector experts were conducted. The interviews focused on challenges in the context of the MFA phaseout and the global economic crisis as well as generally in entering and upgrading within global clothing value chains.

The study is structured in five chapters. After this introductory chapter, chapter 2 discusses global dynamics in the global clothing value chain and how they relate to possibilities for LICs to enter these chains and upgrade within them. The following three chapters (chapters 3 to 5) assess country-specific experiences of important clothing-exporting LICs from different regions—SSA, Southeast Asia, and South Asia—in the post-quota and post-crisis world and show distinct types of integration into global clothing value chains, related outcomes, and challenges. The country-specific chapters are structured along similar lines and may have some overlap. However, this is necessary to allow for reading them independently from each other. The conclusions in chapter 6 bring together the global and country-specific developments and challenges, and discuss what they mean for entering global clothing value chains, upgrading within them, and for using the sector as a stepping stone for export diversification and industrial development in LICs today. The sections below present short overviews of the remaining chapters of this study.

The Global Clothing Value Chain: Global Buyers, the MFA Phaseout, and the Global Economic Crisis

In chapter 2, main developments in the global clothing sector are discussed. The global clothing sector has expanded rapidly since the early 1970s and many LICs have been integrated into the global clothing value chain. However, there are important recent developments in the global clothing sector driven by (i) changes in the regulatory system, in particular the phaseout of the MFA; (ii) the global economic crisis; and (iii) changes in the strategies of global buyers and their sourcing policies, which have accelerated in the context of the MFA phaseout and the global economic crisis. These developments have had crucial implications for the role of LICs in the global clothing sector and on their possibilities to enter this sector and upgrade within it. Furthermore, there are underlying structural challenges, namely changing global supply and demand structures and asymmetric market and power relations within global clothing value chains, which have created a difficult context for clothing suppliers to capture gains and upgrade in global clothing value chains. The chapter examines the impact of these developments on the global clothing value chain, on import and export patterns, and on the possibilities of LICs to enter global clothing value chains and upgrade within them.

Clothing Exports in Sub-Saharan Africa: From Footloose to Regional Integration?

Chapter 3 assesses the clothing sector in SSA in the post-quota and post-crisis world. Over the past decade several SSA countries have developed export-oriented clothing sectors, in particular Kenya, Lesotho, Madagascar, Swaziland, and Mauritius (where the process had already started in the 1970s). This took place (i) within a policy framework of 'export-led growth' as governments hoped that the sector would play a central role in (starting) the industrialization process; and (ii) in light of MFA quota restrictions in large

Asian producing countries and based on agreements securing preferential market access to developed countries, in particular the African Growth and Opportunity Act (AGOA). Despite exceptional growth of these countries' clothing sectors in the beginning of the 2000s, the industry has declined quite drastically since 2004 in terms of production, exports, employment, and number of firms in all of the main SSA clothing exporter countries (although to different extents). The chapter presents an overview of recent developments of clothing exports in SSA and the specific ways SSA LICs have been integrated into global clothing value chains based on MFA quota hopping and preferential market access dominated by foreign investments and a disintegrated clothing industry with limited local or regional linkages. It also discusses main internal challenges of clothing exporters in SSA LICs, which are strongly linked to their specific integration, and identifies policy recommendations to increase the competitiveness and sustainability of the clothing sector. The last part focuses on regional integration. In particular, it assesses opportunities for and challenges of (i) using the region, in particular South Africa, as an end market by analyzing sourcing strategies of retailers in South Africa; and (ii) creating regional production networks by analyzing intraregional trade in cotton, yarn, and fabric.

Cambodia's Clothing Exports: From Assembly to Full Package Supplier?

Chapter 4 assesses the clothing sector in Cambodia in the post-quota and post-crisis world. Cambodia is a latecomer with regard to exporting clothing. But since its start in the mid-1990s the sector has played the leading role in Cambodia's development process and developed rapidly into the largest export sector, accounting for more than 80 percent of Cambodia's export revenues. The growth of the sector was driven by foreign direct investment (FDI), which was motivated by MFA quota hopping and preferential market access as well as by Cambodia's low labor costs. Although expectations on the impact of the MFA phaseout on Cambodia's clothing exports had been pessimistic, Cambodia was able to increase export value and market share after 2004. However, Cambodia's clothing industry has declined quite drastically since 2008 in the context of the global economic crisis and the phaseout of the China safeguards. This chapter traces the recent developments of Cambodia's clothing exports and discusses the specific way in which Cambodia has been integrated into global clothing value chains based on quota hopping and—at least partly—preferential market access dominated by foreign investments, cut-make-trim (CMT) production, and a disintegrated clothing industry with limited local or regional linkages. It further discusses main internal challenges of Cambodia's clothing exporters and identifies policy recommendations to increase the competitiveness and sustainability of the clothing sector.

Bangladesh's Clothing Exports: From Lowest Cost to Broader Capabilities?

Chapter 5 assesses the clothing sector in Bangladesh in the post-quota and post-crisis world. Bangladesh's clothing export sector started in the late 1970s and early 1980s when Korean and other East Asian manufacturers invested in and sourced from Bangladesh, motivated by MFA quota hopping and access to Bangladesh's abundant supply of low-cost labor. In the mid-1980s a period of rapid export growth started and clothing became the main export product of Bangladesh in the late 1980s. Foreign investment, the MFA quota system, and preferential market access to the EU as well as specific government support policies and local entrepreneurs have played central roles in the development of the Bangladeshi clothing sector. Although the sector had been thought to be negatively affected by the MFA phaseout, Bangladesh was able to increase export value and market share after 2004. Also, during the global economic crisis Bangladesh has been one of the few winners and increased market shares in both the U.S. and EU markets. Despite continued growth of the sector and important competitive strengths, Bangladesh's clothing sector faces challenges that need to be addressed should the growth of the clothing sector be sustained in the future. The chapter presents an overview of recent developments of Bangladesh's clothing exports and highlights the specific way Bangladesh has been integrating into global clothing value chains. Based on this assessment, the main internal challenges of Bangladesh's clothing sector are discussed and policy recommendations are identified to enhance the sector's performance.

Conclusions: How to Compete in the Post-quota and Post-crisis World?

Chapter 6 presents main conclusions with regard to global and country-specific dynamics as well as common challenges of LIC clothing exporters and main policy recommendations to address these challenges. It concludes that the clothing sector still provides opportunities for export diversification and industrial development in LICs but that the global clothing value chain and related entry and upgrading possibilities look different in the post-quota and post-crisis world. Entry barriers for first-tier suppliers have increased and low labor costs and preferential market access are not enough to compete in the clothing sector today. This provides opportunities for some suppliers that provide broader capabilities, but challenges marginal and potential new suppliers. The latter group may still be able to enter global clothing value chains but only through intermediaries, where entry barriers are lower while upgrading opportunities are limited. Two underlying structural challenges have limited possibilities to capture gains at the supplier level: (i) changing global supply and demand structures, and (ii) asymmetric market and power relations within global clothing value chains. Associated with these challenges is heightened competition between LICs. However, new global developments, including the emergence of powerful intermediaries and first-tier suppliers, shifting end markets, and the increasing importance of developing countries' buyers as well as China's move to higher-value exports, at least potentially challenge traditional competitive and power structures in global clothing value chains. Besides these global trends, country-specific dynamics related to the respective type of integration into global clothing value chains are crucial and can lead to very different outcomes. Notwithstanding important differences, there are common internal challenges that LIC clothing exporters face in the post-quota and post-crisis world. The chapter identifies main policy recommendations for LIC governments, industry associations, and clothing firms to face these challenges. These policy recommendations are crucial to sustain and increase competitiveness of LIC clothing exporters and to secure a sustainable impact of clothing exports on export diversification, industrial development, and economic growth. The chapter concludes that, although entry and upgrading in global clothing value chains have become more difficult for LICs in the post-quota and post-crisis world, the clothing sector still offers a pathway to export diversification and industrial development—granted that proactive policies to increase the competitiveness and local embedding of LIC clothing exporters are adopted.

Notes

1. Large retailers in the United States and in the EU from the discount and the mid-market segment, involving general retailers as well as specialized clothing retailers, were interviewed. In the United States, also one branded marketer and one branded manufacturer were interviewed. Mail-order companies and super/hypermarkets were not part of the sample.

2. Five of the six largest retailers in South Africa were interviewed.

3. Due to the political crisis it was not possible to visit Madagascar—the remaining main LIC clothing exporter from SSA—for fieldwork in summer 2009. Thus, the information on Madagascar is based only on secondary sources. Although Mauritius and South Africa are not LICs, they play an important role in the clothing sector in SSA and, thus, are often included in the analysis.

CHAPTER 2

The Global Clothing Value Chain: Global Buyers, the MFA Phaseout, and the Global Economic Crisis

Introduction

Export diversification into higher value-added products and away from primary commodities remains a major development objective for low-income countries (LICs). The clothing sector has traditionally been a gateway to export diversification for LICs and is generally regarded as a first step for developing countries embarking on an export-oriented industrialization process. In most developed countries of today and newly industrialized economies (NIEs), the clothing (and textile) sector was central in the industrialization process (Dickerson 1999). This was the case in the United Kingdom, the United States, and Germany during the early nineteenth century; in Japan in the first half of the twentieth century; and in the NIEs Hong Kong SAR, China; Taiwan, China; and the Republic of Korea in the 1950s. More recent cases are Malaysia, Thailand, Indonesia, Sri Lanka, China, Vietnam, Bangladesh, Cambodia, and Mauritius. In particular, the sector played three important roles in the industrialization process (Palpacuer et al. 2005). First, as the clothing sector has low fixed costs, requires relatively simple technology, and is labor intensive, it absorbed large numbers of unskilled, mostly female, workers. Second, despite low investment requirements, it served to build capital and knowhow for upgrading into more technologically advanced and higher value-added activities within the sector and in other sectors. Within the sector, the clothing sector can be diversified into more complex production processes, and it allows building forward linkages to product development, design, merchandising, and branding as well as backward linkages to the more capital-intensive textiles sector. Third, through export earnings, it financed imports of more advanced technologies.

Related to this role, the clothing sector is one of the largest export sectors in the world and has become increasingly globalized. In 2008 global clothing exports accounted for US$340 billion, making clothing one of the world's most traded manufactured products. Even more significantly, clothing exports increased at a compounded annual rate of 7 percent between 1995 and 2008. Developing countries have accounted for a rising share of this growth and the clothing sector constituted the first manufacturing sector where exports became dominated by developing countries. In the mid-1960s developing countries accounted for around 25 percent of worldwide clothing exports. In 2000 their share was above 70 percent (Morris 2006a). For most LICs, clothing exports are by far the main manufacturing export. The share of LICs in global clothing trade increased from 6.5 percent in 1995 to 14 percent in 2008 driven by an annual average growth rate of 16 percent. Comparing this figure to the total share of LICs in world's merchandise exports (0.63 percent) underlines the importance of the clothing sector for LICs.

As in many other sectors production and trade in the clothing sector are organized in global value chains where production of components and assembly into final products is carried out in intra-firm networks on a global scale. The clothing sector is particularly suited for these global production arrangements as most (intermediate) products can be exported at each stage of the chain (Morris and Barnes 2009). The clothing value chain can be roughly divided into five stages that are intertwined with the textile sector (Appelbaum and Gereffi 1994): (i) raw material supply, including natural fibers (such as cotton and wool) and synthetic fibers (such as polyester, nylon, and acrylic); (ii) yarns and fabrics production (textile sector); (iii) clothing production; (iv) export channels; and (v) marketing networks at the retail level. Natural and synthetic fibers are produced from raw materials such as cotton, wool, and chemicals. These fibers are spun to yarn, which is used to produce woven or knitted greige fabric. The fabrics are then finished, dyed and printed, and used to produce clothing, home furnishing, and industrial and technical textiles. The clothing sector is a significant consumer of textile products but other sectors such as mining, motor vehicles, and construction are also important buyers of textile products (Morris and Barnes 2009). A large part of clothing production—which includes cutting, sewing, and finishing activities—remains labor intensive, despite various attempts at automation (Jones 2006), has low start-up and fixed costs, and requires simple technology. These characteristics have encouraged the move to low-cost locations, mainly in developing countries. In contrast, textile (yarns and fabrics) production is more capital and scale intensive, requires workers with higher skills, and has partly remained in developed countries or shifted towards middle-income countries. However, the production of clothing fabrics is less complex compared to household and industrial textiles; thus, relocation of textiles to developing countries has concentrated in clothing fabrics (Morris and Barnes 2009). Beyond these tangible aspects of production there are a variety of activities such as design, marketing, distribution/logistics, and sales that link producers to consumers.

The strategies of lead firms, in particular their global sourcing policies, importantly shape production and trade patterns in the clothing sector. The clothing value chain is the classic example of a buyer-driven value chain. Gereffi (1994) differentiates governance forms in global value chains between producer- and buyer-driven. In producer-driven chains (which are common in capital and technology-intensive products such as automobiles, electronics, and machinery) large, integrated (often multinational) firms coordinate production networks. Control is generally embedded in the lead firm's control over production technology. In contrast, buyer-driven value chains (which are common in labor-intensive, consumer goods industries such as clothing, footwear, toys, and consumer electronics) are characterized by decentralized, globally dispersed production networks, coordinated by lead firms who control design, marketing, and branding at the retail end but are generally not involved in production (Gereffi 1994, 1999; Appelbaum and Gereffi 1994; Gereffi and Memedovic 2003). Although, these firms are not directly involved in production, they control global production networks, yield significant power over manufacturers, and stipulate often detailed supply specifications. Their sourcing strategies have a profound effect on relationships in global clothing value chains, on capabilities expected from suppliers, and on entry and upgrading possibilities. Global buyers in the clothing sectors have been described as 'the organizational motors' and 'the key drivers of globalization in the apparel industry' as they shape the geography of clothing manufacturing by their sourcing strategies (Appelbaum and Gereffi 1994; Gereffi 2005; Palpacuer et al. 2005).

Besides the crucial importance of organizational dynamics, in particular strategies of global buyers and their sourcing policies, institutional and regulatory factors decisively influence global production and trade patterns. In particular, in an industry as highly regulated as clothing, "upgrading prospects, and developmental outcomes more generally, are determined not just by the organizational dynamics of commodity chains but also by several layers of institutional environments" (Bair and Gereffi 2003, 165). The clothing sector continues to be one of the most trade-regulated manufacturing activities in the global economy. Besides tariffs and nontariff barriers, clothing trade had been governed by a system of quantitative restrictions for more than 40 years under the Multi-Fibre Arrangement (MFA).

The global clothing sector has expanded rapidly since the early 1970s and many LICs have been integrated into the global clothing value chain, which provided employment to tens of millions of, mostly female, workers (Gereffi and Frederick 2010). Recently, however, the environment for global clothing trade has changed significantly which may condition the role the sector can play in promoting export diversification and industrial development in LICs today. Main drivers have been (i) changes in the regulatory system, in particular the phaseout of the MFA, which provided access for many LICs to the markets of developed countries, under the Agreement on Textile and Clothing (ATC); (ii) the global economic crisis and the associated downturn in global demand for clothing exports; and (iii) changes in the strategies of global buyers and their sourcing policies, which have accelerated in the aftermath of the MFA phaseout and the global economic crisis. This chapter examines the impact of these developments on the global clothing value chain, on import and export patterns, and on possibilities for LICs to enter and upgrade within global clothing value chains.

Changing Regulations: The MFA Phaseout, Tariffs, and Preferential Market Access

The clothing sector has been one of the most trade-regulated manufacturing activities in the global economy. Until 2005, textile and clothing (T&C) trade had been governed by a system of quantitative restrictions for more than 40 years under the MFA, which was signed in 1974 and renewed several times. It was predated by the Short Term Cotton Agreement (signed in 1961) and then the Long Term Cotton Agreement. Although the objective of the MFA was to protect the major import markets (Europe, United States, Canada) by imposing quotas on the volume of certain imported products and to allow those countries to restructure their sectors before opening up to competition, the quota restrictions led to spreading production to an increasing number of countries and provided many developing countries a way to establish a clothing industry. Seventy-three countries were subject to quotas by the EU, the United States,[1] and Canada, but most countries with quota restraints did not use the full quota to which they were entitled. Thus, when manufacturers, mostly from Japan, Korea, Hong Kong SAR, China, Taiwan,

China, and later China, reached quota limits in their home countries, they searched for producer countries with underutilized quotas or for countries with no quota to set up clothing production there or source from existing clothing firms. In particular, producers in Hong Kong SAR, China, Taiwan, China, and to a lesser extent, Korea spread their operations to other Asian countries; but, particularly in the 1990s, also to Latin America, the Caribbean, and to Sub-Saharan Africa (SSA) countries (Gereffi 1999). Thus, these trade restrictions contributed to the international fragmentation of the global clothing value chain.

In 1994 the General Agreement on Tariffs and Trade (GATT) signatories signed the ATC committing to phaseout the MFA by the end of 2004 and, hence, all quotas on T&C trade between World Trade Organization (WTO) member states would be ended by this date. Although the phasing out of the quota has been planned as a gradual process spanning five years, importing countries backloaded the products they would remove from quotas. Thus, more than 80 percent of clothing imports to the United States and more than 70 percent of clothing imports to the EU were subject to quotas until the end of 2004 (Kaplinsky and Morris 2006). However, while the year 2005 was supposed to mark the end of the quota system, the major importing markets of Europe and the United States, as well as some middle-income countries (Turkey, Argentina, Brazil, and South Africa) introduced a number of temporary restrictions on imports from China under the Safeguard Agreement negotiated as part of China's WTO accession. In June 2005 the EU reached an agreement with China allowing the EU to impose quotas on imported products from China between 2005 and 2007. In December 2005, the United States also signed a Memorandum of Understanding with China allowing the United States to impose similar quotas between 2006 and 2008. Some other countries (such as South Africa) have also imposed quotas against imports of T&C, although the EU and the United States were by far the most important markets to have done so (World Bank 2007). For most products, however, the quotas agreed were much larger and had higher growth rates than those previously applied under the ATC. The safeguard quotas in 2006 were 500 percent larger in the United States and 200 percent larger in the EU than they had been for the same products in 2004 (Martin 2009). The U.S. arrangement specified annual quota growth rates of 12.5 percent for most products in 2007 and 2008. The EU agreement involved increases of the quotas between 10 and 12.5 percent. Although the safeguard quotas had the objective to protect domestic industries from Chinese imports, other Asian producer countries seem to be the primary beneficiaries of Chinese safeguards as they encouraged buyers to diversify their sourcing away from China.

To a large extent in 2005 and totally in 2009, global buyers became free to source T&C in any amount from any country subject only to tariffs (Gereffi and Fredrick 2010). Intensified competition and price pressures, as well as dramatic changes in global production and trade, and in sourcing patterns of global buyers had been expected to take place due to the MFA phaseout. In particular, the phaseout had caused widespread concern that the global T&C market would be swamped by Chinese and to a lesser extent Indian exports with adverse implications for LICs that relied heavily on clothing exports or were seeking to diversify into clothing production. The USITC (2004) stated that China had a major competitive advantage derived from a combination of low wages and high productivity, and the production of high-quality and low-cost inputs. China is regarded "among the best in making most garments and made-up textile articles at any quality or price level" (USITC 2004: xiii). Hence, it is "expected to become the 'supplier of choice' for most U.S. importers because of its ability to make almost any type of textile and apparel product at any quality level at a competitive price" (USITC 2004, xi). Although, the adjustments in production and trade patterns have been less drastic and more differentiated than originally expected, T&C exports from China and to a lesser extent from India but also from Bangladesh, Vietnam, and Cambodia have increased substantially after 2004. In contrast, higher-cost, regional suppliers in Mexico, Central America, and the Caribbean for the United States and in North Africa and Central and Eastern Europe (CEE) for the EU as well as producers in SSA countries and several LICs in other regions have lost export shares leading to significant adjustment (see trade data analysis below).

Although quotas were eliminated, tariffs still play a central role in global T&C trade, in particular in developed countries and in those developing countries that have important T&C sectors as well as large end markets (such as South Africa, China, and India). Average MFN tariffs on imports of textiles are 6.7 percent for the EU and 7.5 percent for the United States and for clothing 11.5 percent and 10.8 percent respectively. However, these tariffs vary considerably for different product categories. In the United States tariffs on clothing products vary between 0 and 32 percent with duties on cotton products ranging on average between 13 and 17 percent and duties on synthetic products ranging on average between 25 and 32 percent[2] (see table 2.1). In the EU tariffs on clothing products vary between 0 and 12 percent; there are no systematic differences between cotton-based and synthetic products. These tariffs exceed the average of manufactured products, which is typically around 3 percent (Brenton and Hoppe 2007). Markets in fast-growing developing countries are also protected by relatively high tariffs exceeding on average 20 percent. In South Africa the average applied tariff on clothing imports accounts for 36.9 percent varying between 0 and 40 percent, in China for around 16 percent varying between 14 and 25 percent, and in India for 10 percent (which is misleading, however). Looking at India's tariff rate for a specific product such as HS 610120 (men's or boys' overcoats, cloaks, anoraks, etc.) shows that although the applied tariff accounts for 10 percent, the estimated total ad valorem equivalent tariff accounts for 108 percent (ITC MacMap 2010).

Table 2.1. U.S. Tariff Rates for Selected Clothing Products

Product	MFN duty (%)
Cotton-based clothing	
knit men's shirts	19.70
knit t-shirts	16.50
woven men's trousers	10.30
woven women's dresses	8.40
Synthetic based clothing	
knit women's skirts	14.90
knit sweaters	32.00
woven men's suites	27.30
woven women's dresses	16.00

Source: General U.S. duty rates: Harmonized tariff schedule, ITC MacMap 2010.

Since clothing exports face some of the highest tariffs on manufactured goods, preferential market access has a substantial impact on global production and trade patterns. Preferential market access is negotiated in different agreements. On the one hand, developed countries, in particular the United States, the EU, and Japan, have negotiated regional and bilateral trade agreements. Examples include NAFTA, the Caribbean Basin Initiative, and DR-CAFTA as well as bilateral trade agreements with Jordan and Israel in the case of the United States; and the EU itself, the Euro-Mediterranean Partnership, and the EU Customs Union in the case of the EU. These agreements further regional production networks and allow domestic producers to outsource labor-intensive production steps to countries with lower labor costs. This was typically achieved by applying—at least in the initial phase—complex tariff schedules and rules of origin (ROO) to protect the more capital-intensive parts of the sectors (textiles) and reduce tariffs on labor intensive stages[3] (clothing) (Kaplinskly 2005; Morris 2006a; Bair and Gereffi 2003; Begg et al. 2003). On the other hand, within the Generalized System of Preferences (GSP) 27 developed countries have provided tariff preferences to over 100 beneficiary countries. Whereas the EU includes T&C products in its GSP scheme, the United States excludes T&C products from GSP preferences. Besides the GSP, trade agreements have been negotiated that should benefit developing countries in giving them preferential access to the markets of developed countries such as the Everything but Arms (EBA) Initiative and the Economic Partnership Agreements (EPAs, which were predated by the Lomé Convention and the Cotonou Agreement) by the EU and the Africa Growth and Opportunity Act (AGOA) by the United States. These agreements generally also cover T&C products and preferential market access is governed by (more or less restrictive) ROO, which have a crucial impact on outcomes.

The United States implemented its GSP in 1976. The ROO requirements of the U.S. GSP stipulate that the value added in the beneficiary country must be at least 35 percent. However, the U.S. GSP excludes most T&C products and thus reduces average tariffs only marginally from 7.54 percent (under MFN) to 7.36 percent for textile and from 10.67 percent (under MFA) to 10.64 percent for clothing. For SSA countries, AGOA was signed in May 2000 and has subsequently been extended and modified three times (from AGOA I to AGOA IV, see below on SSA). The EU implemented its GSP in 1971 and it can be used by all developing countries but Myanmar. For textiles the general GSP reduces average EU tariffs from 6.7 percent (under MFN) to 5.42 percent and for clothing from 11.54 percent to 9.23 percent. The most favorable arrangement under the EU GSP is reserved for least developed countries (LDCs). The EBA amendment that became effective in March 2001 extended duty- and quota-free access to all products originating in LDCs, except arms and ammunition. ROO requirements under EU preferential trade agreements vary. In general ROO under the EU GSP require two significant processes to be performed within the beneficiary country, which often requires a product to be reclassified from one four-digit tariff heading to another. For the clothing sector this means that production, including cutting and sewing, must be combined with another process such as manufacture of fabrics or yarns. Thus, ROO require that clothing items undergo a double transformation in the beneficiary country, that is, assembly plus at least one preassembly operation (spinning and/or weaving/knitting, Gereffi and Memedovic 2003).[4]

The group of African, Caribbean, and Pacific (ACP) countries, now 77 (excluding South Africa), has traditionally received more generous tariff preferences on a broader range of products than those covered under the EU GSP. The Lomé Convention (signed in 1975 and renewed three times) was replaced by the Cotonou Agreement in 2000. The Cotonou Agreement eliminates import duties on clothing meeting its ROO. For textile it reduces average tariffs from 6.7 percent (under MFN) to 0.34 percent. As with the GSP, ROO demand double transformation.[5] A central part of the Cotonou Agreement was the negotiation of EPAs and several countries signed interim EPAs in 2008 and 2009. For countries that signed an interim EPA, ROO changed to single transformation meaning that the clothing production stage is enough to be eligible for preferential market access to the EU.

The crucial impact of preferential market access on trade and production patterns can be shown by the following two examples from Gereffi and Memedovic (2003). (i) Bangladesh is the top supplier of cotton t-shirts in the EU market but does not figure among the top t-shirt suppliers in the United States. This is because the EU grants Bangladesh's clothing exports duty-free entry as a LDC and because of Bangladesh's ability to meet EU's ROO requiring double transformation (see below on Bangladesh). In the United States, by contrast, Honduras is the top supplier of t-shirts followed by Mexico, El Salvador, and the Dominican Republic—all countries that have preferential access to the United States due to regional trade agreements (Abernathy et al. 2005). (ii) SSA clothing exports to the EU and the United States also show the importance of preferential market access a well as ROO. Until 2000, nearly three quarters of SSA clothing exports were directed to the EU market where SSA countries enjoyed duty- and quota-free access under the Lomé Convention. However, only South Africa and Mauritius were important exporters to the EU as preferential market access required fulfilling double transformation ROO. These export patterns have changed dramatically since 2000/01 when the United States signed AGOA and U.S. exports more than doubled while EU exports stagnated. Lesotho, Kenya, Madagascar, and Swaziland became large clothing exporters to the United States due to AGOA and as they (as lesser developed countries) only had to fulfill single transformation ROO (see below on SSA; Gibbon 2005). Table 2.2 shows tariff differences for selected SSA and Asian clothing exporter countries based on preferential market access for exports to the United States, the EU, and Japan of the product category 'men's or boys' overcoats, cloaks, anoraks, etc.' (HS 610120).

However, preferences may erode in the future, which will be a crucial challenge for countries, in particular LICs, whose clothing exports importantly depend on preferential market access. Preference erosion is driven by two developments: First, tariffs on clothing imports may generally decrease through negotiations on Non-Agricultural Market Access (NAMA) within the WTO reducing the value of preferences. Second, developed countries may offer preferential market access to more countries. The EU already provides preferential market access to many Asian LICs (see table 2.2), but the United States only provides preferences to Central American and Caribbean and SSA countries as well as to some individual countries such as Jordan and Israel. There have been discussions to extend preferences to Asian LICs, including Cambodia and Bangladesh.

Table 2.2. Tariff Differences: Men's or Boys' Overcoats, Cloaks, Anoraks, Etc. (HS 610120) (Percent)

	United States	EU	Japan
Kenya	0	0	10.9
	AGOA	EPA Preference	Applied MFN duty
Lesotho	0	0	0
	AGOA	LDC & EPA Preference	LDC Preference
Madagascar	0	0	0
	AGOA	LDC & EPA Preference	LDC Preference
Mauritius	0	0	10.9
	AGOA	EPA Preference	Applied MFN duty
South Africa	0	0	10.9
	AGOA	Trade Agreement	Applied MFN duty
Swaziland	0	0	10.9
	AGOA	EPA Preference	Applied MFN duty
Cambodia	15.9	0	0
	Applied MFN duty	LDC Preference	LDC Preference
Bangladesh	15.9	0	0
	Applied MFN duty	LDC Preference	LDC Preference
China	15.9	12	10.9
	Applied MFN duty	Applied MFN duty	Applied MFN duty
India	15.9	9.6	10.9
	Applied MFN duty	GSP Preference	Applied MFN duty
Pakistan	15.9	9.6	10.9
	Applied MFN duty	GSP Preference	Applied MFN duty
Sri Lanka	15.9	0	10.9
	Applied MFN duty	GSP+ Preference	Applied MFN duty
Vietnam	15.9	9.6	10.9
	Applied MFN duty	GSP Preference	Applied MFN duty
	The United States offers zero tariffs to SSA, NAFTA, Central American and Caribbean, and Andean countries. To qualify for preferences, exporters generally have to satisfy triple transformation ROO (yarn, fabric, and clothing). For SSA lesser developed countries, ROO allow sourcing inputs (yarn and fabric) from third countries undergoing a single transformation.	The EU offers zero tariffs to LDCs, EPA, and GSP+ countries. To qualify for preferences, exporters generally have to satisfy double transformation ROO (fabric and clothing). This changes however in the EPAs where only single-transformation ROO are required.	Japan offers zero tariffs only to LDCs. To qualify for preferences, exporters generally have to satisfy double transformation ROO (fabric and clothing).

Source: ITC MacMap (2010).

The Global Economic Crisis: Reduced Demand and Trade Finance

The global economic crisis has had important direct and indirect impacts on the clothing sector. Direct impacts are the downturn in global demand which has led to reduced demand for clothing exports in major import markets such as the United States, the EU and Japan, declining prices, as well as the reduction of trade finance which has made it difficult for suppliers to finance exports. Retailers in the United States and also in Europe have been hardly hit by the crisis as consumer spending has decreased and many retailers have dealt with tumbling revenues, slow turning inventory, and stressed cash flows (just-style 2009a). The reduction in sales and the tightening of inventory control by retailers have repercussions on the entire supply chain and have been felt by suppliers as orders decreased in 2008 and 2009. Total U.S. clothing imports declined by 3.3 percent in 2008 and by 12 percent in 2009. This is the worst result in 20 years; even in the last recession in 2001 U.S. clothing imports declined only by 1.3 percent (just-style 2009a). Clothing imports to the EU-15 increased slightly by 1.5 percent in 2008 and decreased by 5.2 percent in 2009. According to the International Textile, Garment, and Leatherworkers Federation (ITGLWF) around 11.5 million jobs were lost up to the summer 2009 in the sector and it expected 3 million more losses in the second half of 2009 (MFA Forum 2009: 1). The International Labour Organization (ILO) estimates that 11 to 15 million jobs were lost up to the first quarter of 2010 (just-style 2010e). Higher estimates for job losses attributable to the global economic crisis in different developing countries include 10 million in China, 1 million in India, 200,000 in Pakistan, 100,000 in Indonesia, 80,000 in Mexico, 75,000 in Cambodia, and 30,000 in Vietnam (Forstater 2010, cited in Gereffi and Frederick 2010).

In addition to decreasing orders, prices have commonly decreased in 2008 and 2009 (with important product-level variations), lead-time demands have become tighter, and contract time has been shortened leading to limited planning possibilities on the suppliers' side. With regard to prices, unit-value analysis for United States and EU-15 imports shows that unit values generally declined for woven and knit products in 2008 and 2009.[6] For the United States, unit prices for knit and woven products (where volumes are reported in dozens[7]) declined significantly in 2008 and 2009—for knit by 2.9 and 2.4 percent and for woven by 0.3 and 9.3 percent respectively. Using Otexa data, Textiles Intelligence reports that the average price of U.S. clothing imports has fallen to its lowest level in over 20 years. At US$2.96 per square meter equivalent in 2009, the price was 6.1 percent down on the previous year and 21 percent lower than the average price of around US$3.75, which prevailed for much of the 1990s (just-style 2010b). Mentioned as main causes of this decline were the global economic crisis and the elimination of safeguard restrictions on imports from China at the end of 2008. For the EU, knit and woven unit values for total extra-EU-15 imports declined in 2008[8]—knit by 3.9 percent and woven by 4.7 percent; in 2009 woven unit values declined by 4.2 percent and knit slightly increased by 0.2 percent.

The crisis also led to financing problems as banks have tightened their credit lines for trade finance as well as investment and working capital, and credit lines from suppliers have decreased, in particular from textile mills. A series of surveys conducted in 2009 by the World Bank and others confirmed that trade finance was more expensive and less available, with banks becoming more risk averse and selective in their supply of credit. A recent update suggests that small exporters were the principal victims of this shortage and lost their credit lines when demand for their products declined (Malouche 2009). Generally buyers have not reduced their credit line demands to support their suppliers—some have even demanded longer payment periods or delayed payments. However, there are some cases where lead firms and large intermediaries helped to remedy trade finance shortages. According to Gereffi and Frederick (2010), a number of buyers in the clothing sector offered financial support to their suppliers: Kohl's provided 41 percent of its suppliers a 'Supply Chain Finance' program, Wal-Mart also offered about 1,000 suppliers an alternative to their traditional means of financing, and launched a 'Supplier Alliance Program' for expediting payments. Li & Fung, a Hong Kong SAR, China-based trading company that serves as an intermediary between buyers and suppliers, became a lender of last resort to factories and small importers whose credit was cut off during the crisis (Cattaneo et al. 2010).

Besides these direct demand and finance effects the crisis has had an accelerating effect on changes in sourcing strategies of global buyers. These changes in sourcing policies started earlier but have been accelerated by the MFA phaseout and currently by the global economic crisis (see below on buyers' sourcing policies). In particular the trend towards supply chain consolidation with regard to countries, and more importantly supplier firms, has been accelerated by the crisis as buyers and intermediaries used the reduction in orders to focus sourcing on their strategic and most capable suppliers transferring orders away from marginal suppliers. As Gereffi and Frederick (2010: 20) put it: "The recession has caused lead firms to 'cut the fat' and they are confining their relationships to their most capable and reliable suppliers."

Another critical impact of the crisis might be a change in import structures as import demand for clothing in the United States, the EU, and Japan might stagnate while demand might increase in fast-growing emerging countries. The Economic Intelligence Unit estimates clothing retail demand for selected countries for the period 2008 to 2013. The fastest growth in the period is estimated for China, Eastern Europe (including the Russian Federation), India, Turkey, and Brazil (EIU 2008, cited in Textiles Intelligence 2009). Although the United States and the EU markets will remain the major import markets—at least for some time—emerging and regional markets will gain in importance in the post-crisis world.

Global Clothing Trade Patterns: MFA Phaseout and the Global Economic Crisis

This part discusses global clothing trade patterns with a focus on the implications of the MFA phaseout and the global economic crisis on import and export patterns.

Top Clothing Importers

Consumption and imports of clothing are highly concentrated in three countries and regions: the United States, the EU, and Japan. In 2008 the EU-15 (including intra-EU-15 trade) accounted for 44.5 percent of total world clothing imports while the United States accounted for 22.8 percent, Japan for 7.2 percent, and Canada for 2.2 percent respectively (see table 2.3).[9] Thus, the EU-15, the United States, and Japan together accounted for 75 percent of world clothing imports in 2008, which slightly declined from 79 percent in 2000. The EU-15 increased its share from 35.9 percent in 2000 to 44.5 percent in 2008 while the United States and Japan decreased their shares from 31.9 percent and

9.6 percent in 2000 to 22.8 percent and 7.2 percent in 2008 respectively. Global clothing imports increased on average by 8 percent per year between 2004 and 2007. Growth of global clothing imports slowed down to 5 percent in 2008 and global clothing imports decreased in 2009 (see below). Despite the dominance of the EU, the United States, and Japan, clothing imports are increasing significantly in some new markets. The highest growth rates in clothing imports in the period 2004 to 2008 occurred in Turkey with a growth rate of 36 percent, as well as Russia and the United Arab Emirates with growth rates of 35 percent. This data confirms that, although the United States and the EU will probably remain the major import markets for some time, other markets will catch up leading to partially shifting import structures.

Table 2.3. Top 15 Clothing Importer Countries

	1995		2000		2005		2008	
	Value (US$ million)	Share (%)	Value (US$ million)	Share (%)	Value (US$ million)	Share (%)	Value (US$ million)	Share (%)
EU-15	65,239	42.8	69,556	35.9	110,833	41.3	148,768	44.5
United States	37,790	24.8	61,741	31.9	74,155	27.6	76,364	22.8
Japan	17,656	11.6	18,611	9.6	21,167	7.9	24,216	7.2
Canada	2,395	1.6	3,262	1.7	5,374	2.0	7,451	2.2
Switzerland	3,599	2.4	2,983	1.5	4,143	1.5	5,361	1.6
Russian Federation	—	—	—	—	—	—	4,225	1.3
Korea, Rep. of	941	0.6	1,239	0.6	2,719	1.0	3,993	1.2
Australia	1,110	0.7	1,680	0.9	2,840	1.1	3,901	1.2
Poland	—	—	485	0.3	—	—	3,229	1.0
United Arab Emirates	—	—	800	0.4	1,431	0.5	2,617	0.8
Norway	1,308	0.9	1,206	0.6	1,709	0.6	2,381	0.7
Mexico	1,836	1.2	3,471	1.8	2,319	0.9	2,346	0.7
Singapore	1,549	1.0	1,817	0.9	2,048	0.8	2,127	0.6
China	905	0.6	1,135	0.6	1,510	0.6	2,076	0.6
Turkey	—	—	—	—	—	—	1,992	0.6
Top 15	136,314	96.7	169,267	94.8	234,282	93.2	291,048	91.9
World	140,988	—	178,617	—	251,336	—	316,843	—
Hong Kong SAR, China	11,571	—	14,952	—	17,255	—	17,563	—

Source: UN COMTRADE.
Notes: Clothing represented by HS 61 and HS 62. Top 15 by year; value in million US$. EU-15 values include intra-EU trade. Data for Hong Kong SAR, China not included in table and in world total due to large share of reexports.

Top Clothing Exporters

An assessment of global export patterns highlights the impact of the MFA phaseout and the global economic crisis. China is by far the largest exporter of clothing and it has increased its share from 21.5 percent in 1995 to 38.6 percent in 2008 (see table 2.4). China increased its export share in the context of the MFA phaseout (from 28.3 to 33.5 percent between 2004 and 2005) and in the context of the global economic crisis. Excluding the second largest exporter—the EU-15, which includes intra-EU trade—the other top exporter countries, including Turkey, Bangladesh, India, Vietnam, and Indonesia, accounted together for less than half (17.4 percent) of China's total exports in 2008 (Gereffi and Frederick 2010).

Table 2.4. Top 15 Clothing Exporter Countries

	1995		2000		2004		2005		2008	
	Value (US$ million)	Share (%)	Value (US$ million)	Share (%)	Value (US$ million)	Share (%)	Value (US$ million)	Share (%)	Value (US$ million)	Share (%)
China	32,868	21.5	48,058	24.8	71,149	28.3	89,847	33.5	129,219	38.6
EU-15	37,857	24.8	33,984	17.6	46,666	18.6	47,786	17.8	60,227	18.0
Turkey	5,261	3.4	6,711	3.5	12,397	4.9	12,923	4.8	15,694	4.7
Bangladesh	2,544	1.7	4,862	2.5	7,945	3.2	8,026	3.0	13,424	4.0
India	4,233	2.8	5,135	2.7	7,298	2.9	9,469	3.5	12,076	3.6
Vietnam	—	—	—	—	4,408	1.8	4,737	1.8	9,522	2.8
Indonesia	3,255	2.1	4,675	2.4	5,285	2.1	5,673	2.1	7,595	2.3
Hong Kong SAR, China	10,463	6.9	10,147	5.2	9,296	3.7	8,480	3.2	5,058	1.5
Mexico	2,871	1.9	8,925	4.6	7,285	2.9	6,683	2.5	4,630	1.4
Tunisia	2,400	1.6	2,645	1.4	3,590	1.4	3,476	1.3	4,479	1.3
Morocco	2,250	1.5	—	—	3,476	1.4	3,326	1.2	4,455	1.3
Thailand	2,706	1.8	3,674	1.9	3,965	1.6	3,860	1.4	4,179	1.2
Romania	—	—	2,737	1.4	5,369	2.1	5,172	1.9	4,166	1.2
Cambodia	—	—	—	—	—	—	2,696	1.0	4,036	1.2
Sri Lanka	—	—	—	—	—	—	3,082	1.1	3,803	1.1
Top 15	120,835	79.2	147,062	76.0	194,909	77.6	221,815	82.6	286,060	85.5
World	152,532	—	193,472	—	251,109	—	268,591	—	334,407	—
Asian 12	50,949	33.4	74,758	38.6	106,541	42.4	128,019	47.7	179,962	53.8
LIC	9,952	6.5	17,413	9.0	28,815	11.5	31,391	11.7	46,897	14.0
SSA	1,136	0.7	2,089	1.1	3,233	1.3	2,792	1.0	2,784	0.8
Bangladesh	2,544	1.7	4,862	2.5	7,945	3.2	8,026	3.0	13,424	4.0
Cambodia	—	—	1,214	0.6	2,435	1.0	2,696	1.0	4,036	1.2

Source: UN COMTRADE.
Notes: Clothing represented by HS 61 and HS 62. Top 15 by year; value in million US$. 1995 values not available for Kenya and Swaziland, data for 1996 was used.

With regard to the MFA phaseout, besides China also India increased its market share from 2.9 percent in 2004 to 3.5 percent in 2005. Altogether the Asian 12, including Bangladesh, Cambodia, China, India, Indonesia, Laos, Nepal, Pakistan, Philippines, Sri Lanka, Thailand, and Vietnam, increased their market share from 42.4 percent in 2004 to 47.7 percent in 2005. Turkey, Bangladesh, Vietnam, Indonesia, and Cambodia experienced stable export shares from 2004 to 2005. Mexico, Hong Kong SAR, China, Tunisia, Morocco, Thailand, and Romania experienced declining export shares. LICs as a group increased their global export share slightly from 11.5 percent in 2004 to 11.7 percent in 2005. Figure 2.1 shows the percentage change of clothing exports (in terms of value) for the top 15 exporter countries (plus SSA) between 2004 and 2005. The largest growth rates are attributed to India (30 percent) and China (26 percent), followed by Cambodia (11 percent), Vietnam (7 percent), and Indonesia (7 percent) as well as Turkey (4 percent), Sri Lanka (4 percent), and Bangladesh (1 percent).

Figure 2.1. Clothing Exporter Countries Post-MFA, Percentage Change

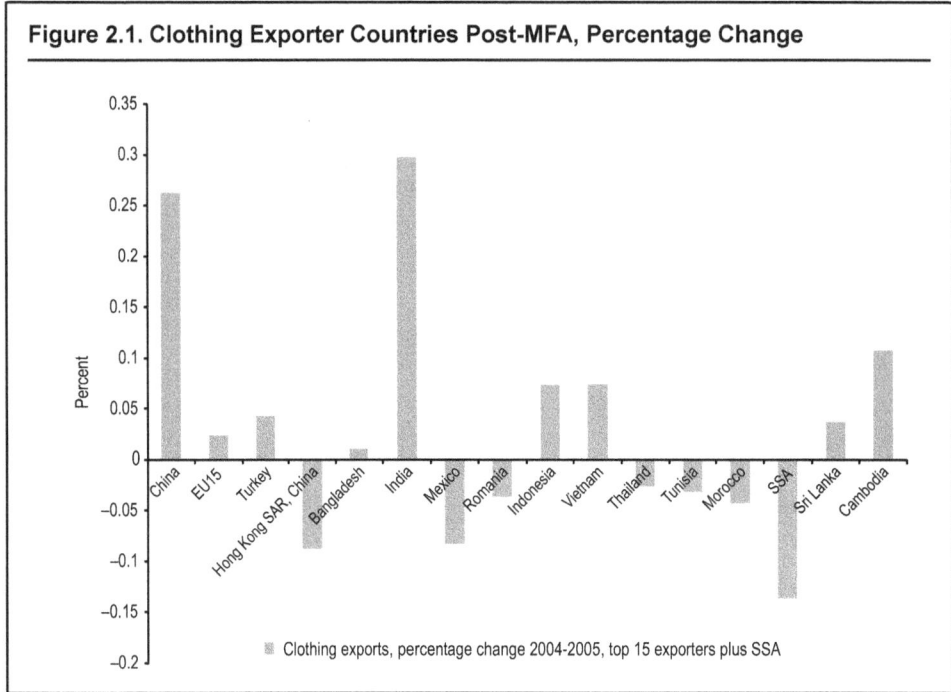

Clothing exports, percentage change 2004-2005, top 15 exporters plus SSA

Source: UN COMTRADE.
Note: Clothing represented by HS 61 and HS 62.

With regard to the global economic crisis, export shares increased for China (from 36.9 to 38.6 percent), Bangladesh (from 3.5 to 4 percent), and Vietnam (from 2.4 to 2.8 percent) between 2007 and 2008. Because data for 2009 is only available for the United States and the EU market (see below) but not for total exports, these developments are provisional as they only capture the initial year of the global economic crisis. Altogether the Asian 12 increased their market share from 51.8 percent in 2007 to 53.8 percent in 2008, which is driven by China, Bangladesh, and Vietnam. India, Indonesia, Tunisia, Morocco, and Cambodia experienced stable export shares in 2008. Turkey, Hong Kong SAR, China, Mexico, Thailand, and Romania experienced declining export shares in 2008. LICs as a group increased their global export share slightly from 13.2 percent in 2007 to 14 percent in 2008.

Generally the top 15 export countries increased their market share from 77.6 percent to 85.5 percent in the period from 2004 to 2008. Over the whole period 2004 to 2008 Vietnam (116 percent), China (82 percent), Bangladesh (69 percent), Cambodia (66 percent), India (65 percent), and Indonesia (44 percent) accounted for the highest export growth rates (in terms of value, see figure 2.2). The Asian 12 increased their market share from 42.4 percent in 2004 to 53.8 percent in 2008. The largest declines in clothing exports in the period 2004 to 2008 were accounted for by Hong Kong SAR, China (46 percent), Mexico (36 percent), Romania (22 percent), and SSA (14 percent). Hence, within the top 15 global clothing exporter countries, low-cost Asian clothing exporters such as China, India, Bangladesh, and Vietnam and to a lesser extent Indonesia and Cambodia increased their export shares in global markets between 2004 and 2008; they were the main winners of the MFA phaseout and up to 2008 had not been strongly affected by the global economic cri-

Figure 2.2. Clothing Exporter Countries 2004–08, Percentage Change

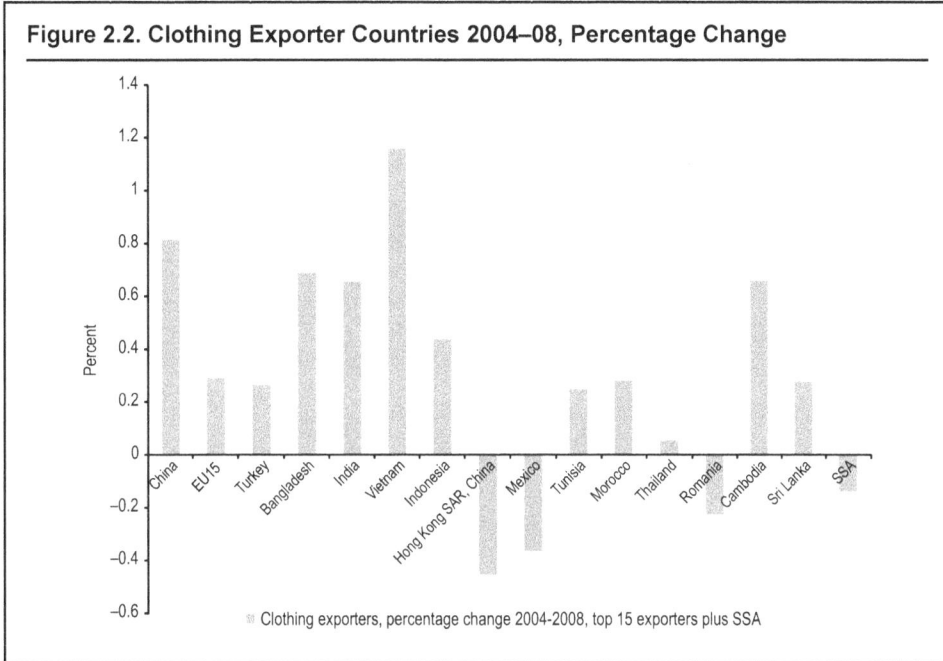

Clothing exporters, percentage change 2004-2008, top 15 exporters plus SSA

Source: UN COMTRADE.
Note: Clothing represented by HS 61 and HS 62.

sis. In contrast, the market shares of higher-cost Asian clothing exporter countries such as Hong Kong SAR, China; Taiwan, China; Korea, Thailand, Malaysia, and the Philippines generally declined. Regional suppliers such as Mexico and Romania as well as SSA countries saw declining growth rates. However, Turkey, Tunisia, and Morocco increased clothing exports. Thus, besides a general trend toward growing market shares of Asian low-cost countries, some other countries also increased exports and market shares.

In the following, clothing import patterns in the two largest markets—the United States and the EU-15—are discussed. In the United States the estimated overall clothing import penetration ratio accounted for 94 percent in 2006 (Clothesource 2008, cited in Gereffi and Frederick 2010). Table 2.5 shows the top clothing importers to the United States. China increased its import share from 10.5 percent in 2000 to 37.9 percent in 2009. Thus, China significantly increased exports to the United States in the context of the MFA phaseout and the global economic crisis. Vietnam, the second largest importer in the United States, experienced a stable market share of 3.8 percent between 2004 and 2005 but increased its market share afterwards, reaching 7.8 percent in 2009. The third largest exporter to the United States, Indonesia, increased its market share from 3.6 to 4.1 percent between 2004 and 2005 and later to 6 percent in 2009. Mexico is still the fourth largest importer country but its import share declined dramatically from 14.6 percent in 2000 to 5.4 percent in 2009. The import share of the DR-CAFTA—which includes the Dominican Republic and the five countries in the Central American Free Trade Agreement (Guatemala, El Salvador, Nicaragua, Honduras, and Costa Rica)—also fell from 13.9 percent in 2000 to 9.6 percent in 2008 (Gereffi and Frederick 2010). Other winners of the MFA phaseout and the global economic crisis in the U.S. market are Bangladesh, which increased its import share from 2.8 percent in 2004 to 5.2 percent in 2009, and

Table 2.5. Top 15 U.S. Clothing Importer Countries

	1995		2000		2004		2005		2008		2009	
	Value (US$ million)	Share (%)	Value (US$ million)	Share (%)	Value (US$ million)	Share (%)	Value (US$ million)	Share (%)	Value (US$ million)	Share (%)	Value (US$ million)	Share (%)
China	4,646	13.0	6,193	10.5	10,685	16.0	16,774	23.7	23,983	32.9	24,337	37.9
Vietnam	—	—	—	—	2,502	3.8	2,664	3.8	5,147	7.1	4,998	7.8
Indonesia	1,190	3.3	2,059	3.5	2,390	3.6	2,868	4.1	4,028	5.5	3,867	6.0
Mexico	2,778	7.8	8,617	14.6	6,843	10.3	6,230	8.8	4,129	5.7	3,482	5.4
Bangladesh	1,000	2.8	1,940	3.3	1,872	2.8	2,268	3.2	3,353	4.6	3,345	5.2
India	1,161	3.3	1,846	3.1	2,257	3.4	3,064	4.3	3,110	4.3	2,878	4.5
Honduras	932	2.6	2,415	4.1	2,743	4.1	2,685	3.8	2,668	3.7	2,113	3.3
Cambodia	—	—	—	—	—	—	1,703	2.4	2,369	3.3	1,866	2.9
EU-15	1,699	4.8	2,224	3.8	2,277	3.4	2,158	3.1	2,054	2.8	1,394	2.2
Pakistan	—	—	—	—	—	—	—	—	1,510	2.1	1,319	2.1
El Salvador	—	—	1,600	2.7	—	—	—	—	1,533	2.1	1,297	2.0
Thailand	1,041	2.9	1,839	3.1	1,821	2.7	1,831	2.6	1,691	2.3	1,245	1.9
Sri Lanka	918	2.6	—	—	—	—	1,650	2.3	1,487	2.0	1,217	1.9
Guatemala	—	—	—	—	1,948	2.9	1,816	2.6	1,388	1.9	1,103	1.7
Philippines	1,486	4.2	1,877	3.2	1,770	2.7	1,820	2.6	—	—	1,010	1.6
Top 15	27,145	75.4	43,423	73.5	46,570	69.8	52,869	74.8	60,003	82.2	55,472	86.4
World	36,018		59,092		66,757		70,718		73,010		64,224	
Asian 12	12,100	33.6	19,170	32.4	27,510	41.2	35,979	50.9	48,084	65.9	46,114	71.8
LIC	4,838	13.4	9,468	16.0	13,420	20.1	14,513	20.5	18,333	25.1	16,840	26.2
SSA	387	1.1	747	1.3	1,757	2.6	1,464	2.1	1,151	1.6	922	1.4
Bangladesh	1,000	2.8	1,940	3.3	1,872	2.8	2,268	3.2	3,353	4.6	3,345	5.2
Cambodia	—	—	800	1.4	1,417	2.1	1,703	2.4	2,369	3.2	1,866	2.9

Source: USITC.
Note: Clothing represented by HS 61 and HS 62. Top 15 by year; value in million US$.

India with an increase from 3.4 percent to 4.5 percent. Cambodia increased its import share in the context of the MFA phaseout from 2.1 percent to 2.4 percent but decreased its share from 3.2 percent in 2007 to 2.9 percent in 2009. SSA was negatively affected by the MFA phaseout and the global economic crisis. Although, it increased its import share in the U.S. market from 1.3 to 2.6 percent between 2000 and 2004, which was driven by AGOA (see below), from 2005 onwards, it has lost market share, reaching 2.1 percent in 2005 and 1.4 percent in 2009. Figures 2.3 and 2.4 show the percentage change of clothing imports (in value) to the United States for the top 15 importer countries (plus SSA) between 2004 and 2005 and between 2007 and 2009. The largest growth rates between 2004 and 2005 are attributed to China (57 percent) and India (36 percent) followed by Bangladesh (21 percent), Cambodia (20 percent), and Indonesia (20 percent) and to a lesser extent Sri Lanka (6 percent), Vietnam (6 percent), and the Philippines (3 percent). The only growth rates between 2007 and 2009 were attributed to Vietnam (16 percent), Bangladesh (12 percent), and China (2 percent). All other countries' U.S. clothing exports declined between 2007 and 2009.

Generally the top 15 exporters decreased their share in U.S. imports from 1995 to 2004 (from 75.4 to 69.8 percent) but then increased their share reaching 74.8 percent in 2005 and 86.4 percent in 2009. The diversification of import countries until 2004 can be explained by the MFA system. Clearly, the MFA phaseout and the global economic

Figure 2.3. U.S. Clothing Imports Post-MFA, Percentage Change

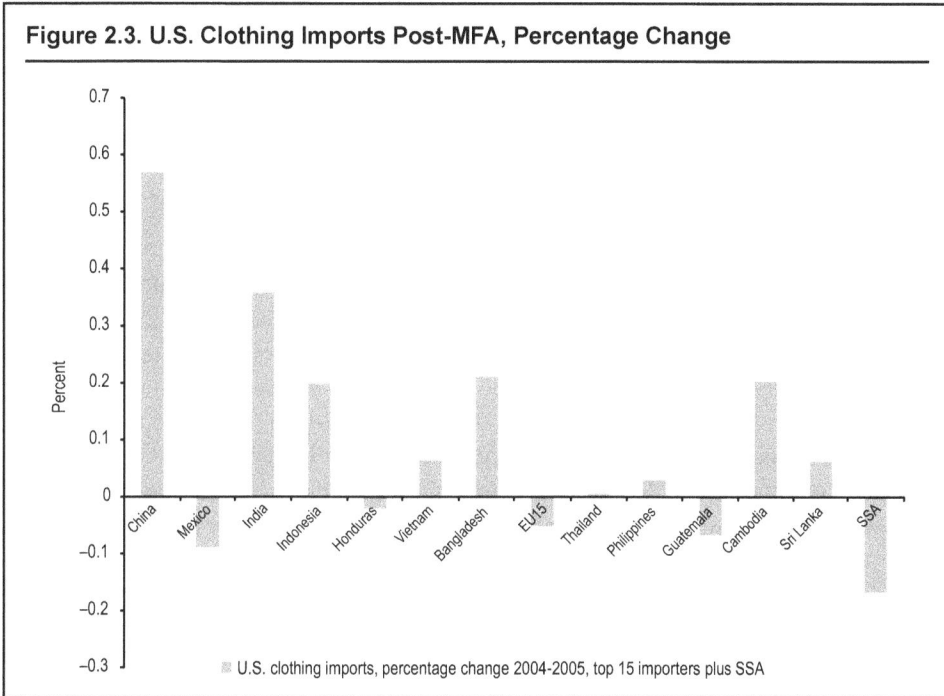

Source: USITC.
Note: Clothing represented by HS 61 and HS 62.

Figure 2.4. U.S. Clothing Imports during the Global Economic Crisis, Percentage Change

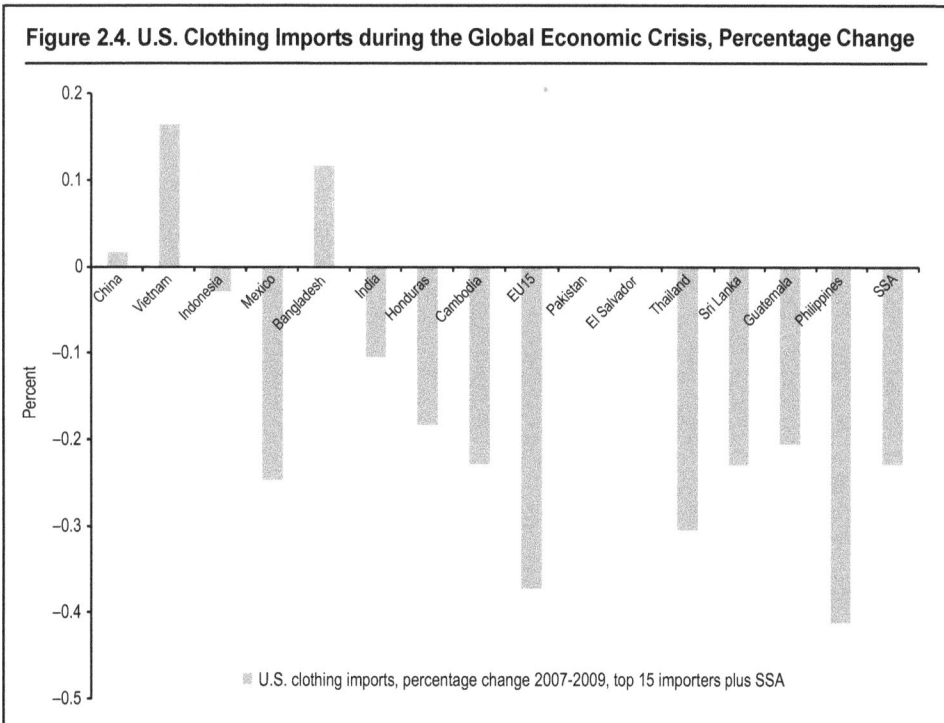

Source: USITC.
Note: Clothing represented by HS 61 and HS 62.

crisis have led to a consolidation of importer countries. The Asian 12 increased their share dramatically from 41.2 to 71.8 percent between 2004 and 2009. LICs as a group also increased their import share from 20.1 percent in 2004 to 26.2 percent in 2009. Consolidation of sourcing countries can be also measured by a modified version of the Herfindahl-Hirschman Index (HHI). It is calculated as follows by taking the total sum of the squared market shares of all countries exporting clothing:

$$HHI_j = \sum_j (S_{ij})^2 \cdot 10,000$$

where S_i is the share of country i expressed as a percentage of total world exports of product j. This measure was used by Mayer et al. (2002), Milberg (2004), and Milberg and Winkler (2010). A decline reflects a decrease in 'concentration' or, more accurately, a greater degree of spatial dispersion of export sourcing in that sector (Milberg and Winkler 2010).[10] Figure 2.5 shows that in the United States the HHI remained quite stable until 2004 but then increased considerably, in particular in 2005 in the context of the MFA phaseout and also in 2009 in the context of the global economic crisis.

The European market differs from the U.S. market and is much less homogeneous due to differences in size, tastes, language, marketing, and the type of retailers supplying different European markets (see Palpacueur et al. 2005 for differences between the United Kingdom, France, and Scandinavian countries). Also, clothing import penetration ratios vary among countries within the EU. In 2006 estimates for the main consuming countries were Germany and the United Kingdom 95 percent, France 85 percent, Italy 65 percent, and Spain 55 percent (Clothesource 2008, cited in Gereffi and Fredrick 2010). Table 2.6 shows the top clothing importer countries to the EU-15. Intra EU-15 trade accounts for the largest import share, which decreased, however, from 43.4 per-

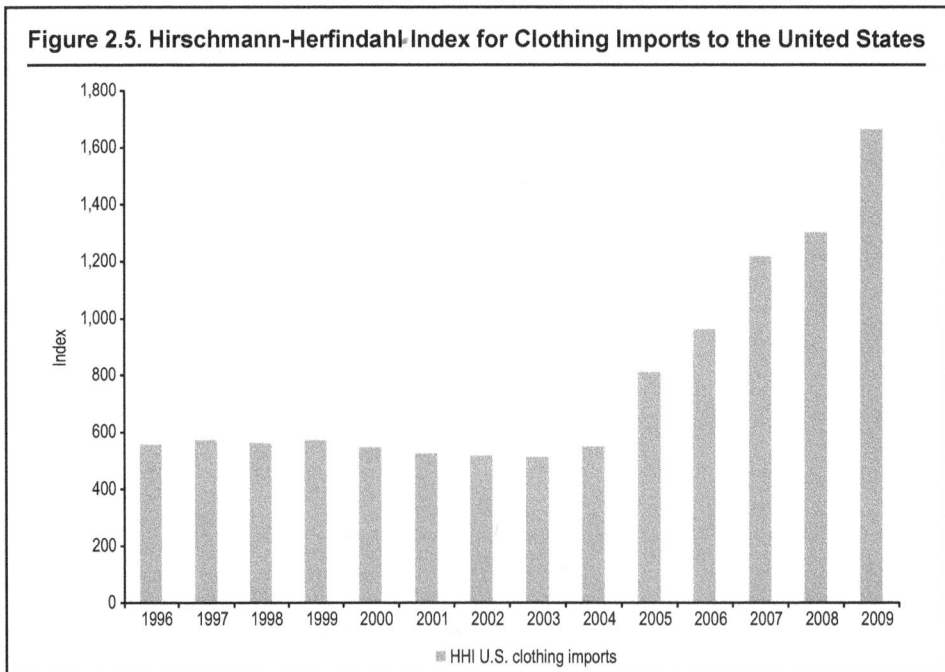

Figure 2.5. Hirschmann-Herfindahl Index for Clothing Imports to the United States

Source: USITC.
Note: Clothing represented by HS 61 and HS 62.

cent in 1995 to 36.6 percent in 2009. China is the second largest importer and increased its import share from 7 percent in 1995 to 25.2 percent in 2009. Thus, China significantly increased exports to the EU-15 in the context of the MFA phaseout and the global economic crisis. Turkey, the third largest exporter, increased its share from 6.3 to 8.8 percent from 1995 to 2004 but then lost export share in the context of the MFA phaseout and the global economic crisis reaching 6.9 percent in 2009. India increased its market share from 2.9 percent in 2004 to 4.2 percent in 2009. Bangladesh experienced a declining market share in 2005 (from 4.3 to 3.9 percent) but afterwards increased its market share to 5.1 percent in 2009. Tunisia, Morocco, and Romania lost market share between 2004 and 2009. Figures 2.6 and 2.7 show the percentage change of clothing imports (in value) to the EU-15 for the top 15 importer countries (plus SSA and Cambodia) between 2004 and 2005 as well as between 2007 and 2009. The largest growth rates between 2004 and 2005 are attributed to China (49 percent) and India (32 percent) and to a much lesser extent to Turkey (4 percent) and Bulgaria (2 percent). All other countries' EU-15 clothing exports declined in 2005. The largest growth rates between 2007 and 2009 are attributed to Poland (48 percent) where exports increased from a very small basis, China (17 percent), Bangladesh (16 percent), Sri Lanka (11 percent), Vietnam (9 percent), India (7 percent), and Cambodia (2 percent).

Table 2.6. Top 15 EU-15 Clothing Importer Countries

	1995		2000		2004		2005		2008		2009	
	Value (US$ million)	Share (%)	Value (US$ million)	Share (%)	Value (US$ million)	Share (%)	Value (US$ million)	Share (%)	Value (US$ million)	Share (%)	Value (US$ million)	Share (%)
EU-15	21,838	43.4	30,375	39.0	32,495	38.1	34,003	37.7	38,502	37.3	35,894	36.6
China	3,542	7.0	7,451	9.6	11,038	13.0	16,420	18.2	24,330	23.5	24,698	25.2
Turkey	3,189	6.3	5,322	6.8	7,520	8.8	7,857	8.7	7,612	7.4	6,754	6.9
Bangladesh	967	1.9	2,567	3.3	3,689	4.3	3,509	3.9	4,667	4.5	5,016	5.1
India	1,588	3.2	2,005	2.6	2,434	2.9	3,201	3.6	3,826	3.7	4,023	4.1
Tunisia	1,729	3.4	2,567	3.3	2,586	3.0	2,454	2.7	2,580	2.5	2,250	2.3
Morocco	1,631	3.2	2,356	3.0	2,417	2.8	2,262	2.5	2,386	2.3	1,992	2.0
Romania	972	1.9	2,558	3.3	3,679	4.3	3,450	3.8	2,348	2.3	1,952	2.0
Poland	1,604	3.2	1,826	2.3	1,153	1.4	998	1.1	1,421	1.4	1,626	1.7
Vietnam	—	—	—	—	—	—	—	—	1,201	1.2	1,163	1.2
Sri Lanka	—	—	—	—	806	1.0	795	0.9	1,113	1.1	1,143	1.2
Indonesia	908	1.8	1,800	2.3	1,320	1.6	1,188	1.3	1,114	1.1	1,076	1.1
Bulgaria	—	—	—	—	1,046	1.2	1,072	1.2	1,114	1.1	985	1.0
Pakistan	—	—	—	—	906	1.1	770	0.9	865	0.8	870	0.9
Thailand	546	1.1	911	1.2	868	1.0	770	0.9	—	—	718	0.7
Top 15	42,896	85.2	65,812	84.4	73,879	86.7	80,430	89.1	93,906	90.8	90,161	92.0
World	50,345	—	77,936	—	85,221	—	90,254	—	103,370	—	97,988	
Asian 12	9,043	18.0	17,679	22.7	22,657	26.6	28,147	31.2	38,718	37.5	39,495	40.3
LIC	3,593	7.1	7,055	9.1	8,976	10.5	9,288	10.3	11,805	11.4	12,246	12.5
SSA	661	1.3	1,078	1.4	763	0.9	686	0.8	672	0.7	592	0.6
Bangladesh	967	1.9	2,567	3.3	3,689	4.3	3,509	3.9	4,667	4.5	5,016	5.1
Cambodia	43	0.1	282	0.4	517	0.6	475	0.5	554	0.5	536	0.5

Source: EUROSTAT.
Notes: Clothing represented by HS 61 and HS 62. Top 15 by year; value in million euro.

Figure 2.6. EU-15 Clothing Imports Post-MFA, Percentage Change

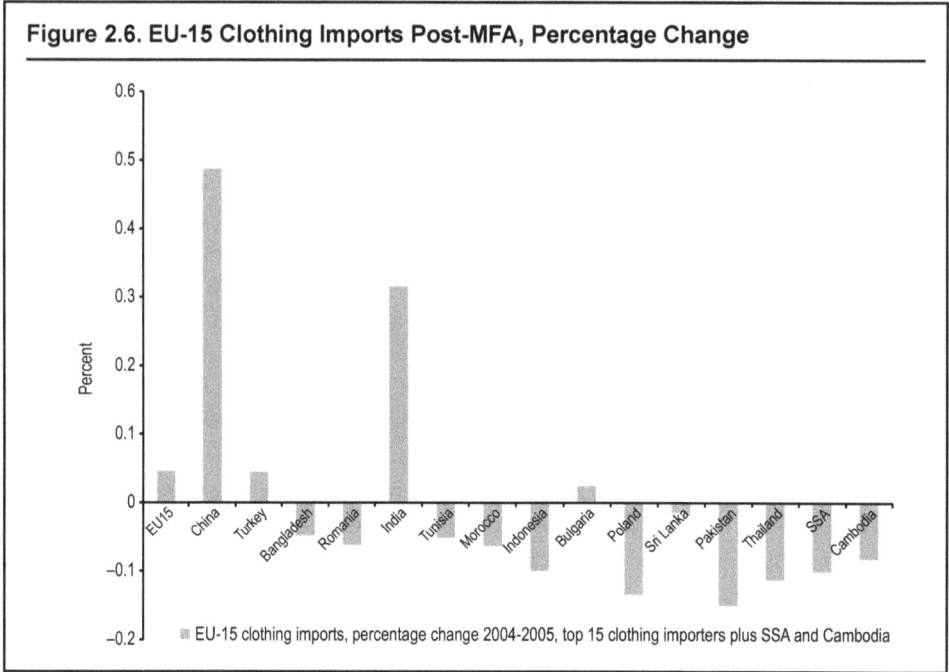

■ EU-15 clothing imports, percentage change 2004-2005, top 15 clothing importers plus SSA and Cambodia

Source: EUROSTAT.
Note: Clothing represented by HS 61 and HS 62.

Figure 2.7. EU-15 Clothing Imports during the Global Economic Crisis, Percentage Change

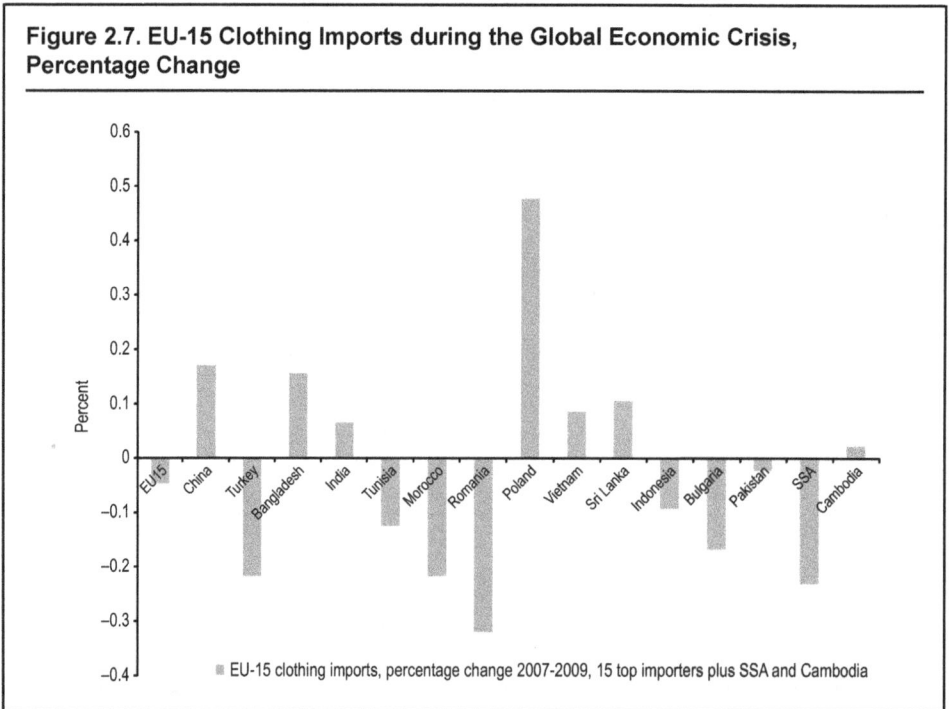

■ EU-15 clothing imports, percentage change 2007-2009, 15 top importers plus SSA and Cambodia

Source: EUROSTAT.
Note: Clothing represented by HS 61 and HS 62.

Generally the top 15 exporters had a stable share in EU-15 imports between 1995 and 2004, reaching on average 85 percent; their share increased after 2004 reaching 92 percent in 2009. Thus, the MFA phaseout and the global economic crisis have led to a consolidation of import countries. The Asian 12 increased their share dramatically from 26.6 to 40.3 percent between 2004 and 2009. LICs as a group also increased their import share from 10.5 percent in 2004 to 12.5 percent in 2009. Figure 2.8 shows the HHI index for the EU-15 and shows that the HHI remained quite stable until 2004 but then increased considerably, in particular in 2005 in the context of the MFA phaseout, and continued to increase until 2009.

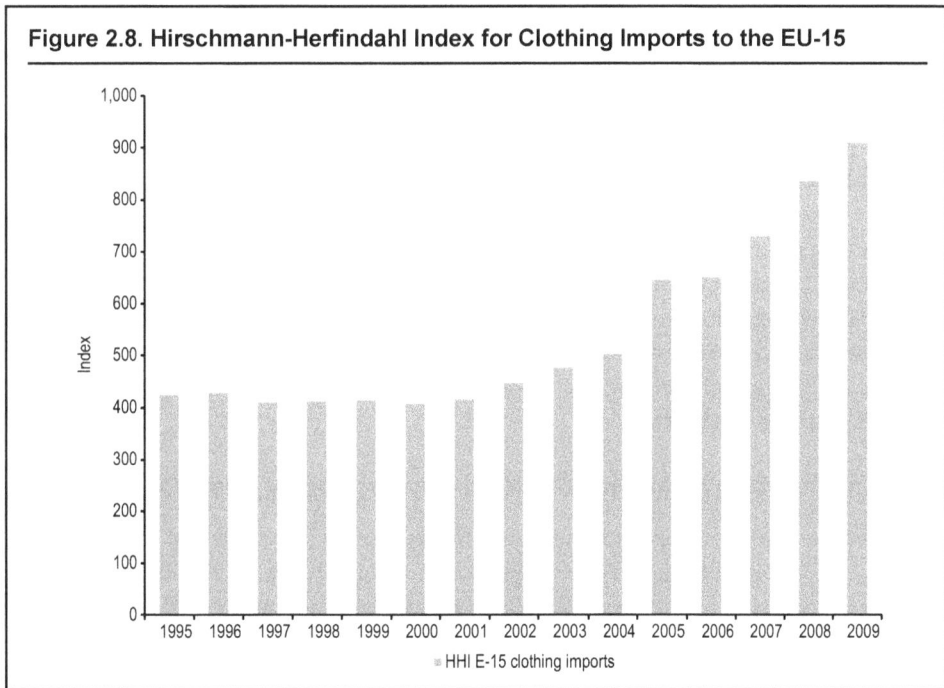

Figure 2.8. Hirschmann-Herfindahl Index for Clothing Imports to the EU-15

Source: EUROSTAT.
Note: Clothing represented by HS 61 and HS 62.

During the global economic crisis, trends accruing after the MFA phaseout have generally been reinforced. Low-cost Asian clothing exporter countries such as China, Bangladesh, India, and Vietnam are increasing their market share in the United States and the EU-15 primarily at the expense of regional supplier countries such as Mexico and Central American and Caribbean suppliers to the United States and North African and CEE suppliers to the EU-15 as well as SSA. Gereffi and Frederick (2010) identify four categories of main clothing exporter countries referring to longer-term developments as well as developments in the context of the MFA phaseout and the global economic crisis: (i) 'steady growth suppliers,' which have shown an increasing market share since the early 1990s and include China, Bangladesh, India, Vietnam, and Cambodia as well as Pakistan and Egypt but with smaller market shares;[11] (ii) 'split market suppliers,' which have experienced divergent developments in different markets and include Indonesia (increasing market share in the United States and decreasing market share in the EU-15) and Sri Lanka (increasing market share in the EU-15 and decreasing market share in the United States); (iii) pre-MFA suppliers, which experienced a sharp decline in the context of the MFA phaseout that has been accelerated during the global economic crisis and include Mexico, CAFTA, Romania, Tunisia, Morocco, Thailand, and SSA; and (iv) 'past-prime suppliers,' which have experienced decreasing market shares since the early 1990s and include Hong Kong SAR, China, Korea, Taiwan, China, and Malaysia, as well as the Philippines, Singapore, and Macau but with smaller market shares.

Despite important consolidation trends and an increase in market share by low-cost Asian countries, in particular China, recent developments have been more nuanced than expected before the MFA phaseout. In particular there have been different developments with regard to the major end markets in the United States and the EU-15 where some countries lost share in one market but could increase share in the other market. Further, although regional suppliers generally lost market shares in the context of the MFA phaseout and the global economic crisis, there continue to be distinct regional sourcing patterns in the United States and the EU-15 markets. Also, different trends at the product level could be observed. Thus, there have remained opportunities for LICs to continue and start exporting clothing. But entry and upgrading in global clothing value chains have become more difficult, which is related to the MFA phaseout, the global economic crisis, and subsequent changes in trade patterns and consolidation trends. However, to understand changes in entry and upgrading opportunities for LIC clothing exporters, global buyers and their sourcing policies have to be assessed as they are the ones who organize and govern global clothing value chains and ultimately decide where and how to source clothing products.

Changing Sourcing Strategies of Global Buyers: Supply Chain Consolidation

A development across different industries is the increasing importance of organizational buyers. The clothing industry is the classic example of a buyer-driven value chain that is characterized by decentralized, globally dispersed production networks, coordinated by lead firms who design, brand, and market the products they sell but where the actual manufacturing is carried out by other firms (Appelbaum and Gereffi 1994; Gereffi and Memedovic 2003). Although buyers are not directly involved in production, they yield significant control over manufacturers and stipulate (often detailed) product and production specifications. Thus, the strategies of these buyers, in particular in the area of sourcing, importantly shape production and trade patterns in the clothing sector. Initially sourcing decisions and related production relocations have been primarily motivated by labor cost differentials. However, sourcing policies have become more complex involving various firm- and country-specific factors, including—besides costs—quality, lead time, production flexibility, nonmanufacturing capabilities (such as input sourcing, product development, and design), risk spreading, and labor and environmental compliance. The MFA phaseout and the global economic crisis have had important impacts on sourcing policies of global buyers and in many areas accelerated earlier trends.

Global Buyers: Retailers, Branded Marketers, Manufacturers, and Intermediaries

Although there are important general trends in buyers' sourcing policies there are differences between different types of buyers. Generally, three main types of lead firms can be identified in the clothing value chain (see figure 2.9; Gereffi 1999; Gereffi and Frederick 2010): retailers, branded marketers, and branded manufacturers.

Within the retailer category there is a distinction between general retailers who sell a broad variety of products and specialty clothing retailers that only sell clothing products. General retailers can further be differentiated between department stores and discounters and include firms such as Wal-Mart, Kmart, Target, Sears, Macy's, and J.C. Penney in the United States and Asda, Tesco, Primark, Marks & Spencer, Debenhams, Galeries Lafayette, Carrefour, Karstadt, and Kaufhof in the EU. Specialty clothing retailers include firms such as Gap, Limited, American Eagle, and Abercrombie & Fitch in the United States and H&M, C&A, Benetton, Mango, New Look, Next, Arcadia, and Inditex (Zara) in the EU[12] (Gereffi and Frederick 2010). Retailers sell products of branded manufacturers and marketers but increasingly (and in particular specialty clothing retailers) have also developed their own private labels. The share of retailers' sales in total clothing sales has become more important and within their sales private label sales have increased. Furthermore, retailers have generally developed greater specialization by product (such as the rise of specialty clothing retailers) and price (such as the growth of high-volume, low-cost discount chains).

Branded marketers are primarily involved in designing, marketing and branding clothing products and are the prime example of buyer-driven value chains and the pioneers of global sourcing. Examples of branded marketers are Nike, Polo and Liz Claiborne in the United States and Hugo Boss, Diesel and Gucci in the EU.

In contrast to retailers and branded marketers, branded manufacturers initially had large in-house manufacturing capacities and only started to outsource manufacturing activities in the 1980s (Bair 2006). Branded manufacturers used to concentrate on regional sourcing but have recently increased their sourcing activities on a global scale. Examples of branded manufacturers are Phillips-Van Heusen Corporation, Sara Lee, Levi Strauss, and Fruit of the Loom in the United States and Giorgio Armani, Adidas, Puma and, to a certain extent, Inditex (Zara)[13] in the EU. Although branded marketers and manufacturers generally did not own the retail channels through which their products were sold, this has changed and today both have increasingly established their own stores (that is, concept stores) besides of selling their brands through external retail outlets. Hence, today all three types of lead firms have increasingly become 'organizational buyers' and have structured their business around the same core activities such as design, branding, marketing, research and development (R&D), and retailing (Gereffi and Memedovic 2003) (figure 2.9). Related to that, all lead firms have been increasingly involved in global sourcing.

An important difference arises from the type of end markets buyers primarily target. Discounters generally sell to the low-market segment where price is the key competitiveness criteria; department stores are generally found in the mid-market segment where quality becomes more important. Specialty clothing retailers target different market segments but generally focus on fashion products; some, such as H&M and Inditex (Zara), focus on fast fashion. Branded marketers and manufacturers can be found in different market segments; some, such as Hugo Boss and Gucci, specialize in high fashion and target the up-market segment where quality and fashion is central. Hence, in these different market segments the weight of sourcing criteria, including price, quality, fashion content, lead time, and flexibility differs, which is reflected in the respective sourcing policies of these buyers.

Figure 2.9. Types of Lead Firms in Clothing Value Chains

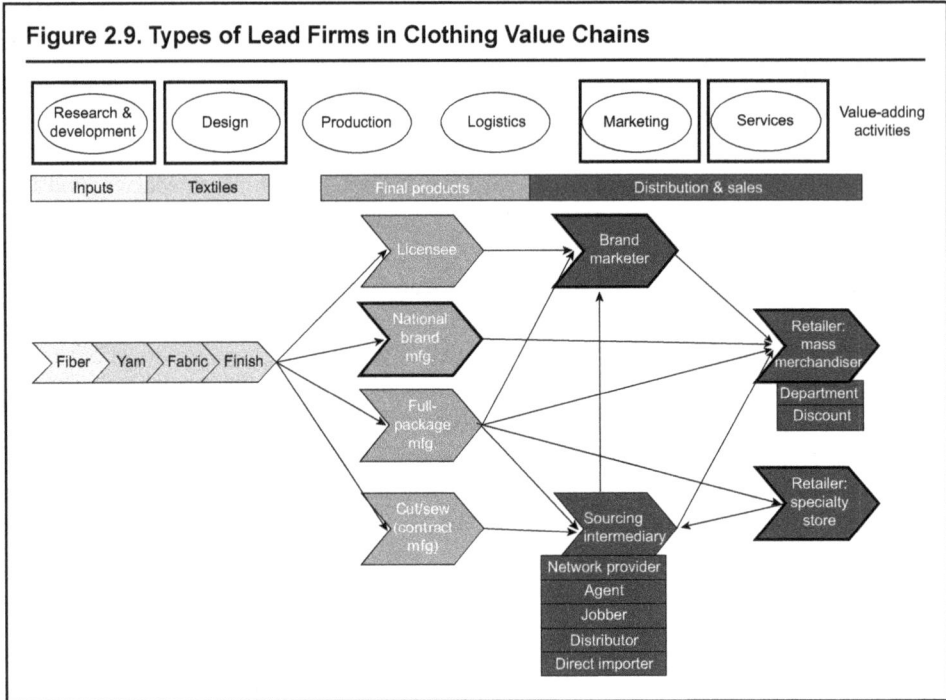

Source: Gereffi and Frederick (2010, 15).

Intermediaries such as importers, exporters, agents, and trading houses play a central role in global clothing value chains and have provided key links between buyers and suppliers. They are generally responsible for coordinating production, including input sourcing and logistics, but increasingly also for providing services in areas such as design, product development, and marketing (Gereffi and Frederick 2010). In the 1990s, a new type of intermediary has evolved. Large full-package manufacturers, in particular in East Asia, have developed from producers to intermediaries organizing far-flung transnational production and sourcing networks (Appelbaum 2008). This trend has been closely related to the MFA and quota hopping, and to changing sourcing strategies of global buyers. Faced with high demands on price, quality, and lead time as well as with large and changing volume demands and technical requirements from global buyers, more capable suppliers have tried to position themselves as globally operating production transnational corporations (TNCs) that coordinate networks with a global supply base. Asian producers headquartered in the 'Big Three' (Hong Kong SAR, China, Taiwan, China, and Korea) are the prototypes in this respect (Appelbaum 2005). These firms gathered experience in coordinating production networks in the Asian region when faced with raising labor costs and quota restrictions in their countries. Although this model was more or less limited to the Asian rim during the 1970s and 1980s (with the exception of Mauritius), in the 1990s it was extended to other continents, in particular to Latin America and the Caribbean and to SSA, mostly driven by quota restrictions and preferential market access. The Asian producers, especially in Hong Kong SAR, China and Taiwan, China, coordinated triangular manufacturing networks (Appelbaum and Gereffi 1994; Gereffi 1999), which usually involved production in a developing country organized by firms in a middle-income country with products sold to final buyers in a developed country[14] (Morris 2006a). Clothing factories that are part of triangular manufacturing networks can be entirely owned subsidiaries of these East Asian manufacturers, joint ventures, or independent overseas suppliers. The latter can be either locally or foreign-owned firms and have sourcing relationships (in contrast to equity relationships) with transnational producers. In this division of labor, skill-intensive activities, which provide higher margins, such as product development and design, sample making, quality control, warehousing, transport, and financing, stayed in East Asia and labor-intensive activities have been relocated. Thus, Taiwan, China, Hong Kong SAR, China, and Korea have maintained their dominant role in the clothing sector for decades. Although they are not important clothing exporting countries anymore (see trade data analysis above), their companies are still the industry leaders, in particular large trading houses and transnational producers that manage far-flung supplier networks located in diverse countries.[15] Later on large manufacturers in other Asian countries such as Singapore, Malaysia, China, India, and Sri Lanka followed the 'Big Three' and have also developed transnational manufacturing and sourcing networks.

Global Sourcing Policies: Supply Chain Rationalization

The activities and strategies of lead firms have a profound effect on relationships in global clothing value chains, on capabilities expected from suppliers, and on entry and upgrading possibilities. Despite variations among different types of lead firms, lead firms from different countries and targeting different end markets and market segments, there are important common trends in sourcing strategies of global buyers with respect to sourcing channels, sourcing geography, supply base, and firm- and country-specific sourcing criteria. These trends in sourcing policies have been mostly accentuated by the MFA phaseout and the global economic crisis. The discussion below is largely based on interviews with large global buyers in the United States and the EU.[16]

Sourcing Channels

While global buyers still use a mix of direct and indirect sourcing channels, the relationship between buyers and suppliers has generally become more direct. Sourcing channels can be classified as direct sourcing where buyers source directly from (overseas) manufacturers and indirect sourcing. In the latter case there can be a variety of intermediaries between buyers and manufacturers such as importers, exporters, agents, trading houses, and transnational producers located in foreign countries or in retailers' home countries (Palpacuer et al. 2005). Intermediaries may own manufacturing operations but most— with the exception of transnational producers—do not. At the very least, intermediaries are responsible for coordinating production, including input sourcing and logistics, but they also have increasingly provided services in areas such as design, product development, and marketing (Gereffi and Frederick 2010).

Global buyers see sourcing as their core competency and key competitive advantage, which is reflected in their increasing involvement in sourcing over the last decade. Main motivations were reducing costs by cutting out the middlemen, reducing lead times, increasing control over product quality and compliance, and mitigating risk.[17] The strategic buying and sourcing decisions are generally made at the headquarters but relationships with suppliers, identifying and negotiating with suppliers, monitoring suppliers' production, and quality control are largely handled by buying offices located in the sourcing country or region. Some buyers are also moving product development and design offices to their buying offices to be closer to their suppliers. Hence, these overseas offices go well beyond their original buying functions and have become engaged in product design, input selection and sourcing, and monitoring production functions handled by supplier firms. Most buyers stated that coordination has increased in sourcing decisions. In the past, individual buying teams had more freedom; nowadays sourcing decisions show a higher degree of coordination and consolidation among different buying teams and follow a central strategy. Intermediaries are still used but mostly for specific, generally higher-value and quality products and when intermediaries can offer extra value with regard to design, post-production services, and so forth.[18] Furthermore, indirect sourcing channels are used to enter new sourcing countries to reduce risks. Smaller buyers, however, seem to still rely much more on indirect sourcing channels and intermediaries. As Gereffi and Frederick (2010) state, the intermediary sourcing model is most popular with buyers that require smaller volumes or large buyers that need small quantities of certain items.

Notwithstanding this general trend to increase direct sourcing, intermediaries are still important. Although traditional intermediaries such as importers and exporters seem to have declined in importance certain types of intermediaries, in particular global trading houses and transnational producers, have continued to play central roles in global clothing value chains. For instance, the global trading house Li & Fung—one of the pioneers in the intermediary sourcing model (Gereffi and Frederick 2010)—has recently achieved a prominent role as the primary purchasing agent for retailers such as Walmart[19] and branded marketers such as Liz Claiborne. Transnational producers and their triangular manufacturing networks have remained important in certain countries and regions, in particular in LICs (such as in SSA countries and Cambodia; see below). Buyers describe sourcing arrangements with transnational producers as direct sourcing because they generally have direct relationships with the headquarters of these transnational producers in Taiwan, China; Hong Kong SAR, China; Korea; Singapore; Malaysia; China; and India. However, the actual plants manufacturing the clothing products do not have direct relationships with buyers and get orders and generally also inputs and products' specifications from the headquarters of transnational producers.

Sourcing Geography

With regard to sourcing geography global buyers have generally consolidated their sourcing countries after the MFA phaseout, which has been accelerated in the context of the global economic crisis. There is a trend that buyers want to concentrate a large share of their intake on fewer sourcing countries where they work with core suppliers and where a large variety of products and inputs can be sourced. However, buyers continuously screen country-specific developments, in particular trade agreements. There are similarities in the sourcing geography of different buyers. All buyers source a large part of their intake from Asian countries; regional supplier countries play an important role but they have generally lost market share in the context of the MFA phaseout and the global economic crisis.[20] Although lead times, production flexibility, and 'fast fashion' have become central in the industry, the role of regional supplier countries has decreased and sourcing from low-cost Asian countries has increased for large buyers in the United States and the EU. Flanagan (2009) states that buyers have managed to get clothes in stores quicker and refresh the range more frequently without moving production to suppliers close to home. A key explanation is that Asian suppliers have partly restructured their firm set-up to be able to produce shorter runs and offer buyers constant streams of new clothes. Thus, geographic proximity to end markets plays a role but location per se does not appear to constitute a major advantage or entry barrier as distance can be compensated by other factors such as infrastructure and logistics, local availability of fabrics and vertical integration, supply chain management capabilities, firm capabilities, and management practices. Spreading risks through some diversification of sourcing countries is an important consideration for buyers, which sets limits to the consolidation of sourcing countries and suppliers. For instance, lead firms continue to source the majority of products from China but they seek to diversify into other countries to avoid 'putting all their eggs in one basket' (Gereffi and Frederick 2010).

Supply Base

There is a general trend towards consolidation of the supply base as global buyers have been striving towards more cost-effective forms of supply chain management and reducing their supply base in order to rationalize and concentrate on core suppliers. As discussed above there is also a trend in consolidating sourcing countries but it seems that consolidation is primarily driven by the objective to reduce the number of supplier firms. Developing long-term strategic partnerships with core suppliers was stated by most buyers as one of the most important sourcing considerations. As just-style (2009b) states: "Regardless of where retailers are sourcing from, the importance of developing strong relationships with a few key strategic suppliers will remain a business imperative." This trend started in the 1990s but has increased in importance since the MFA phaseout and has been accelerated in the context of the global economic crisis. Large buyers interviewed have reduced their supply base and most of them still aim to reduce it further. The objective is to work with few, large, capable and often vertically integrated core suppliers. Buyers demand high capabilities from their core suppliers with regard to manufacturing but also regarding services such as input sourcing on suppliers' account, product development and design, inventory management and stock holding, logistics and financing, and communication and merchandising. Some buyers stated that they prefer multicountry suppliers that have capabilities to produce in or source from different locations and thus can flexibly use their competitive advantages. Furthermore, some buyers prefer to migrate with existing suppliers rather than start working with new suppliers when entering new sourcing countries. Thus, strategic suppliers are increasingly multinational producers or network coordinators that organize production networks and logistics for lead firms and offer a wide range of services to them. As just-style (2010e) states:

> Consolidation of supply chains is making it harder for small apparel producers to remain viable in the global market.… (T)he rise of 'fast fashion' and better inventory control means buyers are increasingly looking for suppliers that can source materials, coordinate logistics, and operate in locations that lend themselves to shorter delivery cycles. Major buyers are increasingly shifting away from sourcing from many small firms towards a smaller number of 'strategic suppliers', either manufacturing groups or agents, who manage production across multiple factories and international locations, providing greater value added services.

The global economic crisis has accelerated this consolidation process. Most large buyers interviewed indicated that the consolidation of their supply base which has been an objective for some time was accelerated in 2009 as they used the reduction in orders to focus sourcing on strategic suppliers. As Gereffi and Frederick (2010, 20) put it: "The recession has caused lead firms to 'cut the fat' and they are confining their relationships to their most capable and reliable suppliers." Birnbaum (2009) divides suppliers—whether firms or countries—into three groups. The first group comprises strategic suppliers or core suppliers on which buyers rely for the most important share of their production. In good times they receive their share of business, in bad times they receive more than their share as buyers channel business to core supplies to keep them busy. Birnbaum (2009) puts China as well as Vietnam and Indonesia in this first group of supplier countries. The second group comprises preferred suppliers that do well in good times but in bad times perform badly as buyers transfer orders to strategic suppliers. This group includes countries such as India, Pakistan, and Sri Lanka. The third group comprises marginal suppliers "which are the national equivalent of subcontractors" (Birnbaum 2009). When business is good they have work, when business turns bad they fall into a state of crisis. "In most industries the marginal suppliers are the little people. Not so in the garment industry.... Our marginal suppliers include DR-CAFTA, the United States' second largest supplier, as well as Cambodia, its eighth largest supplier" (Birnbaum 2009). Birnbaum (2009) explains the marginal status of these suppliers by foreign ownership. Factories in the DR-CAFTA and Cambodia but also in SSA LICs are mostly foreign owned and part of triangular manufacturing networks. To owners in Taiwan, China; Hong Kong SAR, China; Korea; or China, their Cambodian, DR-CAFTA, and SSA production plants are marginal operations—"places to dump low-value adding orders too cheap to produce in their main operation in China. However, when orders become scarce there are no 'too cheap to produce' orders" (Birnbaum 2009). Hence, suppliers that are integrated into triangular manufacturing networks in a marginal position have been particularly hard hit by the crisis as buyers and intermediaries have transferred orders from marginal to core suppliers (see below on SSA LICs and Cambodia).

Firm-Specific Sourcing Criteria

In sourcing decisions, buyers take into account an array of factors that are specific to the sourcing country and to the supplier firm. Central firm-specific criteria in sourcing decisions are the classic firm-specific criteria, namely production costs,[21] quality, and reliability. In addition, other criteria are increasingly shaping sourcing decisions, namely lead times, production flexibility, product range, labor relations and labor compliance, environmental compliance, and certain nonmanufacturing capabilities, including input sourcing on suppliers' accounts, product development and design understanding, inventory management and stock holding, logistics and financing, and communications and merchandising skills. Price, quality, and reliability have always been important and they have become even more important in the context of increased competition through the MFA phaseout and the global economic crisis as suppliers are expected to provide high-quality products at low prices in a reliable manner as a minimum standard. Besides these minimum conditions, short lead times and flexibility, labor and environmental compliance, and, increasingly, nonmanufacturing capabilities have increased in importance (table 2.7).

Table 2.7. Main Firm- and Country-Specific Sourcing Criteria of Global Buyers

Firm-specific criteria	
'Classic' criteria: • production costs • quality • reliability	Newer criteria: • lead times • production flexibility • labor relations and labor compliance • environmental compliance • input sourcing on suppliers' accounts • product development and design understanding • inventory management and stock holding • logistics and financing • communications and merchandising
Country-specific criteria	
• trade agreements and preferential market access • transit time and cost • physical and bureaucratic infrastructure, in particular transport and logistics • access to raw materials—international (duty free imports) • access to raw materials—local or regional • ability to source a wide range of products • labor and management capabilities • stable exchange rate • government incentives • historical, cultural and political ties	

Lead times and flexibility: One of the most influential trends in sourcing is the increasing importance of time factors in sourcing decisions. This is related to the shift to lean retailing and just-in-time delivery where buyers defray the inventory risks associated with supplying clothing to fast-changing, volatile, and uncertain markets by replenishing items on their shelves in very short cycles and minimizing inventories (Abernathy et al. 2006). Lean retailing was made possible by developments in information technology (such as bar coding and point-of-sale scanning, electronic data interchange (EDI), and automated distribution centers) and has been a response to stagnant clothing demand since the early 1980s as well as to rapidly changing consumer preferences. As a result consumers are demanding increased variety and fashionability of products leading to shrinking product life cycles, shorter production seasons, and more rapid production cycles turnover. This trend is underlined by the increasing market-share of 'fast fashion' retailers such as H&M and Zara. This acceleration, however, is not limited to 'fast fashion' retailers but has affected the whole sector and the "days of a couple of collections per year are gone forever … and retailers are getting their clothes into stores more quickly and refreshing their ranges more frequently" (Flanagan 2009). A U.K. managing director states: "Speed to market is last year's news: it is a significant factor for success but it is no longer 'the new thing'. It is just part of the normal way of retailing. You just have to get things from concept to shelf in a shorter time than before. It's not just for fast fashion ranges either; you have to accelerate the lead times right across the business. It's a cultural shift for companies" (just-style 2009a, 6). This trend has important effects on sourcing patterns, as short lead times and flexibility have become key factors in sourcing decisions of buyers.

Lead times have become increasingly important for all types of buyers and products. However, there remain important variations among buyers' and products' lead time requirements, in particular when it comes to balancing short lead time with cost considerations. Basic and fashion basic products that can be sold over the year have commonly longer lead times than fashion products. The lengths of the season is generally declining but there are still differences between mass market retailers where interseasonal changes are limited and often only involve changes in colors, and 'fast fashion' retailers where interseasonal changes are considerable and involve new designs and styles. Thus, time frames still vary importantly between different types of buyers—the quickest 'fast fashion' retailers are able to work with three-week schedules from design to stores; most mass-market U.S. retailers still work with six-month schedules but three-month schedules are increasing in importance. Besides the importance of lead times in the fast fashion segment, lead time is also particularly important for replenishment products. There is a distinction between fast fashion and quick response (Gereffi and Frederick 2010): Quick response is associated with replenishment orders, which are more prevalent for basic and fashion basic products as their demand is more stable (Jassin-O'Rourke 2008). In this case products are ordered on a replenishable basis without changing their styles to reduce inventory on the side of the buyers. An important prerequisite for replenishment products is the introduction of a vendor-managed inventory which entails the determination of the optimum stocking levels at the retail point, and a steady transmission of current sales and stock data to manufacturers so that they can replenish the stocks to maintain them at their desired levels (Jassin-O'Rourke 2008). Fast fashion is quick response in new merchandise, involving smaller but more frequent orders in a larger variety of styles and shorter lead times. Predictions thought fast fashion would importantly increase local and regional sourcing, but this has generally not been the case as Asian suppliers have adapted their capabilities to be able to serve fast-fashion buyers (see above, Gereffi and Frederick 2010).

In the context of the global economic crisis, lead time considerations have further grown in importance. Ken Watson from Industry Forum Consultants and Services (cited in just-style 2009a, 50f) states that time factors have become even more important during the crisis:

> We are now going into a market where nobody knows what's going to happen, but we have to forecast what we're doing. In an uncertain market we have to be more flexible and responsive. It's about having a different supply chain that is responsive and one which can deliver within the season. It's not a question of taking a lead time down to six months, or six months down to six weeks, it's consistently delivering something within four weeks and being able to react within the season.

With regard to production flexibility, large global buyers generally demand large scales and production capacities. This is related to the consolidation process at the buyers' end (see below) and is particularly the case for U.S. buyers as they supply a large homogenous end market. Thus, most large U.S. buyers interviewed stated that a central sourcing criterion is a certain minimum number of employees, such as 1,000. In contrast, for European buyers, in particular specialized clothing retailers and mid-market retailers, the ability to produce short runs quickly and flexibly is demanded. As fashion cycles have decreased and designs are changing fast, buyers prefer ordering smaller volumes of different styles and designs more often. Thus, suppliers are confronted with production flexibility demands that may be contradictory as some buyers demand capabilities to produce long runs while others require short runs.

Labor and environmental compliance: Labor and environmental compliance are gaining importance, which reflects the rising societal expectations global buyers are facing in the light of corporate social responsibility (CSR) campaigns from nongovernmental organizations (NGOs) and compliance-conscious consumers. Labor and environmental compliance has emerged as an important issue in sourcing policies in the clothing sector due to the labor intensity of the clothing industry and the environmental impact of the textile industry (such as high energy use and waste water). Buyers have taken compliance seriously and most have developed Codes of Conduct (CoC) that include labor and environmental standards and conduct regular audits (mostly by their own CSR teams). Fulfilling buyers' CoC often constitutes a precondition for firms to enter sourcing networks. However, with few exceptions there seems to be little institutionalized communication and cooperation between the sourcing and the CSR teams. This can lead to contradictory demands as CSR considerations are not incorporated in the core sourcing business of buyers. Furthermore, a good record in labor and environmental compliance is generally not rewarded with positive incentives, such as longer contracts or a price premium; instead global buyers usually use negative incentives. Compliance to their labor and environmental standards is generally framed as a minimum criterion for being part of their supply chain.

Nonmanufacturing capabilities: Besides manufacturing capabilities suppliers are increasingly expected to perform a number of other services such as input sourcing on their accounts, product development and design, inventory management and stock holding, and logistics, as well as financial services (that is, invoicing on a 60- or 90-day basis) and certain communications and merchandising capabilities. Input sourcing capabilities have generally become minimum criteria as buyers prefer working with free on board (FOB) or even full-package suppliers and not with CMT firms. CMT suppliers (which are also referred to as assembly) are generally only in charge of cutting fabric provided by the buyer (or intermediary) and sewing the cut fabric into clothing products in accordance with the buyer's specifications. Under CMT, a factory is simply paid a processing fee, not a price for the product, and uses fabric sourced by, and owned by, the buyer (Gereffi and Frederick 2010). In contrast to CMT, FOB firms—which are also called OEMs (original equipment manufacturers)—are capable of sourcing and financing inputs and providing all production services, finishing, and packaging for delivery to the retail outlet. In the clothing industry, OEMs typically manufacture according to the buyer's specifications and design, and in many cases use raw materials specified by the buyer (Gereffi and Frederick 2010). Full-package manufacturers—also called ODMs (original design manufacturer)—carry out all steps involved in the production of a clothing product—including design, fabric sourcing and financing, cutting, sewing, trimming, packaging, and distribution. Typically, a full-package supplier organizes and coordinates the design of the product, the approval of samples, the selection, purchasing and production of materials, the completion of production, and, in some cases, the delivery of the finished product to the retail outlet (Gereffi and Frederick 2010). The objective of buyers to concentrate on their core competencies, reduce the complexity of their supply chains, concentrate on core suppliers, and ultimately reduce costs and increase flexibility has spurred the shift from CMT to OEM or ODM suppliers. The global economic crisis has accelerated this development and firms and countries without broader capabilities (besides manufacturing) and in particular without sourcing capabilities face challenges in global clothing value chains (Gereffi and Frederick 2010).

Although buyers demand more capabilities from suppliers, they remain involved in the production process and send 'tech sheets' with detailed specifications to suppliers.[22] Buyers also generally nominate input suppliers that have to be used and in several cases also negotiate prices and conditions with them, given their stronger buying power. In some cases suppliers can use their own input suppliers if they get a better price and fulfill the quality specifications but this has to be confirmed by the buyer. With regard to design capabilities there seem to be varying trends. All buyers stated that design understanding is central but most of them see design as their core competency and do not demand full design capabilities from suppliers. Production development capabilities seem to be more relevant than design capabilities. Related to the trend towards more direct sourcing is the importance of certain service capabilities such as communications (for example, being able to communicate with buyers, replying quickly to e-mails, and so forth) and merchandising skills. Large buyers agreed that capabilities expected from suppliers have increased significantly in the last five years. With regard to selecting new suppliers most large buyers stated that new suppliers have to offer something new (such as significantly reduced prices or fresh design ideas). As a necessary condition, new suppliers need to fulfill minimum standards with regard to prices, quality, and lead times.

When FOB or even full-package capabilities are demanded and suppliers have to be capable of ordering, financing, and stocking inputs, producing a finished product and offering payment periods to buyers typically of 60 to 90 days, access to and costs of credit to finance inputs and production become crucial for suppliers. The global economic crisis has made access to credit very difficult, in particular for trade finance but also for working and investment capital. The general decline in credit availability is affecting all suppliers, but particularly hard hit are small and medium-sized firms and locally owned firms as they normally cannot access transnational finance networks. Large buyers interviewed reported requests from suppliers to provide funds up front or guarantee credit. In some instances buyers extended credit or provided post-shipment financing in partnership with banks. However, buyers are reluctant to step into this area as it represents a move away from their FOB or full-package sourcing model.[23] The global economic crisis brought the importance of suppliers' financial stability to the attention of buyers. Gereffi and Frederick (2010) state that the most lasting effect of the global economic crisis on suppliers may be related to access to finance, because in the future firms will have to prove their financial stability in order to enter sourcing networks of global buyers.

Country-Specific Sourcing Criteria

Most large buyers stated that compared to firm-specific sourcing criteria country-specific criteria are only of secondary consideration. However, this statement has to be put in perspective as the following country-specific factors were named as central: trade agreements and preferential market access, transit time and cost, physical and bureaucratic infrastructure (in particular transport and logistics), access to raw materials (in particular fabric) through duty fee imports, local and regional availability of raw materials, the ability to source a wide range of products, labor and management capabilities, stable exchange rates, and government incentives. Global buyers tend to prefer 'one stop shopping locations' where they can source a critical mass and a wide range of different products in one location or at least region. The availability of suitable fabrics, locally or at least regionally, in the context of shorter lead times and increased flexibility and control of supply chains was stated as central by large buyers. However, fabrics production would need to be competitive in terms of price, quality, lead times, and also variety. The possibility to import inputs duty-free is crucial. Government incentives play a central role, including export processing zone (EPZ) regulations, reduced or zero profit tax rates, and subsidized land and building rents as well as utility rates. Trade agreements are central and most buyers have employees who directly work on screening trade agreements; some are also involved in lobbying activities. Preferential market access often has a larger impact on the final price of the product than labor costs and some country's or regions' competitiveness is seen as largely being based on preferential market access (such as SSA due to AGOA; see below). Concerning infrastructure, buyers stated that transport and logistics are central, in particular ports and customs clearance procedures.[24] In the context of time being a critical element of competitiveness, the quality of transport and logistics services has become increasingly important in influencing trade costs and trade flows. Some firms further stated that geographical location is important; others said that geographical location per se is meaningless and it has to be assessed together with other factors which influence lead times, in particular infrastructure and logistics, local availability of fabrics and vertical integration, supply chain management capabilities, firm capabilities, and management practices. But transit time and cost are clearly central in sourcing decisions and together with these factors geographical location has an impact. A stable exchange rate is also an important sourcing criterion. Exchange rate fluctuations can have large and unpredicted impacts on prices. For instance, the currency appreciation in South Africa probably had a larger impact on clothing exports than the MFA phaseout at the end of 2004 (see below on SSA). Figure 2.10 shows the impact of exchange rates on sourcing costs in selected countries. In the period February 2007 to May 2008 exchange rate fluctuations accounted for an 8.2 percent decrease in costs in Pakistan

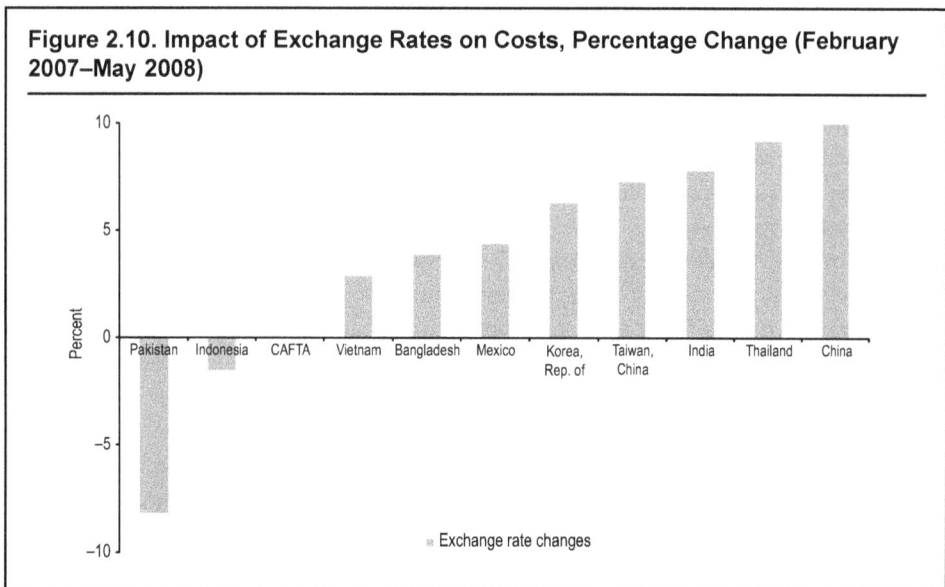

Figure 2.10. Impact of Exchange Rates on Costs, Percentage Change (February 2007–May 2008)

Source: Jassin-O'Rourke Group, LLC (2008).

and a 10 percent and 9.2 percent increase in costs in China and Thailand respectively. Historical, cultural, and political ties as well as informal networks (such as relationships to embassies or the experience of other buyers, agents or core suppliers) also play a role in sourcing decisions, in particular when starting to source from a country.

Conclusions on Global Sourcing Policies

These developments in sourcing policies lead to the conclusion that there is a common trend in sourcing strategies and practices of large global buyers, which can be described as 'supply chain rationalization.' Supply chain rationalization is associated with the centralization and standardization of sourcing decision-making and procedures. Supply chain rationalization strategies result in consolidation of the supply base and sourcing countries, concentration on core suppliers, high demands on suppliers with regard to manufacturing but also other capabilities, detailed performance monitoring, and demanding selection principles for new suppliers (Palpacuer et al. 2005). This trend can be observed for all large buyers interviewed. It can be therefore concluded that global buyers from the United States and the EU are following similar sourcing models post-MFA but have adopted it to different extents. Supporting earlier research by Palpacuer et al. (2005), this trend is most developed in the United States and the United Kingdom, but also large buyers in France and in other European countries are increasingly following this model. However, these conclusions are confined to the largest buyers in the United States and the EU. Crucial differences in sourcing strategies and practices might exist between large buyers on the one side and medium and small buyers on the other side. Along the same lines, medium and small buyers in different end markets may differ in their strategies, and, hence there may still exist more informal, less standardized, and culturally specific sourcing strategies.

Structural Challenges: Global Demand, Supply, and Asymmetric Market Structures

There are two underlying structural challenges that condition the role of the clothing sector in the industrial development process of LICs today: (i) changing global supply and demand structures, and (ii) asymmetric market and power structures within global clothing value chains. These structural challenges are related to and have been accelerated by the MFA phaseout, the global economic crisis, and supply chain rationalization strategies of global buyers.

With regard to supply and demand structures, the second half of the twentieth century was characterized by rising demand in the global clothing sector, albeit with a slower path since the 1970s. At the same time it was characterized by the replacement of production in developed countries by imports, so that demand for imports by developing countries was increasing. However, since the beginning of the 2000s and recently accelerated by the global economic crisis, demand in major end markets has stagnated and import penetration levels in developed countries had already reached high levels of between 80 and 100 percent (Palpacuer et al. 2005). Kaplinsky (2005) points out that these developments have a divisive impact on developing countries with potentially severe implications for late clothing industrializers. The previous period of export growth by NIEs was primarily at the cost of domestic producers in developed countries squeezed out of their domestic markets. All NIEs were able to simultaneously increase their exports to the United States and the EU markets. Today, however, the growth of clothing exports from a few developing countries is largely at the expense of clothing producers in other developing countries (Morris 2006a). The heightened competition between developing countries has been reinforced by overcapacity in the global clothing industry due to the MFA phaseout and related to the entry of large developing countries such as China and India into clothing exporting. The global advance of the two 'Asian Driver' economies of China and India—individually much larger than the Asian forerunners of Japan and the NIEs Taiwan, China; Hong Kong SAR, China; and Korea—and their competitive advantage in many activities relevant for LIC exporters have constrained space for other participants in clothing exporting (see Kaplinsky and Messner 2008; Kaplinsky and Morris 2008). The development of unit prices of U.S. and EU-15 clothing imports underlines this heightened competition—unit values for U.S. and EU-15 imports have generally declined since 2000.[25] For the United States, USITC reports unit prices (customs value/ unit of quantity) for different categories of volumes—dozens, dozen pairs, and numbers. However, due to limited availability of data we can only analyze unit values for products reported in dozens (which account for the majority of clothing imports to the United States, but with country and product variations). Unit prices for knit and woven dozens declined significantly between 2000 and 2009—for knit by 8.8 percent and for woven by 19.4 percent. For the EU, volume is reported in kilograms. Unit values for total extra-EU-15 clothing imports also declined significantly between 2000 and 2009—knit products by 20.2 percent and woven products by 26.8 percent. Stagnant demand in traditional end markets, overcapacity, and related price pressures have created a difficult context for suppliers to capture margins and upgrade through participation in global clothing value chains (Palpacuer et al. 2005).

However, price pressures may not only be explained by stagnating demand and overcapacity but also by asymmetric market and power structures in global clothing value chains. In the context of heightened competition at the supplier level, rents do not derive from relatively standardized and commodified activities such as manufacturing that are globally available. They are associated with design, branding, marketing, R&D, and retailing (Gereffi 1994), which are the core competencies of buyers and protected by high entry barriers. By controlling these high-rent activities—and via them access to consumers—buyers yield significant power over other actors in the chain. Power at the buyers' level has further increased due to consolidation among retailers resulting from mergers and acquisitions and the emergence of large discount chains and specialty clothing stores (Morris and Barnes 2009). In the United States, between 1987 and 1991 the five largest retailers increased their share of retail clothing sales from 35 to 45 percent, by 1995 their share had increased to 68 percent, and a further 24 chains controlled 30 percent of the market (Gereffi and Memedovic 2003). In 2001, the five largest retailers in the United States (Wal-Mart, Sears, Kmart, Dayton Hudson Corp., and J.C. Penney) accounted for around 56 percent of sales among the top 20 retailers (Weathers 2003, cited in Morris and Barnes 2009). Wal-Mart is the single largest retailer representing 32 percent of total United States demand in the retail sector (National Retail Foundation 2008, cited in Morris and Barnes 2009). The European clothing retail sectors are similarly concentrated. The top five retailers in the United Kingdom accounted for 35 percent of total clothing sales in 2007 (London Economics 2008, cited in Morris and Barnes 2009). In Germany in 1992, five retailers (C&A, Quelle, Metro and Kaufhaus, Karstadt, and

Otto) accounted for 28 percent of the clothing market (Gereffi and Memedovic 2003). In France and Italy with a long tradition of independent stores, independent retailers have declined in importance since the mid-1980s and specialized clothing retailers and hyper/supermarkets have grown rapidly (Kaplinsky 2005). This consolidation trend has been accelerated by the global economic crisis as large buyers have increased their market shares through mergers and acquisitions while several of their competitors have gone bankrupt. These asymmetric market and power structures—related to high entry barriers to buyers' core activities, consolidation among buyers and intense competition among suppliers—create an asymmetric distribution of value along the value chain and further impede the capture of margins and upgrading of suppliers to higher value and rent activities within global clothing value chains.

However, new global developments may signal a partial shift in competitive and power structures in global clothing value chains. First, some intermediaries and first tier suppliers, in particular global trading houses and transnational producers, have captured high value-added activities and control far-flung production and sourcing networks. These large global suppliers have reached powerful positions in global clothing value chains, which potentially signal a shift in the governance structure of these chains and a reduction of power of global buyers in relation to some actors (Appelbaum 2008).

Second, global demand structures may change because import demand for clothing in the United States, the EU, and Japan might stagnate while demand will increase in fast-growing emerging countries, as well as in regional and domestic markets. Currently, the large majority of clothing trade is geared towards the EU, the United States, and Japan and, yet, together they only present about 10 percent of the world's population. The wealth of their population and therefore the ability to buy clothing is growing at a much slower pace than that of emerging countries (Morris and Barnes 2010). The Economic Intelligence Unit estimates clothing retail demand for selected countries for the period 2008 to 2013. The fastest growth in the period is estimated for China, Eastern Europe (including Russia), India, Turkey, and Brazil (EIU 2008, cited in Textiles Intelligence 2009). Thus, although the United States and EU markets will remain the major import markets at least for some time, global demand is shifting to new markets where demand for clothing increases at an even higher rate than economic growth (Morris and Barnes 2009). This shift in end markets may also lead to changing governance structures as the role of traditional developed country-based buyers may decline and developing countries' buyers may increase in importance. Traditional buyers from the United States and the EU have increased sales outlets and stores in fast-growing emerging markets and have gained market share. This has however taken place to different extents. Large markets in Latin America are dominated by foreign retailers, but in China, India, and South Africa local or regional retailers play an important role. It will be central to understand sourcing policies and power structures within clothing value chains of these new buyers and associated entry and upgrading possibilities. In particular in regional and domestic markets there may be increased opportunities for suppliers to upgrade their activities to design, marketing, branding, R&D, and even retailing (Gereffi and Fredrick 2010).

Third, there is insecurity about China's future as a competitor to LIC clothing exporters. In the 2000s China at least partly upgraded its production to higher-value products supported by government incentives. This happened within the clothing sector but also across sectors as the Chinese government aims to shift the country's workforce from low-margin industries like clothing towards more highly skilled jobs in higher-technology sectors. Faced with the global economic crisis, this policy was put on hold, and subsidies were used to support the clothing industry to reduce job losses. This is reflected in export data where the trend to higher-value clothing exports has been partly reversed. It is not clear how fast China will move into higher value-added products again in the post-crisis environment. Furthermore, labor costs are rising in China and the exchange rate has gradually appreciated. Industry experts say that eventually prices will rise in China: "Over the next five years, China's apparel and textile industry will be getting fewer and fewer subsidies, while wages will be rising far faster than consumer inflation. The timing's not so predictable—and Chinese factories' ability to keep their prices down shouldn't be underestimated. But without a lot of hard work and investment in new technology, China's clothing prices are set to rise at least 20 percent faster than its competitors' over the next five years" (Flanagan 2010a). Such developments would change supply structures and increase the space for LICs in clothing exporting, at least in the low-value basics market segment. However, the speed with which China's wages and prices rise depends on the size of the rural labor reserves. China has a massive rural labor force yet to be tapped; 750 million people still live in the countryside with the average rural income only one third of its urban counterpart (Ozawa and Bellak 2010).

First Conclusions on Entry and Upgrading in Global Clothing Value Chains

The main arguments for the clothing sector as a springboard for export diversification and industrial development in LICs are that (i) entry barriers are low and LICs with large supplies of unskilled labor can quickly participate in clothing manufacturing, and (ii) clothing manufacturing can be a launching pad for upgrading into higher value-added and more skill- and technology-intensive activities within and across sectors. Upgrading is defined as moving to higher-value activities in global value chains in order to increase the benefits (such as security, profits, skill, technology, or knowledge transfer) from participating in global production (Bair and Gereffi 2003; Bair 2005). Upgrading in global value chains is generally classified in four types (Gereffi et al. 2001, 2005; Humphrey and Schmitz 2002): process upgrading (improving technology and/or production systems), product upgrading (producing more sophisticated goods with higher unit prices), functional upgrading (taking over more functions beyond production such as design, input sourcing or distribution/logistics), and chain upgrading (moving from one industry to another). For the clothing industry functional upgrading can be conceptualized as a trajectory where firms start as assemblers (CMT) but subsequently learn about the production process which allows them to develop more capabilities and take over more functions associated with original equipment manufacturing (OEM, also called FOB) and original design manufacturing (ODM, also called full-package). The last upgrading step in this trajectory is original brand name manufacturing (OBM) where suppliers develop their own brands and are thus also in charge of branding and marketing (Gereffi 1999). But are these assumptions with regard to entry and upgrading still valid for the clothing sector and LICs today?

The global clothing sector has expanded rapidly since the early 1970s and many LICs have been integrated into the global clothing value chain. However, recently the environment for global clothing trade has changed significantly. Main drivers have been (i) changes in the regulatory system, in particular the phaseout of the MFA, (ii) the global economic crisis, and (iii) changes in the strategies of global buyers and their sourcing policies. Beyond the need to adjust to the MFA phaseout and the global economic crisis, longer-term trends in sourcing policies have been accelerated by these two events. Developments in sourcing policies have lead to 'supply chain rationalization,' which is associated with consolidation of the supply base and sourcing countries, concentration on core suppliers, and high demands with regard to manufacturing but also other capabilities. Hence, all three developments have lead to global consolidation whereby leading clothing supplier countries and firms have strengthened their position in the clothing value chain (Gereffi and Frederick 2010). On the country level, low-cost Asian clothing exporter countries such as China, Bangladesh, India, and Vietnam are increasing their market share in the United States and the EU-15 primarily at the expense of regional supplier countries such as Mexico and Central American and Caribbean suppliers to the United States as well as North African and CEE suppliers to the EU-15. Also, SSA clothing suppliers and smaller LICs in different regions have lost market share post-quota and during the crisis. On the firm level the shift to 'supply chain rationalization' has benefited larger and more capable suppliers at the expense of smaller and marginal suppliers in all countries. Thus, in addition to consolidation processes at the lead firms' level, including retailers, branded marketers, and branded manufacturers, consolidation has taken place at the intermediary as well as first-tier supplier level.

Global consolidation has critical implications for possibilities to enter and upgrade within global clothing value chains and questions previous assumptions that see clothing exporting as an easy avenue with regard to entry and upgrading. Global consolidation has increased entry barriers at the country and firm level, which challenges LIC suppliers. The MFA phaseout led to increasing entry barriers at the country level as quotas no longer secure market access for LICs. Preferential market access is still central and provides windows of opportunities for LIC clothing exporters. But preferences have been eroding due to generally decreasing tariffs, and because preferences have been enjoyed by and negotiated for a larger group of countries. Thus, preferential market access alone does not secure clothing exports in the medium term. On the firm level, global buyers' supply chain rationalization strategies have resulted in increased entry barriers as more capabilities and higher standards are expected from suppliers. Thus, firms are only able to enter supply chains of global buyers if they can offer high manufacturing capabilities, including low costs, high quality, short lead times, production flexibility, and labor compliance. In addition buyers increasingly demand nonmanufacturing capabilities, including input sourcing on suppliers' accounts, product development and design understanding, inventory management, logistics, and communications. Suppliers increasingly need to provide FOB or even full-package services to buyers, and suppliers providing only assembly services (CMT) are at a disadvantage (Gereffi and Frederick 2010). These capabilities require financial and human resources at the firm level as well as reliable and low-cost infrastructure and backbone services, education and training facilities, and access to finance at the country level. Integration at the first-tier level has become more difficult for smaller, marginal and less competitive firms that lack capabilities, as well as less-developed and competitive countries. Further, supply chain rationalization leads to reductions in the number of suppliers, which lowers global buyers' propensity to integrate additional suppliers in their sourcing networks. Buyers also tend to use existing suppliers rather than start working with new suppliers when entering new sourcing countries (Palpacuer et al. 2005). For LICs who want to use the clothing sector as a route to export diversification and industrial development, these new developments are challenging. Low labor costs and preferential market access are not enough to be competitive in the clothing sector post-quota and post-crisis.

On the positive side, core suppliers that can provide broader capabilities may develop closer and more strategic relationships with global buyers where learning and further upgrading may be possible. Strategic relationships with core suppliers have become key in buyers' sourcing strategies. This trend has been accelerated in the context of the MFA phaseout and the global economic crisis as buyers have confined relationships to their most capable suppliers. However, as examples from different countries show, buyers tend to support and 'allow' suppliers' upgrading only to a certain extent and as long as it does not encroach on their core competencies. The different types of upgrading described above seem to be differently accessible to suppliers and upgrading in the clothing sector has often been limited to process and product upgrading, because this sort of upgrading is in the interest of lead firms that define and enforce product and process standards (Altenburg 2006). Functional upgrading seems to be accepted up to a certain level, namely into activities buyers do not see as their core competencies. But upgrading into critical areas such as design, branding, marketing, and R&D that buyers see as their core competencies is contested. Thus, first-tier suppliers seem to face learning and upgrading opportunities in process and product and to a certain extent functional upgrading. However, an important part of this upgrading will already be necessary to enter global buyers' supply chains in the first place.

A related question is whether due to increased capabilities of suppliers and more strategic supplier-buyer relationships, first-tier supplier-buyer relationships have become considerably stickier and suppliers' positions more powerful. As more suppliers offer efficient manufacturing processes, higher-quality and value products, and broader capabilities and services, these standards may become the new minimum standard and not 'extra services' that can be the basis for higher rewards and for closer and long-term relationships with buyers. This new minimum standard can be seen with regard to input sourcing and product development functions, which used to be capabilities that firms could add to differentiate themselves from other suppliers and increase value added. But nowadays these capabilities are the basic standard for entering certain chains. Thus, it is questionable to what extent supply chain rationalization leads to closer relationships and more powerful positions of core suppliers. Clearly, however, the emergence of powerful intermediaries and first-tier suppliers such as global trading houses and transnational producers that have captured high value-added activities and control far-flung production networks has at least partially changed power structures in global clothing value chains (Appelbaum 2008).

Hence, on the one hand it has become more difficult for firms in LICs to enter and upgrade within global clothing value chains. On the other hand, if firms should achieve upgrading and be able to offer broader capabilities there seem to be potential gains, at least for some large global first-tier suppliers. However, marginal and new suppliers that lack broader capabilities and only offer basic manufacturing functions may still be able to enter supply chains through intermediaries. The persistence of intermediaries implies that despite of global buyers' supply chain rationalization strategies, there remains a role for second-tier suppliers that are integrated into global supply chains via intermediaries. In particular in triangular manufacturing networks of transnational producers, entry barriers at the firm level are substantially lower. However, upgrading opportunities may also be limited and the sustainability of these suppliers is questionable. Second-tier suppliers are generally in marginal positions as they don't have direct relationships with buyers. This limits upgrading possibilities, in particular functional upgrading, because learning and upgrading is restricted by the intermediaries' control over key functions and services that they see as their core competencies (Palpacuer et al. 2005), such as input sourcing, product development and design, logistics, merchandising, and the relationship with buyers. Transnational producers are even involved in functions more closely related to production such as sample making, which may reduce the role of second-tier suppliers to CMT production. Moreover, the long-term prospects of second-tier suppliers are questionable as orders for second-tier suppliers will be cut first if demand declines, as can be seen during the global economic crisis when orders have been shifted from marginal to core suppliers.

Related to and accelerated by the MFA phaseout, the global economic crisis, and supply chain rationalization strategies, there are two underlying structural challenges which condition the role of the clothing sector in the industrial development process of LICs today. First, with regard to supply and demand structures, the second half of the twentieth century was characterized by rising demand in the global clothing sector and the replacement of production in developed countries by imports from developing countries. However, since the beginning of the 2000s and recently accelerated by the global economic crisis, demand in major end markets has stagnated as import penetration levels in developed countries had already reached high levels (Palpacuer et al. 2005). Thus, today the growth of clothing exports from a few developing countries is largely at the cost of clothing producers in other developing countries (Morris 2006b). The heightened competition between developing countries has been reinforced by overcapacity in the global clothing industry due to the MFA phaseout and related to the entry of large developing countries such as China and India into clothing exporting (Kaplinsky and Morris 2008). The decline in unit prices of U.S. and EU-15 clothing imports underlines this heightened competition. In this context it has become difficult for suppliers to capture margins and upgrade through participation in global clothing value chains (Palpacuer et al. 2005).

Second, with regard to asymmetric market and power structures, rents in the global clothing value chain do not derive from manufacturing but from design, branding, marketing, R&D, and retailing (Gereffi 1994), which are the core competencies of buyers and protected by high entry barriers. By controlling these high-rent activities buyers yield significant power over other actors in the chain. Power at the buyers' level has further increased due to consolidation among retailers resulting from mergers and acquisitions and the emergence of large discount chains and specialty clothing stores (Morris and Barnes 2009).

However, new global developments may signal a partial shift in competitive and power structures in global clothing value chains. First, some intermediaries and first-tier suppliers, in particular global trading houses and transnational producers, have captured high value-added activities and control far-flung sourcing networks. This potentially signals a shift in the governance structure of global clothing value chains (Appelbaum 2008). Second, global demand structures may change as import demand for clothing in the United States, the EU, and Japan might stagnate while demand will increase in fast-growing emerging countries, as well as in regional and domestic markets. This may also lead to changing governance structures as the role of traditional buyers may decline while developing countries' buyers may increase in importance. It will be central to understand sourcing policies and power structures within clothing value chains of these new buyers and associated entry and upgrading possibilities. Third, there is insecurity about China's future as a competitor to LIC clothing exporters. In the 2000s China at least partly upgraded its production to higher value-added products, a trend that was reversed, however, in the context of the global economic crisis. It is not clear how fast China will move into higher value-added products again in the post-crisis environment. Such a development would increase space for LIC clothing exporters, at least in the low-value basics market segment.

Besides these global trends with regard to entry and upgrading in the global clothing value chain, country dynamics and the specific type of integration into these chains are crucial and can lead to very different outcomes. Thus, after giving an overview of global developments, in particular of the impact of the MFA phaseout, the global economic crisis, changing sourcing policies of global buyers, and changing structural dynamics on the global clothing value chain, on import and export patterns, and on possibilities of LICs to enter and upgrade within global clothing value chains, the following three chapters discuss country-specific experiences. The country studies assess the experience of important clothing exporting LICs from different regions—SSA, Southeast Asia, and South Asia—in the post-quota and post-crisis world and show distinct types of integration into global clothing value chains, associated outcomes, and challenges. The conclusions in chapter 6 come back to the question of what these global and country-specific developments mean for entry and upgrading in global clothing value chains and for using the sector as a springboard for export diversification and industrial development in LICs today.

Notes

1. The United States maintained quotas on T&C imports from 46 countries, the EU from 21 countries.
2. Kaplinsky and Morris (2006) point out three explanations for the higher tariffs on synthetic products. First, synthetics are the area of specialty of the U.S. T&C industry. Second, the U.S. industry considers cheap synthetics as competitors of its cotton products. Third, synthetics were incorporated into the MFA later and the U.S. industry used this to dampen potential future competition in synthetics.
3. These regulations were referred to as "807" and later "9802" in the United States and outward processing trade (OPT) in the EU.
4. Regional cumulation of inputs is allowed in four regional groupings—ASEAN, CACM, the Andean Community, and SAARC. For SSA there is no regional cumulation provision under the GSP (World Bank 2007).
5. The Cotonou Agreement allows for full regional cumulation in all regions.
6. It has to be taken into account that this is an aggregate analysis that masks product- and country-specific variations.
7. USITC reports unit prices (customs value/unit of quantity) for different categories of volumes—dozens, dozen pairs, and numbers. However, due to limited availability of data we can only analyze unit values for products reported in dozens.
8. Eurostat reports volume data in net kilograms.
9. Within the EU-15, the main importer countries were Germany (9.1 percent), the United Kingdom (7 percent), France (6.6 percent), Italy (4.9 percent), Spain (4.4 percent), Belgium (2.9 percent), and the Netherlands (2.5 percent).

10. The HHI can range between $1/n2*10,000$, that is, all countries have the same share, and 10,000, that is, one country exports all, where n designates the total number of countries exporting this product.

11. Cambodia and Pakistan however lost market share in the context of the global economic crisis.

12. In Europe also mail order companies such as Otto Versand, Quelle, Great Universals Stores, and Pinault Printemps Redoute are important in clothing sales but their market share has stagnated.

13. Inditex (Zara) can be classified as a specialty clothing retailer or as a branded manufacturer. It originally disposed of significant in-house manufacturing capacities which have been reduced, however, and today only a small part of quick turnaround and fast fashion products are manufactured in-house.

14. U.S. buyers have developed closer links with global Asian manufacturers than European buyers which have predominantly used the service of domestic and global Asian trading houses (Palpacuer et al. 2005).

15. For example, the trading house Li & Fung, based in Hong Kong SAR, China, is the world's second largest clothing supplier after China (just-style 2009a, 23). Li & Fung is the largest company in Hong Kong SAR, China but there are others in the same league. Korea and Taiwan, China are home to the vast majority of the world's 50 largest clothing exporters (just-style 2009a). Unfortunately, no interviews were conducted with these large global trading houses and transnational producers, although they are importantly involved in sourcing decisions.

16. Large retailers in the United States and in Europe from the discount and the mid-market segment, involving general retailers as well as specialized clothing retailers, were interviewed. In the United States also one branded marketer and one branded manufacturer were interviewed. Mail-order houses and super/hypermarkets were not part of the sample. The interview guidelines and topics were elaborated based on previous studies, in particular Palpacuer et al. (2005), Gibbon (2002a), and Palpacuer (2004).

17. However, direct sourcing involves significant investment in overseas offices. Consequently, resorting to intermediaries may occur to reduce overhead costs and minimize the risks involved with direct sourcing.

18. There are also differences with regard to sourcing countries. For instance the use of overseas agents is particularly common in sourcing from India which Palpacuer et al. (2005) explains by the smaller average size of firms in India compared to most developing countries. Intermediaries are also often used in sourcing from CEE due to the lack of financial depth and thus input sourcing capabilities of most firms there.

19. Although Walmart is using Li & Fund for a large share of its intake Walmart still plans to become more direct in the next years.

20. In European countries there are different regional focuses with regard to regional supplier countries due to different historic, cultural, and language contexts: French buyers focus on Maghreb countries, U.K. buyers on Turkey, and German buyers on CEE countries

21. Production costs consist of different factors, in particular the wage rate, which, together with working days, working hours, and productivity, results in unit labor costs. However, the costs of utilities (such as electricity and water), inputs (in particular fabrics), and transport are also central.

22. Buying departments produce technical specification sheets for each product they purchase. These 'tech sheets' specify the size of the order, the size breakdown, delivery date, fabric, trims, seam measurements, tolerance measurements, printing, embroidery, washing, packaging, and other data (Salm et al. 2002).

23. Some buyers and intermediaries offered financial support to their suppliers. For example, Kohl's provided a 'Supply Chain Finance' program, Wal-Mart launched a 'Supplier Alliance Program,' and Li & Fung became a lender of last resort to factories and small importers (Gereffi and Frederick 2010). But others—in contrast to supporting suppliers—demanded longer payment periods or delayed payments during the crisis due to their own financing problems.

24. Other infrastructural areas (besides transport and logistics) such as electricity and water are seen as 'the business of the suppliers' but buyers see the large effect they have on operational costs and their centrality in suppliers' competitiveness.

25. It has to be taken into account that this is an aggregate analysis which masks product and country specific variations.

CHAPTER 3

Clothing Exports in Low-Income Countries in Sub-Saharan Africa: From Footloose to Regional Integration?

Introduction

This chapter assesses the development of the clothing sectors in the main Sub-Saharan Africa (SSA) low-income country (LIC) clothing exporters and their challenges in the post-quota and post-crisis world. Over the past decade several SSA countries have developed export-orientated clothing sectors, in particular the LICs Kenya, Lesotho, Madagascar, and Swaziland, as well as the middle-income country Mauritius where the process had already started in the 1970s. This took place, first, within a policy framework of 'export-led growth' as governments hoped that the sector would play a central role in (starting) the industrialization process as it did in other countries and, second, in light of quota restrictions in large Asian producing countries and based on agreements securing preferential market access to developed countries, in particular the African Growth and Opportunity Act (AGOA).

Despite exceptional growth of these countries' clothing sectors in the beginning of the 2000s, since around 2004 the industry has declined quite drastically in terms of production, exports, employment, and number of firms in all of the main SSA clothing exporter countries (although to different extents). Direct reasons for this decline are significant changes in the environment for global clothing trade, in particulate the phaseout of the Multi-Fibre Arrangement (MFA) at the end of 2004, as well as changing sourcing strategies of global buyers. The global economic crisis has accelerated these developments through a downturn in global demand and through its accelerating effect on changes in sourcing strategies of global buyers. Besides these 'external' reasons, 'internal' factors are also important in explaining the decline, in particular the specific integration of SSA LICs into global clothing value chains based on MFA quota hopping, and preferential market access dominated by foreign investments and a disintegrated clothing industry with limited local or regional linkages. This specific integration of SSA LICs limits the role the sector can play in promoting export diversification and industrial development and strongly challenges the sustainability of this process. The implementation of suitable policies has therefore become central and urgent for the survival and development of the clothing sector in SSA LICs as well as for the industrial development prospects of these countries more general.

The chapter is structured in the following way. The first and second parts present an overview of recent developments of clothing exports in SSA and the specific ways these countries have been integrating into global clothing value chains; the discussion focuses on export-oriented industrialization, MFA quota hopping, preferential market access, and foreign ownership. In the third part main internal challenges of the clothing sector in SSA LICs are discussed, which are strongly linked to their specific integration into global clothing value chains, and policy recommendations are pointed out. The fourth part focuses on regional integration. It assesses opportunities for and challenges of (i) using the region, in particular South Africa, as an end market by analyzing sourcing strategies of retailers in South Africa, as well as of (ii) regional production networks by analyzing intraregional trade in cotton, yarn, and fabric. The fifth part concludes.

Recent Development of Clothing Exports in SSA: Five Phases

After independence, SSA countries (with the exception of South Africa[1]) adopted two distinct approaches to develop their clothing sectors (Traub-Merz 2006): The first phase, the period of import substitution, lasted in most cases from the end of colonialism until the 1980s and targeted a domestic value chain linking raw materials, textiles, and clothing production for the local market. This approach supported industrialization in several SSA countries but reached its limits due to uncompetitive producers and a missing export focus, monopolistic markets, unsustainable trade and public deficits, and deteriorating public infrastructure. In a second phase some countries opted for an export-orientated industrialization strategy in clothing where export processing zones (EPZs) played a key role. Mauritius was the first SSA country to take this industrialization path, beginning in the 1970s.[2] The industry was started by foreign investment (mostly from Hong Kong SAR, China), which assembled imported textile inputs into clothing. But over the years Mauritius managed to establish backward linkages into textile production and today much of the local production chain is controlled by local capital, in particular since the MFA phaseout when most firms owned by Hong Kong SAR, China left. Other SSA countries followed Mauritius' example and established EPZs or similar regulations and offered incentives to foreign investors for export clothing production. Motivated by MFA quota hopping considerations and preferential market access, foreign direct investment (FDI) increased in the clothing sectors in several SSA countries, in particular when AGOA came into force in 2000/01, and clothing exports expanded considerably. These exports are however concentrated in a small number of countries: Kenya, Lesotho, Swaziland, Madagascar, and Mauritius, and earlier also South Africa (which, today, mostly produces for its domestic market), together account for more than 90 percent of total SSA clothing exports. With the exception of South Africa and Mauritius, production in these countries is largely focused on assembly of imported textile inputs with limited local linkages, and plants are foreign owned and largely integrated into triangular manufacturing networks of Asian-based transnational producers.

Gibbon (2008) divides the recent history of SSA's international clothing trade into three periods—pre-AGOA, AGOA, and post-MFA. Two further periods can be identified—global economic crisis and post-crisis.

Phase 1: Pre-AGOA

The first period extends from 1990 to 1999 (Gibbon 2008). During this phase, besides the MFA quotas (which secured market access for countries with unused quotas), the main preferential treatment offered was duty- and quota-free access to the EU market under the Lomé Convention for African, Caribbean, and Pacific (ACP) countries. Preferential market access to the EU required, however, fulfilling double transformation rules of origin (ROO), which proved to be difficult for most SSA countries. Over the 1990s SSA clothing[3] exports roughly doubled, reaching around US$2 billion in 1999 (see table 3.1). Around 60 percent of the exports went to the EU, mostly to the United Kingdom and France; the remainder went almost exclusively to the United States. The majority of exports originated from Mauritius (nearly 50 percent of total SSA clothing exports in 1999). South Africa and increasingly Madagascar were the only two other significant clothing exporters to the EU market. Mauritius and Madagascar traditionally supplied the U.K. and French markets and South African firms typically exported to the United Kingdom. All three countries have local textile mills and thus were capable of satisfying EU double transformation ROO required to obtain preferential market access.[4] Mauritius also dominated U.S. exports but in the second half of the 1990s Kenya, Lesotho, Madagascar, and South Africa also became important exporters to the United States.

Phase 2: AGOA

The second period started with AGOA in 2000/01 and lasted until 2004. SSA clothing exports increased to around US$3.2 billion in 2004 (see table 3.1) and dramatically changed its composition. Exports to the EU stagnated while those to the United States more than doubled peaking at US$1.8 billion for all SSA AGOA beneficiaries in 2004 (see figure 3.1). The share of SSA clothing exports in global clothing exports increased to 1.3 percent in 2004; in the United States SSA's import share increased from 1 percent in 1996 to 2.6 percent in 2004. However, only a handful of the eligible countries have been able to take advantage of these preferences: around 95 percent of clothing exports to the United States from SSA originated in Lesotho, Madagascar, Kenya, Swaziland, Mauritius, and South Africa (see table 3.2 and figure 3.2). Of these countries, South Africa and Mauritius were existing exporters before AGOA. Thus, AGOA has mostly benefited Lesotho, which became the largest SSA clothing exporter to the United States, followed by Kenya, Madagascar, and Swaziland (see table 3.3 and figure 3.3). The vast majority of clothing exports (with the exception of Madagascar) from these countries went to the United States, which implies that the clothing sector in these countries is highly dependent on AGOA preferences. Until 2004 the growth of the clothing sector in the latter group was spectacular. Lesotho's exports grew over 500 percent since 1996 whereas Kenya, Madagascar, and Swaziland's exports grew more than 10-fold. In contrast, EU exports stagnated after 2000 and continued to be dominated by Mauritius; only Madagascar and South Africa were other significant exporters to the EU (see table 3.4 and figure 3.4).

Table 3.1. SSA's Clothing Exports

	1995	1998	2001	2002	2003	2004	2005	2006	2007	2008
Total exports (US$ million)	1,623	1,999	2,253	2,287	2,876	3,235	2,794	2,764	2,991	2,791
Growth rate (%)		7.3	7.8	1.5	25.8	12.5	–13.6	–1.1	8.2	–6.7
Global share (%)	1.1	1.1	1.2	1.1	1.3	1.3	1.0	1.0	0.9	0.8
U.S. share (%)	34	39	44	51	56	58	55	49	46	44
EU-15 share (%)	58	54	45	37	33	31	33	38	39	40
Woven (%)	54	50	46	46	45	42	43	42	41	42
Knit (%)	46	50	54	54	55	58	57	58	59	58

Source: UN COMTRADE.
Note: Values in million US$.

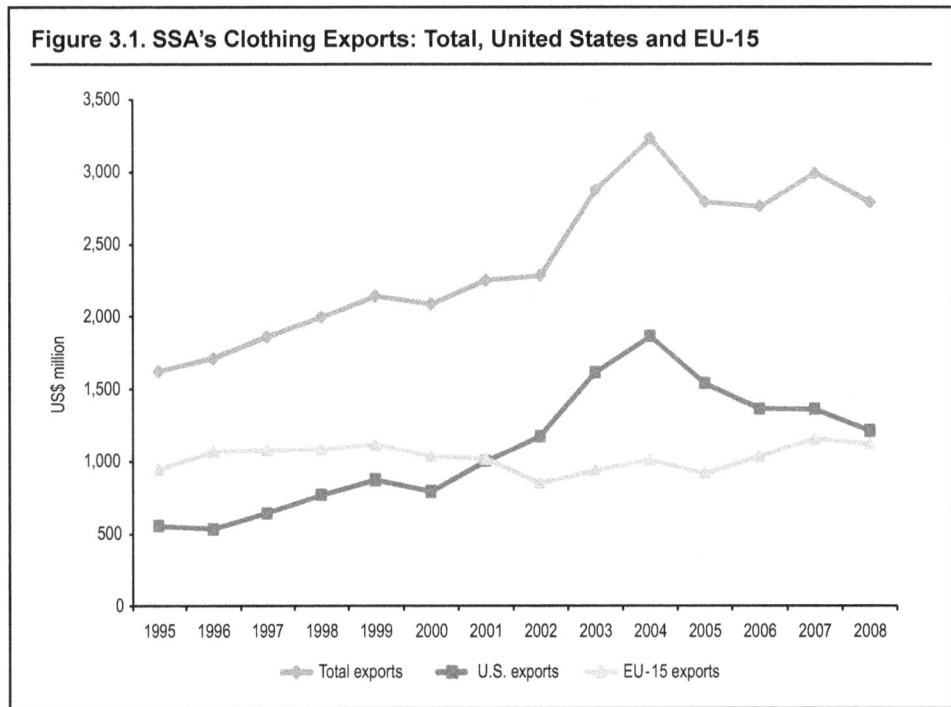

Figure 3.1. SSA's Clothing Exports: Total, United States and EU-15

Source: UN COMTRADE.
Note: Values in million US$.

Figure 3.2. SSA's Main Clothing Exporters

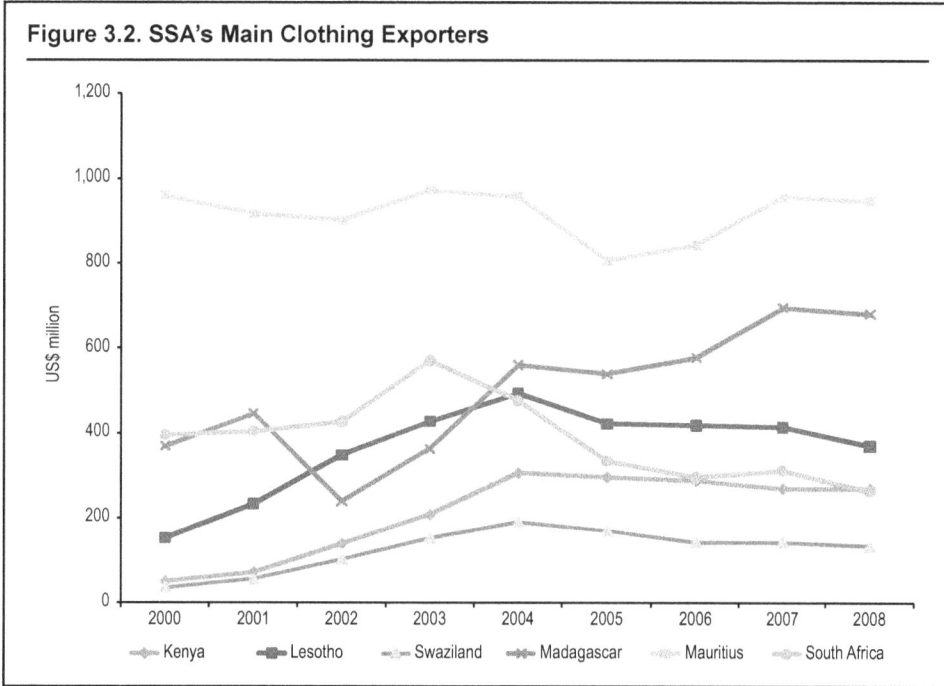

Source: UN COMTRADE.
Note: Values in million US$.

Table 3.2. SSA's Main Clothing Exporters

	2000	2001	2002	2003	2004	2005	2006	2007	2008
Total exports (US$ million)	2,090	2,253	2,287	2,876	3,235	2,794	2,764	2,991	2,791
Global share (%)	1.1	1.2	1.1	1.3	1.3	1.0	1.0	0.9	0.8
6 exporters (US$ million)	1,964	2,129	2,159	2,696	2,986	2,569	2,568	2,792	2,666
SSA share (%)	94.0	94.5	94.4	93.7	92.3	91.9	92.9	93.3	95.5
Mauritius (%)	46.0	40.7	39.5	33.8	29.6	28.9	30.5	32.0	34.0
U.S. share (%)	23	21	20	21	24	26	31	31	29
Madagascar (%)	17.6	19.8	10.5	12.6	17.3	19.3	20.9	23.3	24.4
U.S. share (%)	31	42	40	58	62	55	44	44	43
Lesotho (%)	7.3	10.4	15.2	14.9	15.3	15.1	15.1	13.8	13.3
U.S. share (%)	96	96	98	98	98	97	97	97	97
Kenya (%)	2.4	3.2	6.1	7.3	9.5	10.6	10.4	9.0	9.7
U.S. Share (%)	93	95	97	97	97	96	97	96	96
South Africa (%)	19.0	17.9	18.7	19.9	14.7	12.0	10.7	10.4	9.5
U.S. share (%)	12	10	8	5	16	24	27	39	40
Swaziland (%)	1.8	2.5	4.5	5.3	5.9	6.1	5.2	4.8	4.8
U.S. share (%)	91	90	93	98	99	99	100	99	99

Source: UN COMTRADE.
Note: Values in million US$.

Figure 3.3. SSA Clothing Exports to the United States

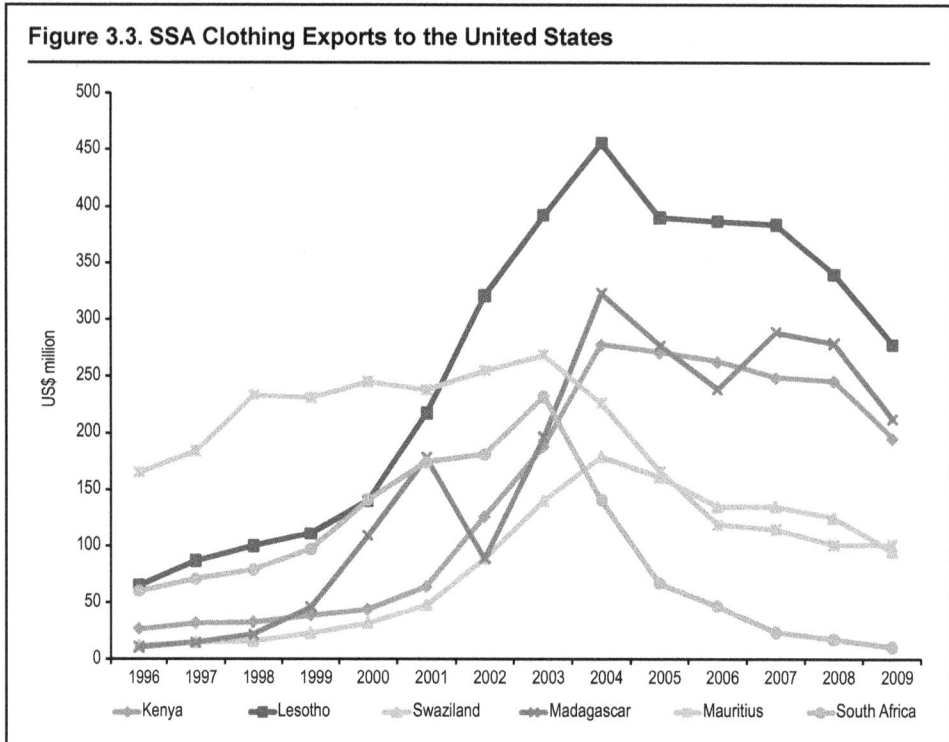

Source: USITC.
Note: Values in million US$.

Table 3.3. SSA's Clothing Exports to the United States

	1996	2000	2001	2002	2003	2004	2005	2006	2007	2008	2009
Total exports (US$ million)	360	747	953	1,098	1,510	1,757	1,463	1,291	1,294	1,151	922
U.S. share (%)	1.0	1.3	1.6	1.9	2.4	2.6	2.1	1.8	1.7	1.6	1.4
Six exporters (US$ million)	340	711	919	1,061	1,417	1,603	1,332	1,190	1,196	1,109	892
SSA share (%)	94.4	95.2	96.4	96.6	93.8	91.2	91.0	92.2	92.4	96.4	96.7
Lesotho (%)	18.1	18.7	22.8	29.2	26.0	26.0	26.7	30.0	29.7	29.5	30.2
Madagascar (%)	3.1	14.6	18.7	8.1	13.0	18.4	18.9	18.5	22.3	24.2	23.0
Kenya (%)	7.5	5.9	6.7	11.5	12.5	15.8	18.5	20.4	19.2	21.4	21.1
Mauritius (%)	45.8	32.8	25.0	23.2	17.8	12.9	11.3	9.2	8.9	8.8	11.0
Swaziland (%)	3.3	4.3	5.0	8.1	9.3	10.2	11.0	10.5	10.4	10.9	10.3
South Africa (%)	16.7	18.9	18.3	16.5	15.4	8.0	4.6	3.6	1.9	1.6	1.2

Source: USITC.
Note:Values in million US$.

Figure 3.4. SSA Clothing Exports to the EU-15

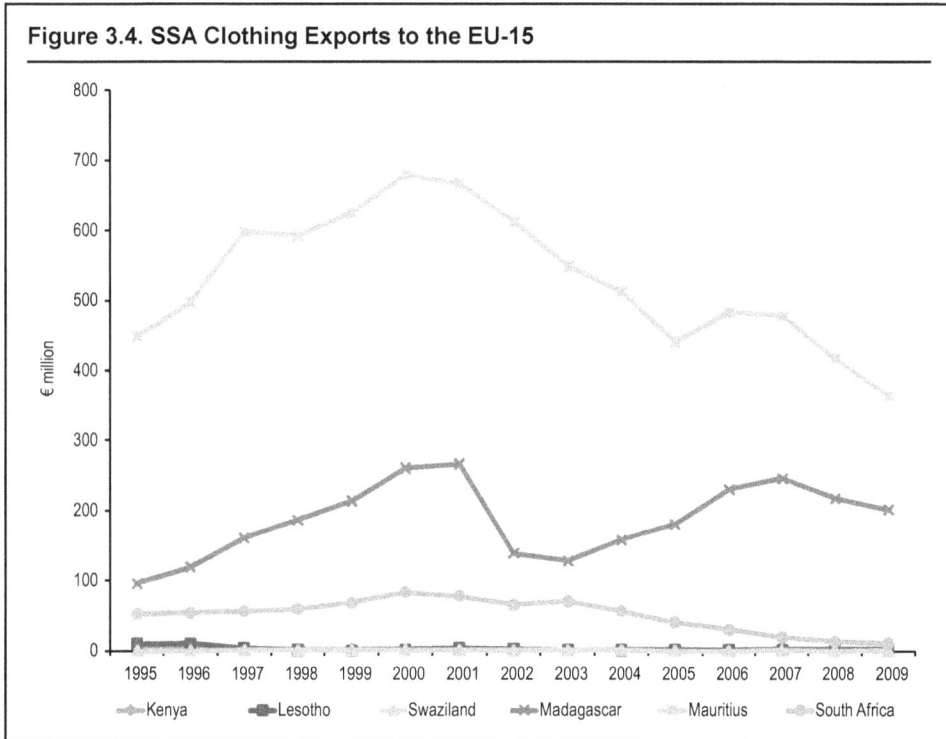

Source: EUROSTAT.
Note: Values in million euro.

Table 3.4. SSA's Clothing Exports to the EU-15

	1995	2000	2001	2002	2003	2004	2005	2006	2007	2008	2009
Total exports (€ million)	661	1,078	1,072	860	783	763	686	770	770	672	592
EU-15 share (%)	1.3	1.4	1.3	1.1	1.0	0.9	0.8	0.8	0.8	0.7	0.6
Six exporters (€ million)	611	1,029	1,018	820	750	732	665	746	745	651	579
SSA share (%)	92.4	95.4	94.9	95.4	95.8	95.9	96.9	96.8	96.8	96.8	97.8
Mauritius (%)	67.8	63.0	62.2	71.2	70.1	67.2	64.2	62.7	62.0	62.1	61.5
Madagascar (%)	14.4	24.2	24.9	16.1	16.4	20.7	26.3	29.9	31.9	32.3	34.0
South Africa (%)	7.9	7.8	7.3	7.6	9.0	7.4	5.9	3.9	2.5	2.0	1.8
Lesotho (%)	1.5	0.2	0.4	0.2	0.1	0.1	0.1	0.1	0.2	0.3	0.3
Kenya (%)	0.7	0.2	0.2	0.1	0.2	0.3	0.4	0.1	0.1	0.2	0.1
Swaziland (%)	0.0	0.1	0.1	0.0	0.0	0.1	0.0	0.0	0.0	0.0	0.0

Source: EUROSTAT.
Note: Values in million euro.

The impact of AGOA on the industrialization process and wage employment creation in several SSA countries is clear from the rapid increase of clothing exports after 2000/01. While in Lesotho, Kenya, Swaziland, and Madagascar the large majority of U.S. clothing exports used AGOA (in 2004 between 97 and 98 percent), Mauritius, and South Africa were not that strongly relying on AGOA. Until 2003 they only exported 50 percent and 55 percent respectively through AGOA, partly because they had to fulfill triple transformation ROO. This started to change in 2004, when the proportion of AGOA-qualifying clothing exports as a percentage of total clothing exports rose to 81 percent in South Africa and 65 percent in Mauritius. However, in both cases and even more in South Africa, this can be explained by a large reduction of non-AGOA clothing exports to the United States (see below, Morris 2006b).

For all SSA countries together the share of clothing and textile exports in their total exports is rather low, accounting for 2.8 percent and 0.5 percent respectively, which is mainly due to the large share of raw materials, minerals, and oil in exports from the region. However, clothing has been by far the most significant manufactured export from SSA, in particular since AGOA came into force in 2000/01. If South Africa is excluded, just over one half of all SSA manufactured exports comprise clothing (Kaplinsky and Morris 2008). For some SSA countries clothing exports are particularly significant, including Lesotho (accounting for 97 percent of total exports), followed by Mauritius (51 percent), Madagascar (41 percent), Swaziland (25 percent), and Kenya (12 percent). In 2002 clothing exports accounted for virtually all manufactured exports in Lesotho and Swaziland and for 50 percent of Lesotho's GDP. In Kenya in 2004 clothing firms accounted for nearly 20 percent of all formal sector manufacturing employment (Kaplinsky and Morris 2006).

Phase 3: Post-MFA

The third period started around 2004/05. There was uncertainty in 2004 due to the first scheduled phaseout of the AGOA Third Country Fabric (TCF) derogation,[5] but more importantly due to the MFA phaseout, which heightened competition from large Asian producer countries such as China, India, Bangladesh, and Vietnam. After slower growth in 2004 SSA clothing exports fell in 2005 in all main SSA clothing exporter countries. From 2000 to 2004 the share of SSA clothing exports in total global clothing exports increased from 1.1 percent to 1.3 percent but in the following years it decreased again reaching 1 percent in 2005 and 0.8 percent in 2008. Total SSA clothing exports decreased by 15 percent between 2004 and 2006 and 20 percent between 2004 and 2008 (see table 3.1). With regard to the United States, exports declined by one third between 2004 and 2008 (see table 3.3 and figure 3.3). SSA clothing exports to the EU decreased by 12 percent between 2004 and 2008 (see table 3.4 and figure 3.4). Hence, besides generally decreasing exports, the dynamics in the U.S. and EU markets were different, which can be seen in Mauritius and Madagascar. While many Asian owned firms serving the U.S. market have left Mauritius in the context of the MFA phaseout, locally owned firms have fared comparatively well by offering more capabilities and exporting higher-value products to the EU market. Overall, exports to the EU from Mauritius had already started to decrease in 2001 but increased in 2006 and 2007. Exports to the EU from Madagascar increased between 2003 and 2007 as the country switched its export focus from the United States to the EU (Gibbon 2008).

Despite a significant general decline in SSA clothing exports after 2004 there have been different developments in the main SAA clothing exporter countries. The highest export decline in the context of the MFA phaseout took place in South Africa. Clothing exports peaked in 2003 in South Africa and then declined by 17 percent and 26 percent in 2004 and 2005, which led to a decline in clothing exports by over 50 percent between 2003 and 2008. Clothing exports to the United States declined by 92 percent between 2003 and 2008. Besides the MFA phaseout, the appreciation of the rand had an important role in declining exports in South Africa. Mauritius clothing exports also peaked in 2003 and decreased by 17 percent between 2003 and 2005. Exports to the United States decreased by 62 percent between 2003 and 2008 but exports to the EU remained relatively stable. Madagascar's clothing exports only declined by 4 percent in 2005 as they declined significantly in 2002 (by nearly 50 percent) due to political instability. U.S. exports declined by 14 percent between 2004 and 2008 but exports to the EU increased, which led to a diversion of exports to the EU. In Madagascar the depreciation of the currency in 2004 could cushion the impact of the MFA phaseout. In Kenya, clothing exports to the United States declined by 3 percent in 2005 and 2006, in Lesotho by 14 percent and 1 percent, and in Swaziland by 10 percent and 15 percent, respectively. Over the period 2004 to 2008 total exports declined by 12 percent, 25 percent, and 30 percent in Kenya, Lesotho, and Swaziland respectively. The declines in Kenya, Lesotho, Swaziland, and Madagascar were less dramatic than expected and once the 'quota hopping firms' had left, the decline came to an end in 2006 and 2007. These countries (with the exception of Madagascar) had also appreciating exchange rates but wage rates are lower than in South Africa and Mauritius and the TCF derogation was expanded, which gave investors some security.[6] However, despite different immediate impacts of the MFA phaseout, over the whole period 2004 to 2008, clothing exports and in particular AGOA clothing exports declined significantly in all SSA main clothing exporting countries.

Competition in the clothing sector has increased significantly since the MFA phaseout, which has affected SSA clothing exporters not only through reduced orders but also through decreasing prices. In particular, prices for basic woven, including denim, and knit products—which China produces in abundance—have decreased considerably since 2005. Thus, one of the most pronounced effects of the MFA phaseout has been a reduction in prices received by clothing manufactures (Morris 2006b). Most firms interviewed reported receiving lower prices for the same product in 2005 and later years than in 2004. Price reductions reported for different products ranged between 5 to 20 percent from 2004 to 2005/06.

The reduction in clothing exports from SSA has had huge consequences with regard to the number of firms and employment. Although exports have been already affected severely by the MFA phaseout, the impact on employment has been even more critical, particularly for Lesotho and Swaziland (Kaplinsky and Morris 2006). In Lesotho employment declined from 54,000 to 40,000 between 2004 and 2005, which accounts for a 26 percent decline, in Swaziland from 28,000 to 16,000 (43 percent, Kaplinsky and Morris 2008) and in Kenya from 32,000 to 28,000 (13 percent). It is not just the degree of job losses that is alarming but the nature of the jobs lost. It mostly involves unskilled and female jobs where the impact on the family income and on poverty is large (Kaplinsky and Morris 2006).

Phase 4: Global Economic Crisis

A fourth phase can be added to Gibbon's (2008) classification, which started in 2008. Since 2008/09 there have been further declines in exports associated, first, with the abolition of safeguard quotas on U.S. and EU imports of clothing from China, and, second, with reductions in U.S. and EU clothing imports as a result of the global economic crisis. Overall U.S. clothing imports decreased by 3.3 percent in 2008 and by 12 percent in 2009. In the EU slower growth of clothing imports of 1.5 percent in 2008 was followed by a reduction of 5.2 percent in 2009. Total SSA clothing exports declined by 7 percent in 2008 (see table 3.1). For the United States and the EU there is also data available for 2009, which shows that SSA clothing exports to the United States declined by 11 percent in 2008 and 20 percent in 2009 and to the EU by 13 percent in 2008 and 12 percent in 2009 (see tables 3.3. and 3.4). Similar to the impact of the MFA phaseout, the country-level impacts of the crisis on SSA clothing exports are nuanced. Exports from Mauritius to the United States declined by 12 percent between 2007 and 2009, and to the EU by 24 percent. Exports from Madagascar to the United States declined by 27 percent and to the EU by 18 percent. Swaziland, Lesotho, and Kenya accounted for export declines to the United States of 30 percent, 28 percent, and 22 percent between 2007 and 2009 respectively. These declines are in the same magnitude and for some countries larger than declines related to the MFA phaseout.

In the case of the EU there was also a positive development in 2008/09 as those countries that have initiated an interim Economic Partnership Agreement (EPA) with the EU[7] have been able to export clothing under single transformation ROO without losing preferential status since 2008. Despite these simplified ROO, EU imports of clothing from SSA countries have declined since the beginning of 2008 as shown above. However, it is difficult to disentangle the impact of the phaseout of the China safeguards, the global economic crisis, and the EPAs. It can be concluded that there is not any compelling evidence yet that simplified ROOs for clothing in the EU market have brought the gains from similar provisions provided under AGOA. However, this has to be seen in the context of the crisis as buyers are reducing orders and consolidating their supply base, which makes it difficult to enter sourcing networks and increase exports—irrespective of which ROO requirements are in place.

Besides decreasing orders, prices decreased again in 2008 and 2009, which accelerated trends in the context of the MFA phaseout. All firms interviewed reported that the pressure on prices from buyers has increased due to the crisis and that they had to reduce prices on average by 5 to 10 percent (with important product-specific variations). Besides prices, lead times also have been reduced and contract time has been shortened; this has increased flexibility on the buyers' side but limited planning possibilities on the suppliers' side. The crisis also led to financing problems as access to credits from banks has become more difficult, costs have increased, and credit lines from suppliers have decreased, in particular from textile mills. Except for a handful of incidences, buyers have generally not reduced their credit line demands to support suppliers.

Phase 5: Post-Crisis?

Industry dynamics and the competitive situation in the global clothing industry may change after the crisis. Earlier trends such as increased importance of lead times and flexibility, demanding more services and capabilities from suppliers, as well as generally supply chain rationalization strategies have been accelerated in the context of the global economic crisis (see chapter 2). Price reductions demanded during the crisis will likely become permanent. Competition in the low-value segment where SSA LICs are concentrated has further increased as some more advanced countries (in particular China) that had moved up to higher-value products in the 2000s have moved again to lower-end production in the context of the global economic crisis. It is not clear how fast China will move into higher value-added products again in the post-crisis environment. In addition, import structures may also change post-crisis as the way out of the global economic crisis may be driven by developing countries. Although the United States and EU markets will remain the major import markets, at least for some time, other markets will gain in importance. In particular, clothing imports may increase in fast-growing emerging countries such as China, India, Brazil, and the Russian Federation. In this context, regional end markets, in particular South Africa in the case of SSA, also may become central to substitute for reduced exports to developed countries' markets.

The above discussion shows that after exceptional growth of SSA's clothing exports from 2000/01 to 2004, which can be mainly attributed to AGOA, exports have declined drastically since 2005. This has had a large impact on production, the number of firms, and employment in all main SSA clothing exporter countries. The clothing sector in SSA LICs faces critical challenges that have to be addressed to increase competitiveness and exports. These challenges are closely related to the specific integration of SSA LICs into global clothing value chains, which is discussed next.

SSA LICs and the Global Clothing Value Chain: Quota Hopping, Preferences, and Foreign Ownership

The recent rapid development of export clothing sectors in some SSA LICs has been based on export-oriented industrialization strategies where EPZs played a central role as well as quota hopping and preferential market access. It has been characterized by a strong reliance on mostly Asian investment and by limited local involvement and linkages. This specific integration into global clothing value chains has led to vulnerability as evidenced by the decline of the sector in the context of the MFA phaseout and the global economic crisis. It further limits the role the sector can play in promoting export diversification and industrial development and strongly challenges the sustainability of this process.

Export-Oriented Industrialization and EPZs

Following the example of Mauritius in the 1970s, in the 1990s some SSA countries opted for an export-oriented industrialization strategy in clothing. The establishment of EPZs played a key role in these strategies. EPZs are special zones that are isolated from the domestic economy. In these zones, investors are either not or only to a limited extent allowed to supply local consumers as production is geared towards exports. Domestic investors may be granted access but EPZs are usually schemes to attract FDI. EPZs are a legal framework for export production where governments commonly provide a package of incentives such as tax holidays, duty free imports, provision of infrastructure, lower fees for public services like water and electricity, and subsidized land and factory shells (Traub-Merz 2006). These incentives should correct for administrative, infrastructure-related, and utility supply problems investors face in the rest of the country. Several SSA countries have adopted such policies since the 1990s (following Mauritius, which signed the first EPZ law in 1971), including Kenya (1990), Madagascar (1995), Zimbabwe (1995), Malawi, Namibia, and Zambia. Overall EPZs in SSA have not been very successful in attracting investment and generating production and employment (see Farole 2010). This is problematic as EPZs are expensive policies to host countries due to direct costs in form of infrastructure investments and indirect costs in form of lost tax revenue. Further, although EPZs were meant to attract a range of manufacturing industries, they have usually been dominated by clothing factories. Apart from Zimbabwe, where agro-businesses are dominant, all other SSA EPZs show a clear bias towards clothing production, which accounted for two thirds of all EPZ employment and possibly an even higher share of output in 2005 (Traub-Merz 2006). Hence, in the clothing sector in SSA EPZs have played an important role in attracting investment, initially in Mauritius and later in Kenya and Madagascar. The two other important clothing exporters, Lesotho and Swaziland, have no EPZ laws but do have regulations that offer similar incentives called industrial zones, which have also been critical for investments in the clothing sector. However, besides the importance of EPZ-like regulations and investment-friendly environments in host countries, two other factors are the main drivers of recent clothing export growth in several SSA countries—MFA quota hopping and preferential market access.

MFA Quota Hopping

The recent development of export-oriented clothing sectors in several SSA countries was based on FDI. The main motivation of FDI in the clothing sector in SSA in the 1980s and 1990s was MFA quota hopping as predominantly East Asian producers took advantage of SSA's unused quota access to the United States and the EU[8]—initially in Mauritius in the 1970s and later on in South Africa, Lesotho, Swaziland, Madagascar, and Kenya.[9] Subsequently, preferential market access further increased the sector's attractiveness for FDI. For few countries preferential market access to the EU already played a role in the 1980s and 1990s—South Africa, Mauritius, and to a lesser extent Madagascar (and for a short period also for Lesotho due to its special ROO derogation with the EU until 1997). Since 2000/01, preferential market access to the United States under AGOA and the TCF derogation have become the main motivations of clothing FDI in SSA. However, the quick response to AGOA was only possible because investors were already located in SSA countries. In Lesotho, and to a lesser extent in Swaziland, the existence of investors from Taiwan, China in 2000 allowed quick expansion of existing capacities and use of existing networks to establish new firms. The same was true in Kenya and Madagascar, where in particular foreign-owned firms were already exporting to the United States before AGOA.

Thus, until the end of 2004 SSA clothing exports were protected by secured market access and the cost-of-buying import quota, as well as by the percentage duty rate due to preferential market access to the EU and later the United States. In most quota-bound countries quota was traded for product categories, which added a cost to the landed price. For instance, quota prices for the U.S. market accounted for around US$32.5 and US$39 per dozen for knit men's shirts and woven men's trousers respectively in China in July 2003[10] (see table 3.5, Gibbon 2003a). Estimates state that the MFA quotas provided SSA firms with a cost advantage of around 20 percent in addition to preferences. With the phaseout of the MFA at the end of 2004 and the phaseout of the safeguard measures at the end of 2008, the quota hopping motivation for FDI was gone. Producers in SSA can no longer depend on displaced production from quota-bound countries and many Asian-owned firms left in the context of the MFA phaseout.

Table 3.5. China-U.S. Quota Costs, July 2003

Item	Quota price per dozen, in US$
Cotton based clothing	
knit men's shirts	32.50
knit t-shirts	32.50
women men's trousers	39.00
woven women's dresses	30.50
Synthetic based clothing	
knit women's skirts	35.00
knit sweaters	23.50
woven men's suites	90.00
woven women's dresses	37.00

Source: www.chinaquota.com, Gibbon 2003a.

Preferential Market Access

Although quotas are gone, tariffs remain important in the clothing sector. Hence, preferential market access plays a decisive role for SSA clothing exports—for the EU from the 1970s/80s and for the United States from 2000/01 onwards. In the case of the EU, relevant agreements include the EU Generalized System of Preferences (GSP), the Everything but Arms Initiative (EBA) for least developed countries (LDCs) as well as the Lomé Convention and its successors, the Cotonou Agreement and the EPAs (see chapter 2 for a discussion of these agreements). Generally preferential market access to the EU requires fulfilling double transformation ROO.[11] However, this changed with the EPAs. Thus, for countries that signed interim EPAs in 2008 and 2009, including the five main SSA clothing exporter countries, ROO requirements changed to single transformation. Only South Africa has not signed an interim EPA and still has to fulfill double transformation ROO. Relevant agreements for the United States include the GSP (which however excludes most T&C products) and AGOA. AGOA was signed in May 2000 and has subsequently been extended and modified three times (from AGOA I to AGOA IV). The current program extends until 2015. The principal element of AGOA is an enhanced set of trade preferences with increased commodity coverage beyond that of GSP (additional 1,800 tariff lines). In order to be eligible for AGOA[12] countries must be eligible under GSP. 45 of 48 SSA countries are today GSP eligible and 37 of those are AGOA eligible. In terms of improved market access the potential impact of AGOA differs between lesser developed countries (defined as countries that had a GNP per capita of less than US$1,500 in 1998)[13] and others. For lesser developed countries it matters whether they are able to access the preferences on clothing products[14] because most other products liberalized under AGOA had already been liberalized under the GSP. To be eligible for AGOA's clothing rules, countries need to fulfill additional requirements: they need procedures in place to prevent transshipments and use of counterfeit documents, which requires an export visa system approved by U.S. Customs.[15] AGOA ROO requirements state that clothing has to be made 85 percent from yarns, fabrics, and thread from the United States or produced in AGOA beneficiary countries (limited to a maximum of 3.5 percent of all U.S. clothing imports). Thus, ROO stipulate a triple transformation (raw material to yarn to fabrics to clothing, which involves spinning, weaving/knitting, and clothing production). However, a special rule applies to lesser developed countries that allows them duty-free access for clothing made from fabrics originating anywhere in the world—the TCF derogation, which was initially granted until September 2004 but then extended twice to September 2007 and September 2012. Of the 37 AGOA-eligible countries, 26 are eligible for clothing benefits and 24 for the TCF derogation.[16] The only major countries that were initially not eligible for the use of the TCF derogation are Mauritius and South Africa. However, Mauritius received a derogation for one year in 2004–05 and could extend this derogation to the period 2009 to 2012. Thus, only South Africa requires triple transformation to qualify under AGOA. A large majority of clothing exports currently eligible for AGOA preferences uses the TCF derogation. In 2003, of all clothing products shipped under AGOA, 76 percent were exported using TCF; in 2004 this share accounted for more than 90 percent in Lesotho, Swaziland, Kenya, and Madagascar.

Kaplinsky and Morris (2006, 2008) stress that due to the TCF derogation the degree of effective subsidy offered to AGOA exporters in the United States is substantially higher than the nominal tariff rate. Tariff rates on clothing products that AGOA countries export to the United States range between 16 and 32 percent. However, as AGOA clothing products can use (duty-free) fabrics and other inputs from outside of SSA and these imported inputs account for up to 60 percent of costs, the implicit effective rate of subsidy is substantially higher than the nominal rates of protection. These effective rates range between 27 and 84 percent for representative exported products (Kaplinsky and Morris 2008). The same is now the case for the EU market as EPAs allow using third-country imports for clothing exports to the EU. Kaplinsky and Morris (2006) give the examples of two products from two factories in Swaziland: The first product is cotton denim jeans, where the nominal duty preference is 16.6 percent and the second is synthetic women's underwear, where the nominal duty preference is 28.2 percent. The rates of effective subsidy are much higher as the nominal duty applies to the whole value of the product where much is made up of imported material. In the case of denim jeans, the effective rate of subsidy is 27.7 percent, and in the case of synthetic women's underwear, it is 83.9 percent. The effective rate is higher in the case of synthetics due to the higher value of imported inputs as can be seen in the breakdown in table 3.6.

Table 3.6. Effective Rates of Subsidy in Two Swaziland Clothing Factories

	Denim jeans (%)	Synthetic women's underwear (%)
Labor costs	45	30
Fabric and other imported inputs	40	66
Utilities	3	1
Distribution	2	2
Other (agent fee, transport, etc.)	10	1
Total	100	100
Duty preference	16.6	28.2
Effective rate of subsidy	27.7	83.9

Source: Kaplinsky and Morris (2008, 266).

The discussion on ROO has been controversial. Appropriate ROO are critical in any preferential trade agreement to ensure that the actual products of trading partners receive preferential market access and that exporters from third countries do not use transshipment and 'light' processing to circumvent external tariffs (Brenton and Oezden 2009). The official motivation behind restrictive ROO is to support backward integration and also regional integration as cumulation provisions often allow for the use of regionally produced inputs. However, restrictive ROO threaten the competitiveness of beneficiary countries in SSA as they are not able to source inputs from the most competitive source globally. In addition, the textile sector is—partly due to its capital, scale, and electricity-intensive nature—nearly nonexistent or uncompetitive in many SSA countries (see below). Furthermore, it is questionable if investment in textile capacity can be encouraged by ROO on the content of clothing exports (Brenton and Hoppe 2006; Brenton and Oezden 2009). The EU ROO that required double transformation were in place for decades and exports to the EU from SSA were marginal[17] (with the exception of South Africa and Mauritius, which disposed of local fabric production, and later Madagascar, which used Mauritian fabric). In strong contrast to the limited use of EU preferential market access, AGOA led to significant increases in exports and a large part of this came from TCF production. Thus, the experience of AGOA compared to EU preferential trade agreements underlines the central role of ROO on the impact of preferential market access. Moreover, restrictive ROO have become problematic in light of technological changes, global trade liberalization, and the associated fragmentation of production processes and the development of global networks of sourcing. Strict ROO constrain the ability of firms to integrate into these global production networks (Brenton and Oezden 2009).

Nevertheless, there are some examples in SSA where ROO requirements encouraged investment in textile production. In Mauritius ROO requirements encouraged building up a vertically integrated sector. EU ROO demanded double transformation and encouraged the establishment of fabric mills in Mauritius, in particular in the knit segment. Also, the triple transformation ROO of AGOA encouraged some investment in spinning mills, which was supported by the government through fiscal incentives. But the ROO requirement was only one motivation for backward linkages; others were lead times, flexibility, and control with regard to production and quality. All these factors are important for the market segment in which most Mauritian firms are operating—mid-market chains that demand higher quality, shorter lead times, and higher flexibility. Another positive example is the US$100 million investment in a denim fabric mill in Lesotho in 2004. Representatives from Nien-Hsing, the investor from Taiwan, China, stated that one of the main motivations to invest in the denim mill was the expected phaseout of the TCF derogation in 2007.[18] A second Taiwan, China-owned jeans producer in Lesotho (CGM) purchased a denim plant in South Africa in 2002, also motivated by the TCF phaseout. Representatives from the Lesotho National Development Corporation (LNDC) who have tried to attract investment in a knitted fabric mill stated that it would be easier to attract investors if the TCF derogation were phased out. In Swaziland the investment of TexRay in a spinning mill and more importantly in a knitting mill in 2002 and 2006 respectively was also partially motivated by the expected phaseout of the TCF derogation in 2007.

Besides varying ROO (in the past), another difference between United States and EU trade preferences is the value of the duty-free access, which is lower in the case of the EU. As duties on certain clothing products are higher in the United States than in the EU, the preferential access has more value. Average MFN tariffs on clothing in the United States are 10.8 percent but there are considerable variations between product types, with duties on cotton products ranging between 13 and 17 percent and duties on synthetic products ranging between 25 and 32 percent. In the EU average MFN tariffs account for 11.5 percent with tariffs varying, however, only between 0 and 12 percent. Furthermore, EU preferences are accessible for all ACP countries and LDCs, and, thus, for some large Asian clothing producer countries, including Cambodia and Bangladesh. AGOA in contrast is only accessible for SSA countries. Besides the importance of regulatory differences between market access to the United States and the EU (in particular ROO, tariff levels, and access to preferences) in explaining different export developments, another important factor is differences in end markets with regard to consumer preferences, types of retailers, and buyers' sourcing policies (see below).

Preferential market access remains central for SSA clothing exports, in particular AGOA, but the potential impact of single transformation ROO under the EPAs still has to be seen. Quota hopping and preferential market access agreements have led to a specific integration of SSA LICs into the global clothing value chain that is dominated by foreign (mostly Asian) investment.

Foreign Ownership

With the exception of Mauritius (and South Africa), the majority of exporting firms in SSA's main clothing exporting countries is foreign-owned and part of triangular manufacturing networks. In Kenya[19] and Madagascar there are few local firms; in Lesotho and Swaziland there are virtually no locally owned clothing export firms.[20] In Mauritius the situation is different: because most Hong Kong SAR, China-owned firms that had invested in the 1970s and 1980s left after 2004, the majority of firms (around 85 percent) have been locally owned since 2004. Foreign ownership is further very concentrated. Until very recently, in Lesotho and Swaziland nearly all foreign investment came from Taiwan, China,[21] although in the last few years South African investment has increased in importance. In Kenya and Madagascar the picture is more mixed but foreign investment is also dominated by Asian capital, including investors from the NIEs Taiwan, China and Hong Kong SAR, China, as well as from Singapore, China, India, and Sri Lanka. In Kenya investors also come from the United Arab Emirates, and in Madagascar from Europe (in particular France) and Mauritius. Foreign ownership is not a problem per se because—with the exception of the Republic of Korea, Hong Kong SAR, China, and Taiwan, China—all clothing sectors of late-industrializing countries were built by foreigners (Birnbaum 2009). However, most countries have developed and moved from an industry dominated by foreigners to one owned, at least partially, by local industrialists. Up to now, in SSA this shift has only taken place in Mauritius (and South Africa where locals were also involved in starting the sector). With regard to triangular manufacturing networks, in Lesotho and Swaziland, firms owned by Taiwan, China are subsidiaries of transnational producers and part of their manufacturing networks. In Kenya and Madagascar, investment from initial transnational producers located in East Asian NIEs is not dominating. But other foreign-owned firms generally are also part of foreign-governed sourcing and merchandising networks. In Kenya for instance Indian manufacturing networks have an important role.

Ownership structures are important as they determine how supplier firms are linked to global production and distribution networks (Natsuda et al. 2009). Most foreign-owned firms in SSA are local affiliates of large Asian firms and are integrated into triangular manufacturing networks of transnational producers from Taiwan, China, Hong Kong SAR, China, and Korea, as well as from Singapore, Malaysia, China, India, and Sri Lanka. Thus, factories in SSA are integrated into global clothing value chains through their foreign parent or sister companies (see figure 3.5). This type of integration has on the one hand led to access to global sourcing and merchandising networks and made entry into global clothing value chains possible. On the other hand it has limited upgrading possibilities as critical decision-making and certain higher-value functions are located at the headquarters and are not transferred to supplier firms. Unlike locally owned factories, foreign-owned factories in SSA LICs have limited leverage and autonomy in terms of strategic decision making and in attracting orders as negotiations with buyers are generally located at the headquarters (Natsuda et al. 2009). The parent or sister companies are generally in charge of input sourcing (often drawing on their own textile mills or sourcing networks based in Asia), product development and design, logistics, merchandising, and marketing, and have direct relationships with buyers. Production plants in SSA are generally only in charge of manufacturing (CMT). Only a few of those foreign-owned firms have invested in more capital-intensive finishing operations such as washing and embroidery and even fewer—a couple in South Africa and Kenya, one in Lesotho, and one in Swaziland—have integrated backwards into fabric and yarn production (Gibbon 2003a).

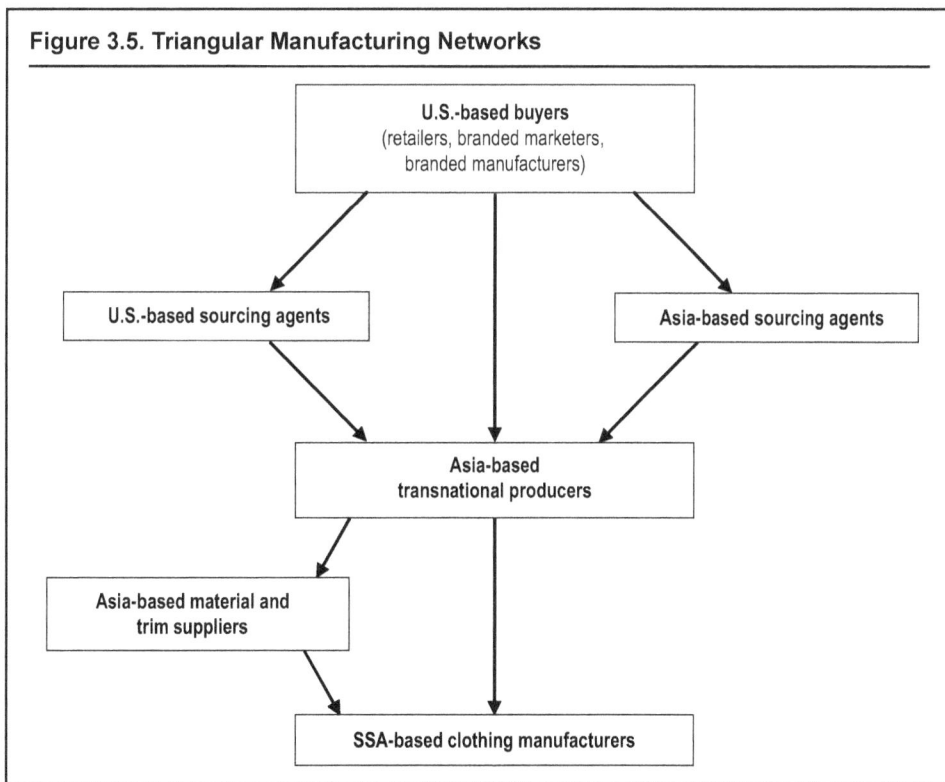

Figure 3.5. Triangular Manufacturing Networks

Source: Adapted from Kaplinsky and Morris (2006, 23).

Transnational clothing producers generally own or source from production units in several countries. They follow a global strategy involving long-run production and specializing in a narrow range of functional activities and basic products made in large plants—normally employing well over 1,000 workers—(Gibbon 2008). Workers were mostly unskilled when investors came to SSA LICs and their long learning curves were offset by long average runs. Workers with higher skills were imported from Asia, including management and supervisors. Sunk costs of investments are generally low. Levels of investment in plant and machinery for a clothing firm employing 1,000 workers are typically between US$1 and US$2 million and shells are generally leased or rented at concessional rates (Gibbon 2008). This global strategy can be seen in the similar set-up of firms in different locations, the nearly exclusive concentration on the U.S. market, the specialization in a limited number of long-run low-value products, the widespread use of foreigners at the management and supervisory level, and the limited linkages to local or regional economies.

These ownership structures and this specific business model have important impacts on embedding, in particular on the location of critical decision-making processes (such as sales and merchandising, and input sourcing), on local linkages to input suppliers and spillovers (such as learning in management or supervisor positions, and skills and knowledge transfer), as well as on export markets (see below). In Lesotho and Swaziland three types of firms can be identified to illustrate the importance of ownership structures (see box 3.1).

Box 3.1. Different Types of Firms in Lesotho and Swaziland

Firm Type 1: Most Taiwan, China-owned firms in Lesotho and Swaziland are part of triangular manufacturing networks of transnational producers based in Taiwan, China. Activities in Lesotho and Swaziland are limited to manufacturing, whereas input sourcing, product development and design, logistics, merchandising and marketing, and the relationship with buyers are located at the headquarters in Taiwan, China. The strategy of these firms is global: they export almost exclusively to the U.S. market and have production plants in different regions, including SSA, Asia, and Central America and the Caribbean. Decision powers based in Lesotho and Swaziland are minimal in these types of firms. There are barely any local linkages as parent companies generally source inputs for all their plants on a global scale given their price advantage. Further, the SSA plants fulfill a role in a global strategy. In interviews managers said that some decisions in Taiwan, China are not in the interest of the plant in SSA. Even if local inputs are available, which would be quicker and more flexible, locally based managers normally do not have the power to make decisions concerning sourcing. Also with regard to marketing, some firms said if interested buyers should approach them directly (for example from South Africa), they have to send them to Taiwan, China as they have no sales and merchandising competencies. Particularly in the context of the global economic crisis as U.S. orders dropped dramatically, firms said they could have exported to South Africa to fill their capacity but parent companies were not interested in a regional strategy and continued focusing on their global strategy of long-run, basic product export to mass-market buyers in the U.S. market. The management in this type of firm consists almost exclusively of foreigners: the top management is mostly from Taiwan, China; the middle management mostly from mainland China; and shop floor supervisors are from China, Sri Lanka, and some local. In the management offices the common language is Chinese. Thus, there are also cultural and language barriers. Further, there is generally quite a negative attitude toward locals in this type of firm. Many problems are attributed to 'lazy workers' and 'their unproductive culture.'

(Box continues on next page)

Box 3.1 (continued)

Firm Type 2: A second type of Taiwan, China-owned firm in Lesotho and Swaziland is more embedded. In Swaziland there are two Taiwan, China-owned firms that seem to be more integrated in the local economy. One example involves an investor from Taiwan, China who is not linked to a parent company in Taiwan, China and who has lived in Swaziland for decades. He was one of the first investors from Taiwan, China in Swaziland and brought several others to the country. He sees Swaziland as his home, intends to stay here, and thus has a long-term interest in the firm in Swaziland. He makes all the sourcing decisions locally and has direct relationships to buyers. Management and also supervisors consist mostly of foreigners, but there is a program in place that tries to support local involvement. Currently, two managers are locals and 17 out of 40 supervisors are locals. The location of the sales and merchandising function relates directly to end markets. The firm exclusively exported to the United States until some years ago. But due to the MFA phaseout and accelerated by the global economic crisis it started to export to the South African market, which now accounts for around 60 percent of its production. Inputs are nearly exclusively imported from Asia. There are only linkages to packaging firms and some trims and a minimal amount of fabrics are regionally sourced.

Another example is a firm in Swaziland that is part of a transnational producer and has its parent company and most decision-making power in Taiwan, China. However, due to decreasing orders in Swaziland and huge investments (they not only own four clothing firms but also one spinning mill, one knitting fabrics mill, and a dye house), the parent company decided in 2008 to send a sales and merchandising person to Swaziland to start exporting to the regional market, in particular South Africa. Since then the firm has exported to South Africa, which accounts today for around 30 percent of its exports. Local linkages are limited as the sourcing decisions are mostly based in the headquarters. There is also no local person in a management position.

In Lesotho there are three to four Taiwan, China-owned firms that are more embedded. Some owners arrived a long time ago and see Lesotho as their home and are more interested in long-term exports, also to South Africa. One of those firms also has a merchandise team located in Lesotho and thus has more autonomy in the decision-making process. Two other firms take on their own orders as well as orders from their headquarters in Taiwan, China.

Firm Type 3: The third type of firm in Lesotho and Swaziland is South Africa-owned firms. South Africans started investing in Lesotho and Swaziland in 2005/06 due to high labor costs in South Africa, and in Lesotho because once-limited space became available as firms from Taiwan, China left in the context of the MFA phaseout. The main motivation was to use low-cost labor close to their end market, which they supply almost exclusively. This type of firm has a very different set-up, is smaller, and is specialized in short-run, quick response and products with higher fashion content. Most management positions are hold by South Africans. Most inputs, in particular fabrics, come from Asia but some firms use regional fabrics, in particular from South Africa and Mauritius but also from Lesotho. Trims are more often sourced regionally. Most firms have headquarters, sales, and merchandise offices as well as their input sourcing, product development, and design teams in South Arica, but some have more decision-making powers in Lesotho and Swaziland. Thus, these firms are not part of a global strategy but are more embedded in the location as owners have their networks in South Africa. Most firms have direct relationships with large South African retailers.

An event that illustrates the different strategies of these types of firms is the dissolution of the Swaziland Textile Export Association (STEA). Twelve firm representatives attended the last meeting of STEA. The vote was 8:4 in favor of abolishing the association. The eight firms voting in favor of the dissolution had no decision power located in Swaziland. The four representatives voting in favor of STEA were the one local firm, one South African firm and the two Taiwan, China-owned firms that are more embedded. The fractionalization of industry associations in Lesotho also highlights the different strategies of these types of firms. There is one association for large firms from Taiwan, China, one for smaller firms from Taiwan, China, and one for South African firms.

Source: Author.

In Kenya most exporting firms in the clothing sector seem to be a mixture of types 1 and 2. Most firms (including the locally owned Indian-Kenyan firms) have parent or sister companies overseas but ownership structures are more diverse than in Lesotho and Swaziland. Parent/sister companies may be from the NIEs Taiwan, China and Hong Kong SAR, China, or from Singapore, China, India, Sri Lanka, Bangladesh, and the United Arab Emirates (see Phelps et al. 2009). Most of the sales, merchandising and marketing functions, and the relationship with buyers are handled in the parent/sister companies. However, some firms also have direct relationships with buyers. Input sourcing is also mostly organized by the parent/sister companies or directly by the buyer but there are several exceptions where input sourcing functions are located in Kenyan firms. The top management mostly consists of foreigners but in middle-management positions there are some Kenyans.

Main Challenges of SSA LIC Clothing Exporters

In this part main internal challenges of SSA LIC clothing exporters are discussed, which are strongly linked to the specific integration of SSA LICs into global clothing value chains. Challenges can be characterized in two types: (i) exogenous factors reflecting changing dynamics in the global economy and in global clothing value chains, including the structure of the industry, global regulations, and global sourcing policies of buyers that were discussed in chapter 2; and (ii) endogenous factors that affect SSA's supply response to global market opportunities, including physical and bureaucratic infrastructure, productivity, skills and capabilities, and entrepreneurship. In all these endogenous factors, with the possible exception of South Africa and Mauritius, all SSA economies face huge challenges (Kaplinsky and Morris 2008).

Preference Erosion

Competition has significantly increased in the clothing sector due to global developments discussed in chapter 2: in particular stagnant demand in major end markets, over-capacity at the suppliers' side, changing sourcing policies of global buyers, the MFA phaseout, and the global economic crisis. In this context preferential market access is central for SSA LIC clothing exporters. SSA LICs enjoy duty-free market access to the EU and U.S. markets. Under AGOA, lesser developed countries in SSA enjoy single transformation ROO as stipulated in the TCF derogation. Large buyers interviewed in the United States say that AGOA is crucial in sourcing from SSA countries. However, most buyers stated that the TCF derogation is even more important for SSA's competitiveness. In the EU SSA countries had to fulfill double transformation ROO for a long time but this changed to single transformation for countries that signed EPAs. Hence, SSA countries enjoy very favorable market access conditions to the two major clothing import markets. Due to single transformation ROO and the important share of (often imported) inputs in total costs, the degree of effective subsidy offered to SSA LIC exporters is substantially higher than the nominal tariff rate (Kaplinsky and Morris 2008). In the United States only Central American and Caribbean countries as well as Mexico, Jordan, and Israel enjoy similar beneficial conditions for market access. For instance, Cambodia and Bangladesh face an average tariff of 10.8 percent on exports to the United States. The EU offers duty-free access to all ACP countries under the EPAs and to all LDCs under the EBA initiative, including Cambodia and Bangladesh. However, for instance Cambodia and Bangladesh have to fulfill double transformation ROO; only EPA signatories enjoy single transformation ROO. Japan, the third largest import market after the EU and the United States, offers duty-free market access to LDCs, including Lesotho and Madagascar (but not Kenya and Swaziland). Cambodia and Bangladesh enjoy also duty-free access due to their LDC status. LDCs in SSA also enjoy preferential market access in Norway, Canada, Australia, and New Zealand.

A central challenge for SSA's clothing sector is preference erosion. U.S. preferences may erode as AGOA is only in place until 2015 and the TCF derogation until 2012. It will probably be extended but there is concern about the unreliability of AGOA and its rules. Certainty beyond 2015 in the form of a permanent trade agreement such as the EPAs would be needed, in particular for long-term, capital-intensive investments into knitting, weaving, and spinning. Also, an extension of the TCF derogation beyond 2012 is critical for a survival of SSA LIC clothing exports, at least in the short run. But more importantly, preferences may erode because of generally decreasing tariffs through NAMA negotiations and access to U.S. tariff preferences for more LDCs if the WTO round should be concluded, and an increase in bilateral as well as preferential trade agreements.

SSA LIC governments need to actively extend favorable market access for clothing exports to its main market, the United States, but they also need to negotiate duty-free market access to more markets to support export diversification, in particular to middle-income and emerging markets such as Turkey, Russia, the Middle East, Mexico, Argentina, China, and India, as market access conditions have an important impact on competitiveness. In market access negotiations emphasis should be put on nonrestrictive ROO as well as regional cumulation provisions in ROO to enable and encourage the integration of regional T&C industries and the leveraging of regional strengths (see below on regional integration). However, it should be taken into account that while SSA LICs face very favorable preferential market access to the main import markets of the United States and the EU, several important competitor countries face tariffs in these markets. As this situation may change due to preference erosion, SSA LICs should not only rely on preferential market access to be competitive but be prepared to compete without it. In the short run, however, preferential market access together with single transformation ROO will remain crucial for SSA LICs to sustain clothing exports. Even in the very favorable preferential environment SSA LIC clothing exporters are operating today they are only marginally competitive.

Foreign Ownership and CMT

As discussed above, with the exception of Mauritius and South Africa, the majority of exporting firms in the clothing sector in the main SSA clothing exporter countries is foreign-owned and part of triangular manufacturing networks. This has important impacts on the functions performed in SSA, on the embeddedness (in particular on the location of decision-making power and on local linkages and spillovers), and on the sustainability of operations. Given the little local involvement in the sector and few local linkages and spillovers, the sectors may not survive if foreign investors should leave. Firms in SSA LICs are generally only in charge of manufacturing; sales, merchandising and marketing, product development and design, logistics, and largely also input sourcing are located at the parent or sister company. This is problematic as SSA firms have no direct access to sourcing and selling networks and thus no direct relationships to buyers and input providers. Foreign ownership and the specific integration of SSA LICs into global clothing value chains through triangular manufacturing networks limits the possibility for taking over more functions with higher value added as these functions are ensured by the headquarters on a regional or global basis. In contrast to locally owned firms, which functions foreign owners decide to locate in SSA LIC plants is not only a question of local capabilities. Rather, it is determined by their strategic choice of what and how to produce in their global sourcing network (Natsuda et al. 2009). SSA LIC clothing firms remain concentrated into a particular set of low-value adding assembly functions (CMT) not only as a result of deficiencies in the countries' operating environment but as a strategy of the parent or sister company. Thus, the upgrading challenge is not only one of developing skills and creating capabilities in SSA LICs but of changing their specific role and integration into global clothing value chains (Barnes and Morris 2010). The concentration of SSA LIC firms in CMT production enforces their second-tier supplier position. As discussed in chapter 2 sourcing policies of global buyers have changed and there is a focus on direct sourcing and a move away from CMT to FOB or even full-package suppliers. Thus, to be able to have direct relationships with buyers, capabilities beyond manufacturing are required. This has happened to a very limited extent in SSA LIC clothing exporters—to a larger extent in Kenya and Madagascar than in Lesotho and Swaziland.[22]

Export clothing factories have been in SSA LICs for more than 10 years and there still has been very limited local initiative. Thus, a central challenge for SSA LIC clothing exporters is to increase local involvement in the industry at the management and/or owner level to embed and upgrade the sector, foster local skill development, linkages and spillovers, and make the sector more sustainable. The limited local involvement in SSA LICs compared to Mauritius and other LICs such as Bangladesh can be partly explained by their late integration into global clothing value chains. When clothing exports started to take off in the 1970s and 1980s in Bangladesh and Mauritius, entry barriers in the industry were still relatively low and local firms were able to start exporting with 20 to 50 sewing machines. Furthermore, market access was guaranteed as those countries had excess quota not only used by foreign investors with quota hopping motivations but also by local entrepreneurs. In the 1990s and 2000s and even more in the context of the MFA phaseout and the global economic crisis, entry barriers and capabilities demanded from supplier firms have increased substantially. In this context, financial and human resources at the firm level, reliable and low-cost infrastructure and backbone services, access to finance and education and training facilities at the country level, as well as relationships to buyers and input suppliers have become much more important. This has made it difficult for local firms in SSA LICs to start exports in clothing since the export sector (with the exception of South Africa and Mauritius) took off on a larger scale only in the early 2000s. But besides timing, institutional factors are central, in particular the existence of a local entrepreneurial class and government support. In Mauritius, which has a long entrepreneurial tradition, particularly in the sugar industry, mostly sugar entrepreneurs who wanted to diversify their business and saw the opportunities of quota access invested in the clothing sector in the 1970s and 1980s. With the exception of Mauritius and South Africa and to a lesser extent Kenya, an entrepreneurial class is missing in many SSA LICs such as Lesotho, Swaziland, and Madagascar. SSA business systems are further fragmented and the parastatal, mostly foreign-dominated formal and indigenous informal sectors are poorly integrated (Pedersen and McCormick 1999). Furthermore, governments or industry associations have not supported local involvement in the clothing sector. There are no explicit programs to support local skills, linkages, and spillovers, as well as locally owned firms taking into account their specific challenges (for example, no access to finance through headquarters; no established relationship with buyers and input suppliers; and skill gaps at the management, technical, and design/fashion level).

End Market and Product Concentration

A major challenge to SSA LIC clothing export growth is the lack of diversification in markets and products. Clothing exports are highly concentrated with regard to end markets. This was been particularly evident during the global economic crisis, as demand in SSA's major export market—the United States—has declined strongly. With regard to concentration in end markets there is a difference between Lesotho, Swaziland, and Kenya on the one hand and Madagascar and Mauritius on the other. In Lesotho, Swaziland, and Kenya exports go nearly exclusively to the United States, accounting for 97 percent, 99 percent and 96 percent respectively in 2008;[23] in Madagascar and Mauritius (and in the past South Africa) exports are divided between the United States and the EU, accounting together for 96 percent (43 percent to the United States and 53 percent to the EU) and for 90 percent (11 percent to the United States and 79 percent to the EU) respectively (see table 3.2 and figure 3.6). Exports to South Africa have increased recently in Mauritius as well as in Lesotho and Swaziland, which is not however shown in the data as it involves trade within the Southern African Customs Union (SACU) (see below on regional integration).

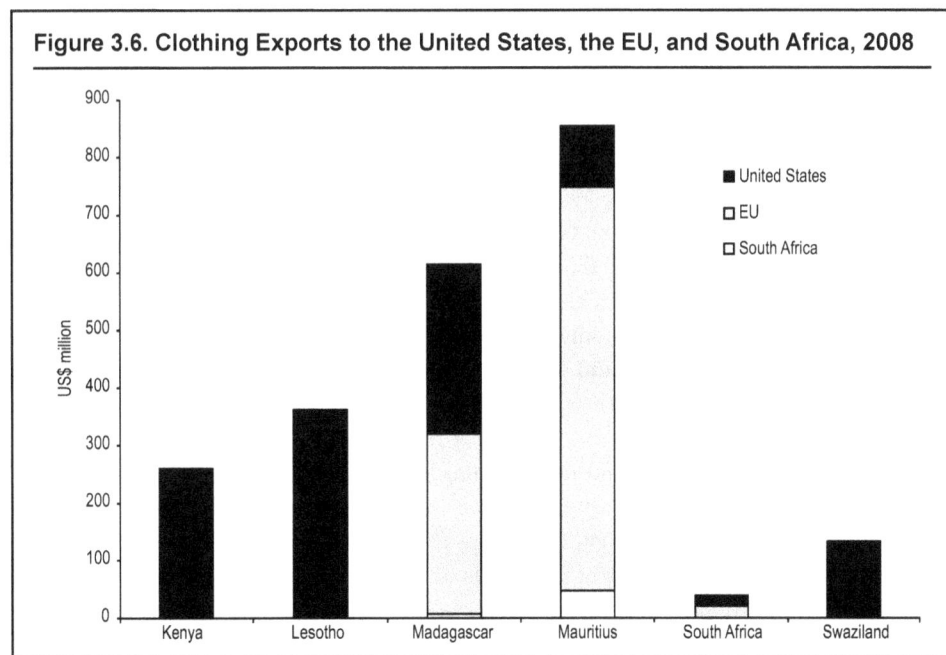

Figure 3.6. Clothing Exports to the United States, the EU, and South Africa, 2008

Source: UN COMTRADE.
Note: Values in million US$.

Gibbon (2002b, 2003a) was the first to state the importance of end-market segmentation for the cases of Mauritius and South Africa, arguing that because of differing end markets and buyers' differing requirements, clothing firms exported either to the EU or the United States. This end-market segmentation was closely related to nationality as Asian-owned firms in South Africa and Mauritius tended to export to the U.S. market and locally or European-owned firms to the EU market. End-market segmentation is even more pronounced in Lesotho, Swaziland, and Kenya. Foreign-owned firms in Kenya and Taiwan, China-owned firms in Lesotho and Swaziland export nearly exclusively to the U.S. market. However, exports from Lesotho and Swaziland to South Africa have increased since 2005/06. But these exports come mostly from South African-owned firms exporting nearly exclusively to the South African market. Gibbon's end-market segmentation argument can be partly supported for Madagascar. Asian firms are more likely to export to the United States and Mauritian and EU firms predominantly export to the EU (Morris and Sedowski 2006b). In Mauritius the situation seems to be more nuanced and the findings of Gibbon (2003, 2008) can only be partly supported. Earlier, Hong Kong SAR, China-owned firms in Mauritius nearly exclusively exported to the U.S. market and Mauritian and European-owned firms concentrated on the EU market. After 2004 exports to the United States drastically declined in Mauritius due to the closure of Hong Kong SAR, China-owned firms, which mostly supplied the U.S. market in the context of the MFA phaseout. Mauritian-owned firms, which are the majority, now still focus on the EU market but some of them also export to the United States and most of them are interested in exporting to the United States. However, Mauritian firms do not export to the same market segment and buyers as the Hong Kong SAR, China firms, which previously exported mostly large volumes of basic products to mass market retailers but are now approaching smaller mid-market retailers.

The two major clothing import markets, the United States and the EU, are quite different and firms follow different strategies to access these markets (Gibbon 2003a).[24] Three main factors behind these differences can be identified. First, end-market segmentation is related to language as well as political and economic history. Firms oriented exclusively or mostly to the U.S. market are almost all Asian-owned (owned by Hong Kong SAR, China in Mauritius; Taiwan, China in Lesotho and Swaziland; and more mixed in Kenya and Madagascar). Generally, these investors also have other plants that were already supplying the U.S. market before they came to SSA. Thus, they know the U.S. market and their global strategies are geared towards it. In contrast, in South Africa, Mauritius, and Madagascar (the only three significant exporters to the EU market), there exist strong historical, cultural and language ties to the United Kingdom in the case of South Africa, and to the United Kingdom and France in the case of Mauritius and Madagascar (Gibbon 2003a).

Second, trade regulations and in particular ROO are central to understanding end-market segmentation. Plants set up by Asian investors to export to the United States are essentially CMT firms. In contrast, firms exporting to the EU market are mostly vertically integrated in Madagascar and Mauritius or use local inputs in South Africa related to the Lomé convention as it demanded double transformation ROO. Furthermore, the duty advantage is smaller in the case of EU preferential market access as tariffs in the EU are lower for most products and as EU preferences are also available to Asian competitor countries.

Third, there are differences between EU and U.S. end markets in sourcing practices and buyers have different expectations on suppliers' functions and capabilities. EU buyers seem to be more interested in flexibility and versatility, expect suppliers to contribute to design and product development, and have the financial capacity to manufacture and independently source inputs (Gibbon 2008). U.S. buyers emphasize the ability to produce to buyers specifications. They nominate specific fabrics and other input suppliers, mostly from Asia, and are generally not interested in suppliers' contributions to design. Supplier firms stated that production for the EU market brings an overhead structure that is uncompetitive for the U.S. market as U.S. buyers and, in particular, transnational producers exporting to the U.S. market generally demand CMT capabilities and no input sourcing and design capabilities from their SSA suppliers (Gibbon 2003a, 2008). Moreover, there is a difference in the size of orders. With regard to volume U.S. buyers demand a higher percentage of total production, making it difficult for producers to have other buyers. European markets are not as unified as in the United States. The EU market is quite segregated and each country has its own retailers and chains with few large cross-border retailers and this translates into smaller orders.[25]

Despite these end-market specificities, end-market diversification is crucial for SSA LIC clothing exports to sustain and grow. Asian-owned firms who nearly exclusively exported to the United States were mostly affected by the MFA phaseout. Also during the crisis firms exporting to the U.S. market were hit hardest. With regard to the EU market the EPAs with their single transformation ROO offer significant opportunities. Furthermore, there is only limited but increasing export to regional markets (see below on regional integration). Other high potential export markets are Norway, Australia, New Zealand, Mexico, Brazil, Argentina, Turkey, Russia, and the Middle East, in particular the United Arab Emirates. However, firms and industry associations are not particularly active in diversifying end markets. For export diversification support at the associations' level is critical. Support for breaking into new markets could include information on different markets, buyers and their sourcing policies, marketing and promotional initiatives, local and international exhibitions to attract foreign buyers, as well as image building and the establishment of a brand 'Made in SSA' at the associations' level. Such support would not only help in regard to new markets but could also enhance SSA's reputation in existing markets.

Diversification with regard to products is also central and related to end-market diversification as different end markets demand different types of products. SSA LIC clothing firms are heavily specialized in basic long-run products, in particular denim jeans, pullovers, and t-shirts, and have seen prices falling for these products due to international competition. For the U.S. market three products accounted for 50 percent of all clothing exports from SSA in 2008: women's woven cotton trousers (22 percent), cotton pullovers (14 percent), and men's woven cotton trousers (13 percent). Thus, exports to the United States are dominated by few, generally low-price basic items such as trousers (jeans) and sweaters. These items typically have long production runs, low labor content, and few styling changes; price-based competition is toughest (USITC 2009). For all SSA countries, exports of trousers and pullovers to the United States accounted for over half of their clothing exports in 2008. There is a very similar pattern of clothing exports across the main SSA clothing exporting countries, with the notable exception of Mauritius (which also exports shirts) and South Africa (which also exports socks, t-shirts and jackets). The top five exports to the United States account for 72 percent of total U.S. clothing exports in Lesotho, 76 percent in Kenya, 65 percent in Swaziland, 92 percent in Mauritius, and 61 percent in Madagascar (see table 3.7). For Mauritius and Madagascar export products to the United States and the EU are very similar; only one and two respectively of the top five export products don't overlap. For all SSA countries, exports of cotton t-shirts to the EU account for over one-quarter of EU clothing exports. There are also small flows of cashmere pullovers (from Madagascar), shirts and blouses, pullovers, and jeans. The top five exports to the EU account for 44 percent of total EU clothing exports in Madagascar and 66 percent in Mauritius (see table 3.8).

Table 3.7. AGOA Countries' Top Five Clothing Exports to the United States, 2008

Country	Main clothing exports		% of total clothing exports to United States	% of total merchandise exports to United States
	HS	Description		
All AGOA countries	62046240	Women's woven cotton trousers	22	0.3
	61102020	Cotton pullovers	14	0.2
	62034240	Men's woven cotton trousers	13	0.2
	62052020	Men's woven cotton shirts	7	0.1
	61103030	Man-made fiber pullovers	7	0.1
Lesotho	62034240	Men's woven cotton trousers	23	21
	61102020	Cotton pullovers	22	20
	62046240	Women's woven cotton trousers	12	11
	61103030	Man-made fiber pullovers	8	7
	61046220	Women's knitted cotton trousers	7	6
Madagascar	62046240	Women's woven cotton trousers	29	25
	61102020	Cotton pullovers	11	9
	62034240	Men's woven cotton trousers	7	6
	62034340	Men's woven synthetic fiber trousers	7	6
	61046220	Women's knitted cotton trousers	7	6
Kenya	62046240	Women's woven cotton trousers	41	30
	62034240	Men's woven cotton trousers	13	9
	61102020	Cotton pullovers	9	6
	61046220	Women's knitted cotton trousers	8	5
	61103030	Man-made fiber pullovers	6	4
Swaziland	62046240	Women's woven cotton trousers	17	16
	61102020	Cotton pullovers	14	13
	61103030	Man-made fiber pullovers	13	12
	62034240	Men's woven cotton trousers	11	10
	61046220	Women's knitted cotton trousers	10	10
Mauritius	62052020	Men's woven cotton shirts	66	38
	62046240	Women's woven cotton trousers	11	6
	62034240	Men's woven cotton trousers	10	6
	61051000	Men's knitted cotton shirts	4	2
	61102020	Cotton pullovers	2	1
South Africa	61102020	Cotton pullovers	36	0.1
	61159690	Socks of synthetic fibers	23	0.0
	61091000	Cotton t-shirts	21	0.0
	62063030	Women's cotton blouses	4	0.0
	62043350	Women's suit jackets	4	0.0

Source: USITC.

Table 3.8. Top Five Clothing Exports from SSA to the EU, 2008

| Country | Main clothing exports | | % of total clothing exports to EU | % of total merchandise exports to EU |
	HS	Description		
All Sub-Saharan Africa	61091000	Cotton t-shirts	26	0.0
	61101290	Cashmere pullovers	7	0.0
	62052000	Men's woven cotton shirts	6	0.0
	61102099	Women's cotton pullovers	6	0.0
	62034231	Men's jeans	5	0.0
Mauritius	61091000	Cotton t-shirts	39	17
	62034231	Men's jeans	8	3
	62052000	Men's woven cotton shirts	7	3
	61051000	Men's knitted cotton shirts	6	3
	61102099	Women's cotton pullovers	6	2
Madagascar	61101290	Women's cashmere pullovers	20	8
	61101130	Men's woolen pullovers	8	3
	61102099	Women's cotton pullovers	6	3
	61102091	Men's cotton pullovers	5	2
	61101190	Women's woolen pullovers	5	2
South Africa	61124190	Women's swimwear of synthetic fibers	12	0.0
	61091000	Cotton t-shirts	8	0.0
	61159900	Knee-length socks	7	0.0
	61034200	Men's knitted cotton trousers	7	0.0
	62033390	Men's jackets of synthetic fibers	4	0.0
Lesotho	61051000	Men's cotton shirts	17	0.2
	61091000	Cotton T-shirts	14	0.2
	62034231	Men's jeans	12	0.1
	62033310	Men's jackets of synthetic fibers	8	0.1
	62034235	Men's woven cotton trousers	7	0.1
Kenya	62034235	Men's woven cotton trousers	19	0.0
	61091000	Cotton t-shirts	16	0.0
	62034319	Men's woven trousers of synthetic fibers	14	0.0
	62143000	Scarves of synthetic fibers	8	0.0
	62034390	Men's shorts of synthetic fibers	7	0.0
Swaziland	62034235	Men's woven cotton trousers	32	0.0
	61102099	Women's cotton pullovers	27	0.0
	61091000	Cotton t-shirts	23	0.0
	62092000	Babies' cotton clothing	8	0.0
	62031100	Men's woolen suits	3	0.0

Source: Eurostat.

Thus, all countries are heavily dependent on a few products categories for exporting. This is even more problematic as for most countries these products are also highly important in total merchandise exports. In Lesotho the top five clothing exports to the United States account for 65 percent of total merchandise exports to the United States, in Swaziland they account for 61 percent, in Kenya for 54 percent, in Madagascar for 52 percent, and in Mauritius for 53 percent (see table 3.7). For the EU clothing exports are less important in total merchandise exports. The top five clothing exports to the EU in Madagascar account for 18 percent of total merchandise exports to the EU and for 28 percent in Mauritius (see table 3.8).

At least, part of the export production needs to diversify and upgrade to higher-value products for the following reasons. First, profit margins and value addition is higher in higher-value products and if more production steps are conducted besides CMT such as input sourcing and design. Risk is also lower if export products are more diversified. Second, in basic, long-run production, labor costs are a critical competitiveness factor. SSA countries won't be able to compete solely on price as labor costs and other operational costs are higher than in many Asian countries. Thus, it is central to upgrade to products where price is not the most important competitive factor. Third, as discussed above export market diversification may be related to product diversification as other end markets such as the EU and Japan demand other and, in this case, higher-quality, fashion and design standards. There are few comparable markets to the United States with regard to large orders of basic products. The main challenges to upgrading into higher-value products are quality, lead times, and missing design and technical skills (see below). Firms in Mauritius as well as South African-owned firms in Lesotho and Swaziland and some firms in Kenya and Madagascar already produce for higher market segments. Since market research and R&D is necessary to diversify and upgrade export products, research centers built on public-private partnership could be established. Their role would be to gather and disseminate information to local manufacturers on the latest developments in products, markets, and buyers.

Lack of Backward Linkages and Long Lead Times

Access to raw materials, in particular yarn and fabrics, is crucial for clothing exporters. SSA is a net exporter of clothing but a net importer of textiles. The SSA clothing industry depends almost completely on imported yarn, fabrics, and accessories; local sourcing is very limited with the exception of Mauritius (and South Africa). Most textile imports come from China and other Asian countries. Table 3.9 shows that 57 percent of textile imports come from China followed by India (9.3 percent), Pakistan (2.5 percent), Germany

Table 3.9. SSA Textile Imports: Top 10 Importers in 2008

Country	2000 Value	2000 Share	2004 Value	2004 Share	2006 Value	2006 Share	2008 Value	2008 Share
China	619	22.2	1,830	41.2	2,722	49.8	4,086	57.1
India	430	15.4	432	9.7	490	9	667	9.3
Pakistan	—	—	182	4.1	185	3.4	182	2.5
Germany	77	2.8	134	3	130	2.4	177	2.5
Hong Kong SAR, China	239	8.6	290	6.5	206	3.8	172	2.4
Japan	—	—	79	1.8	105	1.9	162	2.3
Netherlands	63	2.3	—	—	80	1.5	135	1.9
Korea, Rep. of	203	7.3	220	5	127	2.3	131	1.8
United Arab Emirates	69	2.5	162	3.6	145	2.7	118	1.6
Thailand	98	3.5	83	1.9	84	1.5	116	1.6
World	2,784	—	4,442	—	5,461	—	7,152	—

Source: UN COMTRADE.
Note: Values in million US$.

(2.5 percent), Hong Kong SAR, China (2.4 percent), and Japan (2.3 percent). No regional supplier country is in the top 10 list. Only 7 percent and 10 percent of total SSA yarn and fabric imports respectively come from the region (see below on regional integration). The situation differs however in SSA countries (see below for a discussion on regional trade, capacities, and opportunities in textile production).

Becoming a competitive fabric and yarn producer is challenging for a number of reasons. First, investments in the textile sector are much more capital intensive than investments in the clothing sector, in particular for woven textiles. Minimum investments involve US$30–40 million but often up to US$100 million. For comparison, a medium-scale clothing firm requires an investment of around US$2 million. SSA LIC suppliers have a disadvantage due to comparatively limited access to and high cost of finance in the region, which limits new investment and increases the cost of existing production.

Second, investments in the textile sector rely even more on infrastructure than in the clothing sector, in particular on electricity and water. Access to reliable electricity is essential for textile operations and dyeing, washing, and finishing processes require reliable water sources as well as water treatment and solid waste processing facilities. In these areas the textile sector is much more demanding than the clothing sector. Direct electricity costs account for around 35 percent in spinning and for around 20 percent in weaving/knitting of total operational costs compared to around 5 percent in clothing manufacturing. SSA suppliers are at a disadvantage with regard to costs and reliability. The electricity rates of many SSA countries are among the highest in the world (however, with wide variations in the region) and supply is unreliable. Many SSA countries lack abundant supply of clean water. Many countries also lack the ability to treat the wastewater resulting from finishing operations. Increased investment and improved regulation in electricity and water are preconditions for competitive textile sectors and to attract investors in textile production.

Third, the textile sector is more knowledge and skill intensive than the clothing sector. While SSA LICs have an abundant supply of low-skilled labor, the availability of labor with appropriate technical, design/fashion and management skills is limited. There is a limited supply of formal training facilities in the region with the exception of South Africa and Mauritius (see below).

Fourth, the textile sector is scale intensive and needs a critical mass, long runs, and predictability. Thus, a thriving and relatively stable clothing sector is an important competitive factor for the production of textiles as it secures sufficient levels of consistent demand. Due to the comparatively small size of the clothing sector in individual SSA countries an export and a regional perspective is required for the development of a textile sector (see below).

Fifth, existing regional yarn and fabric production is often seen as uncompetitive with regard to costs, quality, and lead times. From a costs perspective, fabrics from Asia are generally significantly cheaper. Quality-wise there are different perceptions but generally the quality of regional yarn and fabric was perceived as good and comparable to third-country imports. Another concern is lead times, in particular for fabric mills in South Africa. In several cases it was reported that lead times for fabric from Asia are similar to lead times for regional fabric. This is highly problematic as this would be the one competitive advantage of fabric mills located in SSA. These competitiveness problems are partly related to infrastructural constraints but also to the prevalence of outdated machines, production techniques, and management practices and low productivity at the firm level.

Notwithstanding the seriousness of these challenges, backward integration will be central to increase competitiveness with regard to lead times, production flexibility, and costs (such as transport, port, and customs clearance) as well as to increase domestic value added and local linkages and spillovers. Furthermore, if the TCF derogation is not extended after 2012, then SSA LICs will be required to use regionally (or prohibitively expensive U.S.) sourced yarn and fabric to maintain AGOA-eligibility for their clothing exports to the U.S. market. In particular reducing lead times is a critical issue in SSA's clothing sector. Success in global clothing trade increasingly depends on short lead times and quick response. Compared to competitor countries, SSA lead times are long. This is related to SSA geographical location with regard to major end markets of the United States and the EU as well as with regard to input supply, which is concentrated in Asia. Thus, SSA faces a double disadvantage. It can take up to four months to complete an order, eliminating most time-dependent fashion lines for SSA producers. Fabric manufacturing and delivery from Asia takes four to five weeks plus the additional time from the port to the factory, which varies depending on the location of the firm. Production can take from three to several weeks depending on the size of the order. To reach the end market in the United States and the EU another minimum of three weeks is needed. Moreover, shipping times are quite infrequent and have been reduced in some cases (for example in Mauritius). Asian competitor firms have a 30-day lead time advantage as fabric mills are closer and Asian firms are approximately only 14 days away from the ports on the West coast of the United States. The market segments that SSA (with the exception of Mauritius) currently serves still allow for relatively long lead times. Lead time will, however, become much more critical as SSA moves into higher value-added clothing and fashion products.

It would not make sense to produce all types of fabrics in SSA. Clothing firms need a large variety of yarns and fabrics and buyers often demand certain types of inputs or nominate mills located in third countries. Thus, it is neither possible nor useful to produce all types of inputs needed by clothing firms in SSA regionally, and the elimination of duties on imported inputs is central to allowing clothing firms to source the most competitive inputs, and to force regional textile producers to become competitive. But there are strong opportunities in basic cotton-based yarn and fabric products, which are broadly used in clothing production and could be produced regionally (see below on regional integration for a more detailed discussion). As a competitive local textile sector contributes to the competitiveness of the clothing sector by reducing costs and lead times and increasing flexibility, a favorable environment for textile investment should be ensured. Policies could involve long-term loans at reduced interest rates for textile investments; attracting FDI specifically to the textile sector; the development of more efficient infrastructure, in particular in the area of electricity and water, which are crucial for textile production; and greater emphasis on skill development in areas that are relevant for textile production. Furthermore, coordinated efforts at the association level and regional level would be important to establish relationships between regional input suppliers, clothing firms, and parent/sister companies and buyers overseas.

The largest lead time reduction would clearly result from vertical integration or local sourcing. But increasing local supply of yarn and fabric to fill the large gap between demand and supply in SSA is challenging and not attainable in the short term. However, there are complementary options to reduce lead times. First, improvements in efficiency and productivity at the factory level, in particular with regard to decision making processes, production structures and supply chain management, can importantly contribute to reducing lead times. Second, improvements in trade facilitation—in particular in the transport infrastructure, logistics, and customs facilities—an also reduce lead times. Third, rather than establishing competitive local yarn and fabric mills at the scale necessary for supplying inputs to the clothing sector, more focus could be put on fabric processing and increasing the capacity of the dyeing and finishing industry. This would make it possible to stock up fabric of the most common constructions in greige form in advance of orders and then dye and finish the fabric once the order and the design is received, which would reduce lead times and increase local value added. However, a close relationship with buyers would be necessary because the type of fabric would need to be known in advance, as only the color and design could be adapted closer to production. Fourth, increased processing capabilities ideally could be combined with establishing central bonded warehouses (CBWs). A CBW could stock up T&C inputs such as fabric in finished and greige form of the most common constructions, accessories, dyes and chemicals, yarn, T&C machinery, and spare parts in amounts determined by expected demand. Manufacturers can then purchase these inputs duty-free from the CBW directly as export orders are received (World Bank 2005a). In this case manufacturers can save on shipping time as they can immediately source the inputs when they receive the order. Once again, for CBWs a close relationship with buyers is required, because buyers generally stipulate the exact fabric they need and often also nominate fabric mills. This information would be needed in advance. CBWs could be organized by industry associations to share costs and reap economies of scales. Fifth, and most importantly, increased regional sourcing could play a central role in reducing input costs and lead times. In SSA regional sourcing is limited, accounting for only 7 percent and 10 percent of total yarn and fabric imports (see below).

Low Productivity and Lack of Skills

Despite low wages (compared to living expenses), SSA is a relatively 'high labor cost' location compared to Asian competitor countries. There are differences between countries, with South Africa having the highest wage rate followed by Mauritius and then Swaziland, Kenya, Lesotho, and Madagascar (see table 3.10). However, this table should be read with caution as data comes from different sources, is reported for 2002, and does not include social charges. It is thus not directly comparable to data for Asian competitor countries for 2008 reported in table 4.13 in chapter 4.[26] However, table 3.10 still shows that minimum wages are high compared to Asian competitor countries such as Cambodia and Bangladesh. For instance, minimum wages in the clothing sector in Kenya accounted for US$97.9 (US$85.1 plus a 15 percent housing allowance) in 2008. In comparison, minimum wages in Cambodia accounted for US$50 per month (which accounts for US$0.24 per hour) and average wages (including overtime and social charges) accounted for US$77 per month (accounting for US$0.33 per hour). In Bangladesh average labor costs per month accounted for US$24 and for US$0.22 per hour in 2008.[27] Another concern for clothing firms is labor flexibility with regard to overtime, flexible work, and piece rate wages, at least in the formal sector. Labor regulations in SSA countries are generally stricter than in many Asian countries and secure some minimum rights for workers, at least in the formal sector and on paper. This should be seen as an opportunity to position SSA as a 'supplier of choice' and not as a problem (see below on labor compliance).

Table 3.10. Average Clothing Manufacturing Labor Costs (Excluding Social Charges) in 2002

Countries	Labor cost (US$/hour)
South Africa	1.38
Mauritius	1.25
Swaziland	0.86
Kenya	0.56
Lesotho	0.5
Madagascar	0.33

Source: Adapted from Fontaine (2008).
Notes: Swaziland estimate based on average monthly wage of US$155 and a 45-hour week. Lesotho estimate based on average monthly wage of US$90 and a 45-hour week. Kenya estimate based on average monthly wage of around US$100 and a 45-hour week.

The largest problem at the labor side in SSA LICs is labor productivity. Factory-level productivity depends on a host of factors, including labor costs, production methods, workers', management and technical skills, and capital and technology. Factors external to factories are also central for productivity such as low-cost, quality and reliable inputs, and infrastructure and logistics (see below). Compared to Asian competitor countries productivity is low.[28] Despite the existence of a clothing export sector for some time, adequate productivity improvements have been lacking. In Lesotho, Kenya, and Madagascar the clothing sector has been present for more than 10 years and in Swaziland for nearly 10 years. Thus, productivity problems can no longer be considered 'teething' problems faced by an industry at the beginning stages. Factories have been in SSA LICs long enough to have realized economies of scale in sewing, and the lack in productivity improvements is indicative of low levels of efficiency and skills at the management and worker level, communication barriers between managers and factory workers, and nonexistent training facilities (Lall 2005).

Managers and supervisors have a crucial role in defining factories' productivity levels, labor relations, and potentials for upgrading. The vast majority of managers and supervisors are foreigners in SSA LIC clothing firms, mostly from China, Bangladesh, South Africa, and Mauritius. These managers have brought experience that was critical for the rapid establishment of the clothing sector in SSA LICs. However, they may now pose a challenge to upgrading and productivity improvements due to their limited training and skills in production processes and industrial engineering, outdated and unsuitable management practices, and communication barriers with regard to language and culture. In Lesotho and Swaziland most middle-management positions are filled by foreigners, mostly from mainland China, who have shop floor but little management experience and are unable to communicate with local workers. Salm et al. (2005, 51) conclude for Lesotho that "operator productivity within the industry was generally low. This was principally due to deficient recruitment policies, inadequately trained operators, poor supervisory management, communication difficulties and cross-cultural mis-understanding." An additional important factor with regard to worker productivity, in particular in Lesotho and Swaziland, is HIV. Estimates state that nearly 40 percent of Swaziland's adult population and 30 percent of Lesotho's is infected with HIV. Firms stated that absenteeism and a high incidence of sick leave are problematic and that every month workers are dying of AIDS—generally younger employees (between 20 and 35) who are most productive. Sickness also interferes with training, making firms reluctant to invest in it.

Generally, training schools for the clothing sector are lacking in SSA LICs, which is a key reason for the high use of expatriates in management, supervisory, and technical positions. With the exception of South Africa and Mauritius very little formal training of skilled personnel, technicians, supervisors, and managers occurs. The skill gap is particularly high in the area of technical and design/fashion skills as well as middle-management skills. Middle management as well as technical and engineering jobs are widely held by foreigners who are expensive compared to locals and who encounter cultural barriers. The design and fashion capacity in SSA is very limited. As buyers increasingly demand design capabilities or at least a design understanding and value added can be significantly increased in the production process if also some design steps are provided by suppliers, the building up of design capabilities is crucial. With regard to sewing operators, training typically occurs informally and in-house on the shop floor. Vocational training schools could play a critical role in improving workers' skills and productivity. In all training initiatives coordination between the government, industry associations, and firms and in certain areas also with buyers is crucial to develop skills that are directly needed in the private sector.

There is an urgent need to increase productivity in SSA's clothing sector. Without a major productivity improvement program that assists clothing firms to remain (or become) internationally competitive, the industry will not be able to compete globally. Education and training at the production workers level, but in particular at the supervisory and management level, will be central to overcome skill deficits that hinder productivity improvements and upgrading. Reducing communication barriers between management and workers is also central in this regard. Firms will have a central role in this effort to increase productivity but a government-supported 'technology upgrading fund' organized at the industry level could support productivity improvements and upgrading by offering low-cost funds for investments in new machinery, technology, and skills that enable more efficient and flexible production processes.

With regard to labor compliance, the situation is generally better in SSA countries (with regard to minimum wages, piece-rate regulations, and overtime), at least in the formal clothing sector and on paper, than in several Asian competitor countries. This should not be seen as a problem but as an opportunity. First, competing on low labor costs and inadequate workers rights is not feasible as labor costs and worker protection is lower in many Asian countries. Second, such practices are not sustainable from a developmental perspective. On the contrary, SSA clothing exporter countries could promote themselves as 'countries of choice' for global buyers. Labor compliance has become central in sourcing policies of global buyers and basic labor standards often constitute a precondition for firms to enter sourcing networks. A program could be developed in SSA together with the development of a brand 'Made in SSA' that secures social compliance in the SSA clothing sector. Departments of labor have generally limited resources to implement and enforce labor compliance. But as in Cambodia's Better Factories Program, SSA governments and industry associations could only provide export licenses to firms that are part of compliance and monitoring programs. SSA governments could further work together with the International Labour Organization (ILO) and the International Finance Corporation (IFC) in their newly established 'Better Works' program. Buyers should also be involved in compliance programs and include labor compliance into their core sourcing policies.

Inadequate Physical and Bureaucratic Infrastructure

An important factor in the competitiveness of the clothing sector with regard to costs and lead times is the efficiency of infrastructure. This includes not just physical infrastructure such as roads, rails and ports, water, electricity, and communications but also bureaucratic infrastructure such as port and customs clearance, company registration and enterprise set-up, the delivery of appropriate certification (including work visa applications), as well as access to finance. The most important areas for the clothing sector include inland (road, rail) and sea (in some cases also air) transport, customs, electricity costs and reliability, availability and cost of factory shells, water, communication, and access to finance. Access to reliable and low-cost infrastructure and backbone services is even more crucial for competitiveness in the post-quota and post-crisis environment where producers are faced with higher and broader demands from buyers and with shorter lead times. Most SSA LICs face problems in these infrastructure areas. There are however differences in governments' support of the clothing sector in SSA LICs and thus also in addressing these infrastructural challenges. In Mauritius and Lesotho the government is very supportive and sees the sector as central in their development process. Also, the Swazi government supports the sector, although to a lesser extent. In Kenya and Madagascar the government is generally not that responsive to clothing exporters' challenges. All main SSA LIC exporters, however, have some type of EPZ-like regulations and most clothing exporting firms are located in these zones. These programs generally include duty-free imports of inputs, machinery and equipment for export production, certain tax incentives, subsidized land and factory shells, and more reliable access and lower costs of utilities.

For Lesotho and Swaziland the transport infrastructure in South Africa is central. Due to inadequate transport infrastructure in these two countries, most firms are located at the border with South Africa, accessing directly South African transport infrastructure. In both countries border crossings operate on a 24-hours basis but there are problems with border crossing and customs, in particular on the South Africa side. In Swaziland internal transport is the largest infrastructural problem. Factory shells provided by the Swaziland Investment Promotion Agency (SIPA) have a high standard. Access to electricity and water is only a challenge in rural areas. In Lesotho availability of land and factory shells that are provided by the LNDC is a problem. In the beginning of the 2000s there was a waiting list as more firms from Taiwan, China were interested in producing in Lesotho; today there is also a waiting list as South African firms are interested in relocating to Lesotho. The main problem is funding. The LNDC does not have enough funds to build more shells and provide the necessary infrastructure (electricity, water, roads). Lesotho's government is very dependent on SACU funds as 60 percent of its income comes from SACU. Furthermore, Lesotho suffers from a lack of water, low water pressure, and unacceptable water quality. Water is in particular central to attract a knit fabric mill for washing and dying. Electricity cuts are generally not a challenge for the industry as zones are largely shielded from power failures. A major challenge for both Lesotho and Swaziland is the scheduled phaseout of the Duty Credit Certificate (DCC). The DCC scheme was a crucial support in the context of the MFA phaseout and the global economic crisis. The DCC regulation had already been changed in 2006 and 2009, which reduced the traded value of DCCs; in March 2011 the DCC scheme is scheduled to totally phaseout.

In Kenya transport is a large challenge. Road transport for a container from the port in Mombasa to Nairobi where most clothing firms are located costs around US$1,400. There is also a railway between Nairobi and Mombasa that would be cheaper, but there is a lack of carriages and reliability is very low. Port delays are quite common in Mombasa but there have been improvements. Another central challenge in Kenya is the very high cost and the unreliability of electricity. This is particular important for investment in spinning and weaving/knitting. Furthermore, there is quite frequent electricity rationing as the electricity network is predominately hydro-based and thus exposes the country to power shortages in times of drought. But EPZs are only sporadically affected by rationing. Most firms have back-up electricity generators as loss in production time, efficiency, and output from outages and the related uncertainty constitute a severe competitive disadvantage.

In Madagascar transport is also a large challenge. The road between Antananarivo where most firms are located and the port town Tamatave is in bad condition and it can take up to one week for containers to travel between the factory and the port (Morris and Sedowski 2006b). Other transport problems include traffic jams in the capital, lack of road capacity, and the fact that cargo trucks are only allowed to enter the capital at night. Electricity is also an infrastructural challenge in Madagascar as prices have increased and power outages occur frequently. Rent costs for factory shells are high (Morris and Sedowski 2006b).

Another challenge is access to and cost of finance. Kaplinsky and Morris (2008) report that export finance costs in Kenya and Madagascar account for 13 and 18 percent respectively, which is much higher than in China (5.5 percent) and India (10.5 percent). This problem has existed for a long time, in particular with regard to access to investment finance, and is related to the volatile history of the clothing sector in some SSA countries and the negative perception by banks of the clothing sector. However the problem has been accelerated recently due to the global economic crisis and lack of working capital and trade finance. This is particularly problematic for textile mills, which are capital intensive. Moreover, local firms cannot access transnational financing networks and have difficulty financing startup operations, investing in upgrading, or acquiring working capital. Buyers expect from suppliers to be able to finance input sourcing and production processes and offer buyers 60 to 90 days invoicing. Foreign firms can access funds generally through headquarters but during the last two years they also had problems. To establish a locally owned industry, pay for productivity improvements, and upgrade production and products, access to finance through specific mechanisms is crucial. As discussed above a 'technology upgrading fund' could be established to facilitate access and reduce costs of finance for investments into productivity improvements and upgrading.

Codes of conduct of global buyers not only include labor standards but increasingly also environmental standards. In SSA LICs environmental protection and waste management is underdeveloped, which is particularly problematic in textile produc-tion that uses large amounts of water. Water used for washing and dying needs to be treated before disposal. Solid waste from T&C production is often burned, which can be environmentally hazardous. The importance of environmental concerns for buyers can be seen in the August 2009 case in Lesotho where waste-water from a clothing manufac-turer was leaking into a lake. This incidence was covered in the media and buyers sourc-ing clothing from this manufacturer investigated the factory and called urgent meetings with relevant stakeholders. Relationships with the factory were generally not ended but pressure was put on the supplier to solve this issue urgently.

Volatile Exchange Rates

Exchange rates play a key role in the competitiveness of clothing exports from SSA. Most problematic is the unpredictability related to volatile exchange rates, which makes it difficult to plan ahead and enter into contracts with buyers. Buyers do not accept rene-gotiations of prices when exchange rates change;[29] and as prices are paid in the buyers' currency (mostly in U.S. dollars but for Mauritian and Madagascar firms also in pounds or euros), this has huge effects on producers. Their prices are paid in foreign (buyer's) currency but their labor and other operational costs (mostly utilities) and taxes are paid in the local currency. Inputs are mostly paid in U.S. dollars as the majority of inputs are imported. Thus, countries that import a large part of their inputs and export products where the share of imported inputs in value added is high are not that negatively af-fected by appreciations as the downside on the export side is partly compensated by an upside on the import side (Kaplinsky and Morris 2006). But it is highly problematic for countries that source a larger share of inputs locally such as South Africa and Mauritius.

Advantageous exchange rates to the U.S. dollar played an important role in explain-ing growth in clothing exports in Lesotho, Swaziland, and Madagascar in the early 2000s (together with MFA quota hopping and AGOA). However, Lesotho and Swaziland expe-rienced an appreciation in their currencies in 2004 that accelerated the negative impact of the MFA phaseout. Between 2000 and 2002 when many foreign investors arrived in Lesotho and Swaziland the exchange rate between the rand and the U.S. dollar was very advantageous. However, in mid-2003 the rand and thus also the maloti and the lilangeni (which are both pegged 1:1 to the rand) started to appreciate against the dollar rising from R 12 to R 7.5 per US$1 in 2004 and to R 6 to US$1 in 2006 (Morris and Sedowski 2006a). The IMF states with respect to Lesotho: "The Maloti's sharp rise vis-a-vis the U.S. dollar resulted in a 23 percent real effective appreciation from end 2001 to mid 2005." (IMF 2005, 15, cited in Morris and Sedowski 2006a) The USITC speculates that the ex-change rate is one of the reasons that in 2004 investors for a knit fabric mill decided to drop their plans in Lesotho (USITC 2005). In contrast to Lesotho and Swaziland, Mada-gascar's currency (the Franc Malgache) lost half of its value against the dollar and the euro between February and June 2004, which could partly compensated negative devel-opments due to the MFA phaseout (Morris and Sedowski 2006b).

Although high public and foreign debt limit options with regard to exchange rate policies, SSA LIC governments have to decide about their industrial policy and realize that a strong currency and, more importantly, a volatile currency has a strongly nega-tive impact on the export sector and undermines programs to support exports, export diversification, and industrial development.

Regional Integration: Regional End Markets and Production Networks

After discussing main internal challenges of SSA LIC clothing exporters, this part assesses the role of, opportunities for, and challenges of regional integration in the clothing sector in SSA. Regional integration can play a central role in the survival of the clothing sector and the development of thriving T&C sectors in SSA. The potential of regional integration could unfold in two ways. First, the region could develop as an end market; in this regard, South Africa is a largely unexploited source of growth. It has a well-developed retail sector, the highest consumption level in the region, and, in particular, increasing clothing consumption. Second, regional production networks could increase value added and competitiveness within SSA clothing sectors by improving lead times and flexibility, which have become central criteria in buyers' sourcing decisions. Furthermore, if the TCF derogation is not extended after 2012, SSA countries will be required to use regionally (or prohibitively expensive U.S.) yarn and fabric to maintain AGOA-eligibility for clothing exports to the United States.

Regional End Markets: Sourcing Strategies of South African Buyers

Regional end markets

South Africa has by far the largest end market for clothing in SSA, accounting for over half of total SSA clothing imports in 2008. Other important SSA clothing importers are Sudan (8.2 percent), Namibia (6.5 percent), Botswana (6.1 percent), Ethiopia (5.8 percent), Mauritius (3.1 percent), Uganda (3 percent), Kenya (2.5 percent), and Ghana (2.3 percent). The South Africa T&C market had a turnover of R45 billion in 2005 and domestic production accounted for around R17 billion. Domestic production has declined over the past decade in response to competitive pressures from imports and rising (labor) costs. While South Africa's market for clothing has grown substantially in recent years (35 percent between 2001 and 2005), growth in consumption has not been satisfied by increased domestic production (which decreased by 18 percent between 2001 and 2005) but by imports of clothing, particularly from China, which accounted for almost two thirds of South African clothing imports in 2008 (see table 3.11). Only two regional countries are in the list of South Africa's top 10 clothing importers: Mauritius and Malawi. However, South Africa's import data (which involves intra-SACU trade) from Lesotho, Swaziland, Botswana, and Namibia is underreported.[30]

In 2008, South Africa imported 9 percent of its clothing from other SSA countries, down from almost 30 percent at the end of the 1990s.[31] The largest regional suppliers to the South African clothing market are Mauritius, where exports to South Africa increased from less than 1 percent in 2004 to above 5 percent in 2008, and Malawi, where exports to South Africa, however, have declined quite dramatically over the last decade. South Africa has become an increasingly important market for Mauritius since under Southern African Development Community (SADC) duties on T&C imports were removed. Exports of t-shirts and men's shirts have grown so rapidly that, together with wool yarn, they are now Mauritius' three largest exports to South Africa, accounting for 15 percent of its exports in 2008. This export growth has been triggered by the SADC elimination of tariffs but other factors are also important: (i) Mauritius has been successful in meeting the SADC ROO requirements (double transformation) given its vertically integrated clothing sector; (ii) Mauritius has a lead-time advantage because it is only six

Table 3.11. Top 10 Clothing Importers to South Africa, 2000–2008

	2000	2001	2002	2003	2004	2005	2006	2007	2008
China (US$ million)	95,393	86,616	96,463	205,041	419,100	558,372	797,601	554,159	543,447
Share (%)	49.6	50.7	54.5	66.4	74.4	74.2	78.5	61.9	60.7
India (US$ million)	20,257	12,836	11,027	20,079	30,138	52,114	40,855	50,965	50,312
Share (%)	10.5	7.5	6.2	6.5	5.3	6.9	4.0	5.7	5.6
Mauritius (US$ million)	1,145	491	1,731	2,771	4,169	8,610	21,253	36,327	47,251
Share (%)	0.6	0.3	1.0	0.9	0.7	1.1	2.1	4.1	5.3
Bangladesh (US$ million)	198	305	636	1,363	2,155	3,766	7,483	20,114	39,164
Share (%)	0.1	0.2	0.4	0.4	0.4	0.5	0.7	2.2	4.4
Hong Kong SAR, China (US$ million)	13,444	13,397	11,417	14,953	25,777	28,754	27,590	36,675	21,517
Share (%)	7.0	7.8	6.4	4.8	4.6	3.8	2.7	4.1	2.4
Indonesia (US$ million)	4,358	2,833	3,501	3,711	3,967	5,956	7,096	22,748	19,886
Share (%)	2.3	1.7	2.0	1.2	0.7	0.8	0.7	2.5	2.2
Malaysia (US$ million)	228	404	305	402	749	1,316	1,390	16,022	18,232
Share (%)	0.1	0.2	0.2	0.1	0.1	0.2	0.1	1.8	2.0
Vietnam (US$ million)	942	950	325	328	833	1,858	3,648	15,512	17,095
Share (%)	0.5	0.6	0.2	0.1	0.1	0.2	0.4	1.7	1.9
Malawi (US$ million)	17,590	19,307	22,780	17,140	18,986	23,449	21,251	16,434	16,987
Share (%)	9.2	11.3	12.9	5.5	3.4	3.1	2.1	1.8	1.9
Thailand (US$ million)	4,773	4,377	3,839	6,548	8,297	9,075	9,327	14,513	15,613
Share (%)	2.5	2.6	2.2	2.1	1.5	1.2	0.9	1.6	1.7
SSA (US$ million)	24,306	22,710	27,498	23,324	27,383	38,939	51,638	69,121	79,451
Share (%)	12.6	13.3	15.5	7.6	4.9	5.2	5.1	7.7	8.9
Total imports	192,191	170,699	177,098	308,894	563,657	752,247	1,015,651	895,762	894,758

Source: UN COMTRADE.
Notes: Values in US$ million. Data for Lesotho, Swaziland, Botswana, and Namibia are underreported.

days away from South Africa by sea, and because of the vertically integrated production process; (iii) Mauritius has a long tradition in exporting to buyers in European countries that are more similar in their orders (for example, volume) and demands (for example, design capabilities) to South African buyers; and (iv) Mauritian firms have actively approached South African retailers.

Unfortunately, there is no accurate data on clothing exports from Lesotho and Swaziland to South Africa. Data based on qualitative interviews shows that exports from Lesotho and Swaziland to South Africa have increased since 2005/06. This was driven by relocations of South African-owned firms from South Africa to Lesotho and Swaziland due to labor costs advantages (type 3 firms). These firms have continued to supply their 'local' market from Lesotho and Swaziland. In addition, some more embedded firms from Taiwan, China (type 2 firms) in Lesotho and Swaziland started to export to South Africa as a reaction to falling orders from the United States in the context of the global economic crisis. Madagascar has also increased exports to South Africa, at least since 2005 when it ratified the SADC Trade Protocol (although in 2009 it was suspended for political reasons). Most exports from Madagascar to South Africa have come from Mauritian-owned firms and there do not seem to be substantial direct relationships between buyers in South Africa and firms located in Madagascar. Kenya's exports to South Africa are still marginal due to Kenya not being a SADC member and thus facing tariffs of 40 percent for clothing exports to South Africa.

Thus, the South African market has grown in importance for some SSA countries—in particular Mauritius, Lesotho, and Swaziland—since 2005 and particularly 2007. This development was driven by the elimination of SADC duties on clothing (in the case of Mauritius and to a lesser extent Madagascar), relocations of South African firms to Lesotho and Swaziland, and the search for new export markets by some more embedded firms from Taiwan, China in Lesotho and Swaziland. However, compared to total South African clothing imports, regional clothing imports have remained relatively marginal, reaching only 9 percent. Thus, there is a large potential for increasing regional exports to South Africa, although the South African market could not replace the United States and EU market in terms of magnitude. To understand further opportunities for and challenges to regional sourcing in South Africa, insights into the South African retail sector are required, in particular into sourcing strategies of South African retailers.

Sourcing policies of South African retailers

South Africa has a large and sophisticated domestic consumer market, which sets South Africa apart from other SSA countries where little production is sold domestically and consumer demand is not as diverse (Morris and Einhorn 2008). The South African formal clothing retail sector resembles sectors in developed countries in terms of variety of retail operations (Gibbon 2002b). However, there is an extremely high level of concentration within the sector. The top six retailers (Mr. Price, Edcon (Jet and Edgars), Pepkor (Pep and Ackermans), Woolworths, Foschini, and Trueworths) together account for 70 percent of the market share[32] (Morris and Einhorn 2008). This is much higher than the level of concentration in the United States, the United Kingdom, and other European markets, which are generally already regarded as highly concentrated. There has been a rise in discount formula retailing that has led to increased price competition. Since 1995 South Africa's leading discounter, Mr. Price, more than doubled its market share to over 10 percent—a level higher than the combined share of the four leading discounters in the U.K. market (Gibbon 2002b). There seems to be a bifurcation in strategies of large retailers (Gibbon 2002b): Woolworths (the market leader with a market share of around 16 percent) and another important retailer, Foschini, have developed mid-market orientations. Edcon has a department store line (Edgars) and a discounter line (Jet) that target different market segments. Other retailers have shifted at least parts of their business down-market. Besides discount formulas, supermarkets have also increased market share.

Power relations in the South African textile-clothing-retail value chain have changed considerably since 1995. Until 1995 the T&C sectors in South Africa were isolated by high tariffs. South Africa's clothing sector has a long tradition but the textile sector only developed after World War II in the context of economic and political isolation. Since 1995 the T&C sectors have been liberalized, reducing tariffs on yarns to 15 percent,[33] on fabrics to 22 percent, and on clothing to 40 percent in 2002. Although, duties are still high, retailers started to abandon their exclusive supply relationships with local manufactures and started to import clothing, particularly since 2002. This importing option for retailers has altered power structures considerably in the South African textile-clothing-retail value chain. The clothing and in particular the textile sector have only slowly reacted to this change. This can be seen by the marginal export activity of the sectors and by the increase in imports in domestic sales. This change is also reflected in buyers sourcing policies with regard to sourcing geography, supply base, sourcing channels, and central sourcing criteria, which are discussed next.

Sourcing geography: Three main observations can be made regarding retailers' sourcing geographies. First, with the exception of one smaller mid-market retailer all retailers have significantly increased their imported intake. There are important differences with regard to imported intake from third countries, which varies from 30 percent to 70 percent for the retailers interviewed. The highest share of imports comes from China (including Hong Kong SAR, China), which strongly dominates third-country imports for all retailers. Other sourcing countries named are India, Bangladesh, and to a lesser extent Vietnam, Indonesia, and Pakistan. Regional sourcing varies from around 5 percent to 15 percent, including from Lesotho, Swaziland, and Mauritius, and Madagascar. Local sourcing varies between 15 percent and 70 percent.[34] Five years ago the sourcing geography looked very different for all but one retailer as the majority of intake was still locally sourced.[35] Thus, imports, in particular third-country imports, have increased considerably in the last five years. Retailers have, in particular, taken most of their long-run and basic product business offshore to Asian countries. Local South African and regional manufactures were left with shorter-run, quick turnaround, and time-critical products as well as with testing and replenishment production.

Second, international sourcing is highly concentrated in China (including Hong Kong SAR, China), followed by India and Bangladesh. The other three Asian sourcing countries, which are Vietnam, Indonesia, and Pakistan (which is exclusively used for home textiles), were each only named by one retailer. Two retailers talked about how their international sourcing started and they both said that they were (at least partly) 'forced' to increase international sourcing in the early 2000s. Against the background of a weak currency in South Africa and preferential market access, clothing firms and textile mills started to increase exporting to the United States and the EU as profits were higher supplying these markets than the domestic market. As the currency appreciated, local firms came back to local retailers as they were not internationally competitive anymore. However, this was in some cases too late as the retailers already had established relationships with suppliers in Asia and as imports became very competitive due to the appreciating currency. About five years ago the only Asian sourcing country was China, which accounted for almost 80 percent of total South African clothing imports in 2006, but Asian sourcing has since diversified to some extent. One driver of this diversification was the safeguard quotas on imports from China that South Africa implemented in 2007 and 2008. Retailers said that they started diversifying, in particular to Bangladesh, which increased its share in total South African clothing imports from less than 1 percent in 2006 to over 4 percent in 2008 (see table 3.11). After the quota phaseout in 2009 they remained in these new sourcing countries and moved sourcing from South Africa to China, again reaching pre-safeguard levels there. Thus, the safeguards seem to have been counterproductive and at the end led to reduced local sourcing.

Third, all retailers stated that they see regional sourcing as important. Lesotho and Swaziland have increased in importance mostly because core South African suppliers relocated to these countries due to lower labor costs. Some suppliers were 'encouraged' to relocate to Lesotho or Swaziland by retailers. In the context of the global economic crisis retailers also started sourcing from firms owned by Taiwan, China in Lesotho and Swaziland. Representatives from retailers stated that the large Taiwan, China firms in Lesotho and Swaziland were not interested in them before the crisis but due to reduced orders in the context of the crisis more embedded Taiwan, China-owned firms started exporting to South Africa. With regard to Mauritius, retailers stated that they have increased sourcing due to the elimination of duties within SADC and that they were actively approached by Mauritian firms. Quality and lead times are important considerations in sourcing from Mauritius. Most imports from Madagascar seem to go through Mauritian-owned firms.[36] Retailers further stated that they are generally interested in increasing regional sourcing but that regional suppliers would need to approach them actively. There is generally very limited knowledge about regional suppliers and their capabilities. Only Mauritian firms have actively approached South African retailers.

Supply base: The supply base of the retailers interviewed varies from 120 to 350 to 'a few hundred' suppliers. However, for all retailers the top 20 or 30 suppliers are responsible for the majority of the intake. All retailers interviewed stated that they have the objective to reduce their supply base and want to concentrate on fewer, more capable, and more meaningful core suppliers and build strategic partnerships. Consistent with trends of buyers in the United States and in the EU, this is a new trend in South Africa, however. Gibbon (2002b) conducted interviews with retailers in 2001 and concluded that the emphasis in the early 2000s was on more rather than less arms' length-type relations and some retailers explicitly rejected the relevance of partnerships with suppliers. This can be seen as a move away from the former dominant sourcing system where exclusive relationships with core local suppliers were the rule. After this move to more arms' length relationships in the late 1990s and early 2000s, it seems that South African retailers are again interested in consolidating their supply base and concentrating on core suppliers. However, the power structures in the sourcing relations before 1995 were quite different. Today, retailers are generally the powerful actors and can build long-term relationships with third country as well as with local and regional suppliers.

Sourcing channels: South African retailers source through different channels. Gibbon (2002b) identified 10 distinct channels in 2001. With regard to domestic intake they involve South African full-package manufactures, design houses and their CMTs, in-house manufacturing, self-organized CMTs, and local licenses of branded goods. Today in-house manufacturing does still exist for two retailers but it is only responsible for a very marginal share of their intake (less than 2 percent). The CMT channel is still common for two retailers. Design houses are often used together with CMT firms. Full-package manufacturers that generally have their own design capabilities are also still important but have (with some exceptions) developed away from exclusive relationships with retailers. With regard to imports the channels involve South African importers, agents in Asia, global trading houses such as Li & Fung and LinMark, South African full-package manufacturers' import operations, and international licensees (for branded goods without local licensees; Gibbon 2002b). Today, direct sourcing is also used for third-country sourcing but the other channels, in particular importers, foreign-based agents, and trading houses, are still important. Some South African clothing firms also stated that they not only manufacture clothing but are also used as importers of clothing by retailers. Besides the existence of these different sourcing channels, there is a shift to more direct sourcing for all retailers interviewed. Direct sourcing was already the norm for local intake but intake imported from third countries was nearly exclusively handled through South African-based importers five years ago. All retailers stated that they see sourcing as their core competency and started to be more involved in sourcing some years ago.

Central criteria in sourcing decisions: Sourcing criteria of South African retailers seem to be less sophisticated and formal than those of large buyers in the United States and the EU. All South African retailers stated that they use GMROI (gross margin return on (inventory) investment) calculations, at least for seasonal products, to assess and benchmark different suppliers. But GMROI calculations were only introduced quite recently and it is not clear if all retailers have already implemented GMROI. Before that the central criterion was price. Price is still central,[37] but especially lead times and production flexibility have increased in importance. The main firm-specific criteria stated by firms were price, lead times, on-time delivery, quality, and production flexibility. The smaller retailers demanded capabilities for short runs due to their demand for low volumes and a variety of styles. It was generally expected that suppliers have to be capable of sourcing inputs on their own account (except where self-organized CMTs were used). Product development and design capabilities were generally demanded from regional and third-country suppliers. Only two retailers stated that labor compliance is important in their sourcing criteria.

Generally retailers stated that firm-specific factors are more important than country-specific ones. However, three issues were central in all interviews involving country-specific factors: labor costs and flexibility, availability of finance, and availability of local or regional fabric. Labor costs and flexibility were named as central by all retailers and one of the main concerns with local suppliers. In South Africa and more general in the region, banks see the clothing sector as risky and it is difficult to get credit, a problem that has intensified during the global economic crisis. Access to credit, however, is central for supplier firms as buyers generally demand input sourcing on suppliers' accounts as well as credit lines as a precondition to enter their supply chains. One of the largest problems in South Africa and the region stated by retailers is the lack of regional textile mills (see below).

Opportunities for regional suppliers

Large South African retailers recently have started to consider regional suppliers and Mauritius (in some cases together with Madagascar), Lesotho, and Swaziland have become important suppliers. In Lesotho and Swaziland this has occurred generally through relocations of already-existing South African supplier firms to Lesotho or Swaziland, but imports have also increased from some more embedded Taiwan, China-owned firms. Suppliers from Mauritius actively targeted the South African market and export either from Mauritius or Madagascar. However, despite these developments, there is much more potential for regional sourcing, in particular in the quick response, fashion, and short-run segment where regional suppliers have a potential competitive advantage compared to Asian suppliers. To realize this advantage, however, regional suppliers have to build relationships with South African retailers, restructure, and become capable of supplying short runs of more fashionable products with short lead times. There are several challenges to this strategy (see below) but it offers a huge opportunity to diversify export markets and to increase regional exports, in particular for South African-owned firms in Lesotho and Swaziland, firms in Mauritius, and some firms in Madagascar (and Kenya if trade barriers should be reduced) that are already geared to a greater extent to small-run and more fashionable products.

But not all firms are suited for this type of production. In particular, large Taiwan, China-owned firms in Lesotho and Swaziland that are set up for long-run basic products for the U.S. market are not competitive in the short run, fashion, and quick response business. It is also not useful that all firms in the region concentrate on quick response, fast fashion production, which is suitable for the South African market but not for other export markets such as the United States. But in the South African market there are also opportunities to engage in more basic and higher-volume production, in particular with the largest retailers such as Mr. Price, Woolworths, Edgars, and Pepkor. Some restructuring would be necessary as the volumes would not be comparable with U.S. volumes. However, the successful export experience of some Taiwan, China-owned firms from Swaziland and Lesotho suggests that the firms will be able to cope with these varying demands. Even if the volumes are smaller than preferable, this strategy can be very useful to fill capacity, stabilize seasonal fluctuations, and diversify end markets.

The supply chain rationalization model that became the dominant sourcing model for large global buyers in the United States and the EU has not become as important yet for South African buyers. Interviews with large South African retailers show that passive sourcing strategies, less involvement in sourcing, less formal and standardized rules, and absence of formal procedures of suppliers' performance used to be prevalent. However, this seems to be changing and there is a process of supply chain rationalization underway. All retailers interviewed have started to get more involved in sourcing, and have established sourcing strategies and rules for suppliers' selection and performance monitoring. They are also reducing or plan to reduce their supply base and focus on fewer, strategic relationships with core suppliers. As most retailers are now in the process of developing more formalized sourcing strategies, there is a window of opportunity. However, this window will close when retailers establish strategic relationships with Asian suppliers and develop more professional sourcing policies, which will also allow sourcing of quick response products from third countries.[38] Thus, regional suppliers have to use this window of opportunity and actively approach South African retailers.[39]

Regional Production Networks

Regional integration is not only important with regard to end markets but also with regard to regional production networks. This could increase value added within the region as well as the competitiveness of the clothing sector as lead time and flexibility have become central criteria in buyers' sourcing decisions. Buyers increasingly source from suppliers that are vertically integrated or located in regions that have a competitive textile sector. Furthermore, if the TCF derogation is not extended after 2012, SSA countries will be required to use regionally (or prohibitively expensive U.S.) sourced yarn and fabric to maintain AGOA eligibility for clothing exports to the United States. Thus, a regionally integrated T&C value chain is crucial from a competitive and value added perspective and would ensure AGOA eligibility beyond 2012. However, regional input production has to be competitive to support an export-driven industrialization process and it is neither possible nor useful to produce all types of inputs, including the huge variety of fabric, needed by clothing firms in SSA. Thus, the elimination of duties on imported inputs, including fibers, yarn, and fabric, is central. This will allow clothing producers to source the most competitive inputs, and will force regional textile producers to become competitive.

There are strong opportunities in cotton-based yarn and fabric production in SSA as cotton is produced competitively in SSA and could be directly processed through spinning and weaving or knitting. Due to scale requirements and competitive advantages in different stages of the cotton-textile-clothing value chain, a regional perspective is central to build a competitive textile sector. In this part a short analysis of intraregional trade in cotton, yarn, and fabric (for 2008) sets the stage for a discussion on opportunities for regional production networks.[40]

Regional trade in cotton, yarn and fabric

SSA countries are traditional suppliers of cotton but they have not become significant processors of cotton into T&C products. SSA countries account for more than 10 percent of world cotton lint exports, the top five exporters being Burkina Faso, Benin, Mali, Tanzania, and Zimbabwe, which account together for 60 percent of SSA cotton lint exports. The large majority of the cotton lint production in SSA countries is exported (World Bank 2007) and 90 to 95 percent of the production is processed in other countries (just-style 2010h). More than one fourth of SSA cotton exports go to China (27 percent) followed by Indonesia (12 percent), Thailand (10 percent), Pakistan (9 percent), and the EU (9 percent). Only 9 percent of SSA cotton exports go to the region but around three quarters of SSA cotton imports come from the region. South Africa imports 58 percent of regionally traded cotton, Mauritius 32 percent, and Kenya 5 percent. Thus, three countries account for 95 percent of regional cotton imports and it is these countries that have (together with Zimbabwe) the largest spinning industries in SSA.

The textile industry in SSA, including yarn and fabric production, is very small and concentrated in cotton-based textile products. It is the 'weak link' in the SSA cotton-textile-clothing value chain. The current regional supply of yarn and fabric cannot meet the needs of clothing producers and most yarn and fabric is imported from third countries (see table 3.12). The only regional supplier country in SSA's top 10 yarn and fabric importers is South Africa, which accounts for 5 percent of SSA yarn imports and 3 percent of SSA fabric imports. Yarn and fabric exports represent around 5 percent and 20 percent of total T&C exports from SSA, which has increased in the case of fabric from 10 percent in 2004.[41] Due to the small size of the SSA textile sector in some countries textile exports are the result of activities of only one or two firms such as in Lesotho, Swaziland, and Madagascar. South Africa is the largest SSA exporter of textiles, accounting for over 50 percent of total SSA textile exports. However, textile exports from Mauritius, Kenya, and Lesotho have increased considerably in recent years.

Table 3.12. SSA Imports of Yarn and Fabric, 2008

	SSA yarn imports			SSA fabric imports	
	US$ '000	%		US$ '000	%
Japan	185,423	22	China	768,086	31
China	108,279	13	United Arab Emirates	366,023	15
India	107,330	13	France	133,762	5
Germany	87,632	10	India	110,823	4
South Africa	39,230	5	Pakistan	103,497	4
Taiwan, China	36,323	4	Taiwan, China	99,456	4
Korea, Rep. of	32,561	4	Brazil	87,145	4
Indonesia	27,707	3	Germany	74,061	3
United Kingdom	17,399	2	South Africa	68,741	3
Turkey	16,022	2	Hong Kong SAR, China	49,911	2
Total	851,873		Total	2,481,808	

Source: UN COMTRADE.

Notes: Values in US$ '000. Togo is excluded from the analysis of fabric imports as trade data reported does not seem to be accurate.

SSA countries are net importers of yarn (cotton and man-made).[42] Twenty-two percent of SSA yarn imports come from Japan and 20 percent from the EU, followed by China (13 percent) and India (13 percent, see table 3.12). While almost one third of SSA yarn exports go to the region, only 7 percent of SSA yarn imports are sourced regionally. South Africa (28 percent), Nigeria (26 percent), Madagascar (11 percent), Mauritius (10 percent), and Kenya (8 percent) account for more than 80 percent of total SSA yarn imports. South Africa's imports of yarn from SSA countries account for one third of intraregional trade followed by imports from Zimbabwe (13 percent), Botswana (11 percent), Madagascar (6 percent), Swaziland (6 percent), Kenya (5 percent), Uganda (4 percent), and Mauritius (4 percent). Sixty-two percent of intra-SSA trade in yarn is sourced from South Africa, followed by Zimbabwe (13 percent), Kenya (7 percent), and Mauritius (5 percent). Main exporters of yarn—to the region and to third countries—are South Africa (55 percent), Kenya (10 percent), Tanzania (8 percent), Nigeria (6 percent), and Madagascar (5 percent), which together account for 85 percent of total SSA yarn exports (see table 3.13). This data reveals that South Africa, Kenya, and Mauritius, which are the most important regional cotton

Table 3.13. Yarn Exports from SSA, 2008

	Yarn exports			Yarn exports to the region	
	US$ '000	%		US$ '000	%
South Africa	115,161	55	South Africa	39,230	62
Kenya	21,457	10	Zimbabwe	8,006	13
Tanzania	16,122	8	Kenya	4,524	7
Nigeria	13,292	6	Mauritius	3,254	5
Madagascar	9,501	5	Tanzania	2,198	3
Zambia	8,922	4	Nigeria	1,542	2
Zimbabwe	8,464	4	Zambia	1,085	2
Mauritius	4,901	2	Botswana	815	1
Total	209,338			63,239	

Source: UN COMTRADE.

Note: Values in US$ '000.

importers, also export yarn regionally, together with Zimbabwe and Tanzania. Only five countries account for more than 80 percent of yarn imports, including South Africa, Nigeria, Madagascar, Mauritius, and Kenya, which are all countries with fabric industries.

SSA is also a net importer of fabric (cotton and man-made).[43] Over 30 percent of SSA fabric imports come from China and 12 percent from the EU, followed by the United Arab Emirates (15 percent), India (4 percent), Pakistan (4 percent), Taiwan, China (4 percent), and Brazil (4 percent, see table 3.12). Whereas around half of SSA fabric exports are to the region, only 10 percent of SSA fabric imports are sourced regionally. Nigeria (30 percent), South Africa (23 percent), Madagascar (8 percent), Kenya (6 percent), and Mauritius (5 percent) account for more than 70 percent of total SSA fabric imports. Nigeria's imports of fabric from SSA countries account for more than 70 percent of intraregional trade followed by imports from Madagascar (5 percent), Namibia (3 percent), Botswana (2 percent), Kenya (2 percent), South Africa (1 percent), and Mauritius (1 percent). Forty-five percent of regional trade in fabric is sourced from South Africa, followed by Mauritius (22 percent), Tanzania (8 percent), and Lesotho (7 percent). Main exporters of fabric—to the region and to third countries—are South Africa (59 percent), Mauritius (16 percent), Tanzania (5 percent), Madagascar (4 percent), and Lesotho (3 percent), which together account for almost 90 percent of total SSA fabric exports (see table 3.14). This data reveals that South Africa and Mauritius, two of the most important regional yarn importers, also export fabric regionally in contrast to Kenya, which accounts only for limited regional exports and seems to use most of its fabric for export clothing production. Lesotho, Tanzania, and Zimbabwe also export fabric to the region. Nigeria and South Africa are the most important importers of fabric used for clothing production for the local market. The other important importers—Madagascar, Kenya, and Mauritius—use fabric for clothing production for exports.

Table 3.14. Fabric Exports from SSA, 2008

	Fabric exports			Fabric exports to the region	
	US$ '000	%		US$ '000	%
South Africa	189,563	59	South Africa	68,741	45
Mauritius	53,034	16	Mauritius	32,979	22
Tanzania	15,792	5	Tanzania	12,591	8
Madagascar	13,389	4	Lesotho	10,630	7
Lesotho	11,220	3	Zimbabwe	4,479	3
Total	322,208			151,557	

Source: UN COMTRADE.
Notes: Values in US$ '000. Togo is excluded from this analysis as trade data reported does not seem to be accurate.

The above analysis shows that intraregional trade in cotton and in particular in yarn and fabric is limited and thus regional production networks are only developed to a limited extent. While half of all SSA cotton imports are sourced regionally only 7 percent and 10 percent of SSA yarn and fabric imports respectively come from the region.

Opportunities for regional production networks

Cotton is the fiber most widely used in textile production. SSA produces and exports cotton competitively and has the potential to grow and gin more cotton. World-class cotton producers in the region include Burkina Faso, Benin, and Mali in West Africa; Malawi,

Zambia, and Zimbabwe in Southern Africa; and Tanzania in East Africa. However, it is central in certain regions to modernize agriculture and to bring cotton production out of subsistence farming to improve the livelihood and incomes and to create a competitive cotton sector as a basis for a viable cotton-textile-clothing value chain. Man-made fibers are mostly imported from outside the region. Acrylics and polyester are the most frequently used man-made fibers in the textile sector. They are produced in the region but output falls short of demand and some other man-made fibers such as rayon are not at all produced in SSA (World Bank 2007). South Africa is the main supplier of man-made fibers but its output is insufficient even for its own consumption. Limited production capacity of man-made fiber and also of man-made yarn and fabric in the region is particularly problematic because demand for synthetic fibers has increased due to fashion trends in the main end markets and the U.S. duty structure[44] (World Bank 2007). However, despite the importance of synthetic yarn and fabric, currently the strongest opportunities for SSA are in cotton-based yarn and fabric production. This is because cotton is already produced competitively in the region and could be directly processed through spinning and weaving/knitting, and also because man-made fiber production is one of the most capital-intensive parts in the T&C value chain.

The weak link in the regional value chain clearly is the lack of spinning and weaving/knitting capacity. This ruptures the regional market for cotton and simultaneously prevents the supply of yarn and fabric to clothing manufacturers. As shown above, today most cotton production in SSA is exported to third countries. These exports are then converted into yarn and fabric and imported back to SSA as inputs for clothing manufacturers. Important production steps within the cotton-textile-clothing value chain are being lost to SSA. The trade data analysis above shows that South Africa, Kenya, Mauritius, and Zimbabwe are the most important regional yarn exporters, accounting for almost 90 percent of regional yarn exports. South Africa, Mauritius, Lesotho, and Tanzania are the most important regional fabric exporters, accounting for more than 80 percent of regional fabric exports.

South Africa has the most developed textile sector in the region and produces a wide range of textile products from high-value, specialty fabric to yarn, knit, and woven fabric of cotton or cotton blends (USITC 2009). Unlike in other SSA countries most yarn and fabric mills in South Africa are not vertically integrated into clothing production and thus selling to third parties is their core business. However, in recent years the textile sector in South Africa has contracted considerably and there is only limited competitive production of T&C inputs left. The textile sector in South Africa has historically been concentrated on the local market. With AGOA in 2000/01 there was a great opportunity for the South African textile sector to supply local and regional producers with fabric for clothing exports but textile mills remained mostly focused on the local market or started direct exporting of yarn and fabric under AGOA. Due to South Africa's long tradition and knowledge in the textile sector and its being the only producer of higher-value and more complicated yarn and fabric, the country has a central role in regional T&C production networks. South Africa is still in a position to establish itself as the textile supply base for SSA using regional cotton inputs. However, this would require a dramatic shift in policies at the levels of government, associations, and firms away from the traditional protectionist to a regional perspective, including eliminating regional trade barriers, increasing productivity and competitiveness, and coordinating with other SSA cotton, textile, and clothing producer countries.

The Kenyan textile sector currently produces cotton yarn and certain synthetic yarn, knit cotton fabric, and woven fabric as well as made-up textile products but has contracted since the 1990s (USITC 2009). These products are either exported directly, some also regionally, or used as inputs into clothing manufacturing. In Kenya there is large potential for spinning, knitting, and weaving, partly resulting from the relatively skilled labor and tradition in the textile sector, and there have been several new investments recently. However, a major problem is the cost and reliability of electricity, which needs to be tackled before Kenya can be established as a main location for spinning, knitting, and weaving. Other challenges are limited access to and high cost of finance and poor transport infrastructure.

Mauritius produces mostly knit fabrics and to a lesser extent yarn, including cotton yarn and cotton and manmade fiber-blended yarn, and some denim and cotton shirting fabric (USITC 2009). Mauritius has a large number of knit fabric mills but most are vertically integrated and use fabric for their clothing production. Production could be extended, in particular in the knit fabric and yarn segment. Madagascar has limited textile capacity. Its largest textile producer, Cotona, produces woven cotton fabric mostly for its internal clothing production, but there is also some yarn and knit fabric production. Besides high cost and unreliable electricity supply as well as high cost of capital and poor transport infrastructure, the political instability during the last decade has reduced Madagascar's prospects as an investment destination.

Lesotho produces cotton yarn and woven denim fabrics in its one vertically integrated denim textile mill, Formosa (owned by Nien Hsing). The mill spins and dyes yarn and weaves fabric for use in production of clothing for export but also for local and regional sales. Lesotho has tried to attract investment in a knit fabric mill. A main problem in Lesotho, however, is the shortage of factory shells and availability of suitable water as well as water treatment facilities. Swaziland produces zippers in a YKK subsidiary and a limited amount of yarn and cotton knit fabric in its one integrated textile mill, Tex-Ray, which is mostly used for their own clothing production but also exported regionally.

The discussion above shows that all main SSA clothing exporter countries have capacities in the textile sector, but to different extents. However, textile sectors have contracted, in particular in South Africa—the country with the most developed textile sector—and in Kenya. In Mauritius production is concentrated in vertically integrated knit fabrics and yarns and in Madagascar, Lesotho, and Swaziland production is dominated by one or two large investments. There are important challenges to develop a competitive textile sector in SSA as discussed above. However, it will be central to improve the competitiveness with regard to lead times and production flexibility as well as to increase value added in the region. A complementary strategy in the short term could be to import fabric in greige form from third countries, mostly Asia, and then conduct the dyeing and finishing operations locally or regionally. This could reduce lead times and increase flexibility if buyers (both international and regional) decide in advance on the types of fabric used for their collections. This would allow fabric to be sourced from third countries in advance and dyed and finished shortly before the clothing production.

Main Challenges to Regional Integration in Clothing

In the parts above opportunities for regional integration with regard to the regional end market (South Africa) and regional production networks were discussed. In this part main challenges to regional integration in the clothing sector are pointed out, including regional trade barriers, regional transport and logistics (the weak link in the chain), foreign ownership, firm setup and coordination, and market information.

Regional trade barriers

Intraregional trade barriers are a major challenge to intraregional T&C production networks in SSA and make it difficult to create efficient regional supply chains. Eliminating or at least reducing intraregional trade barriers is a precondition for regional production networks and regional sourcing. Regional trade agreements such as the SADC Trade Protocol, COMESA, and the East African Community (EAC) have promoted intraregional trade and have recently extended trade benefits that encouraged trade in T&C products. However, the slow path of intraregional liberalization and the existence of restrictive ROO have hampered the development of regional T&C sectors. Within SADC, SACU eliminated its tariffs for T&C imports from SADC member countries in 2006. However, the SADC Trade Protocol requires double transformation ROO for clothing. These rules are difficult to fulfill for most regional clothing producers with the exception of SACU members (which are exempted from ROO requirements), LDCs in SADC[45] (which were granted a temporary ROO exemption), Mauritius, and to a lesser extent Madagascar (due to their vertically integrated clothing firms). For yarn and fabric trade single transformation ROO exist and cotton fiber can be traded duty-free among SADC members. Kenya as a non-SADC member still faces duties for clothing exports to South Africa of 40 percent and of 22 percent and 15 percent for fabric and yarn respectively. Kenya has been able to export T&C products and import cotton duty-free since 2009 under the EAC. Several important cotton producer countries face duty and quota restrictions in exporting to SSA countries.

Hence, among the members of trade agreements, duties on regional trade in cotton and T&C have been liberalized and ROO requirements are now the main constraint. To further regional integration with regard to end markets and regional production networks, all duties on intraregional trade, including fibers, yarn, fabric, and clothing, and external duties on inputs, including fibers, yarn, and fabric, should be eliminated and only a common external duty on clothing imports should be applied. Ideally, this regulation should involve all SSA countries and thus include several trade agreements. This would offer preferences for intraregional clothing trade but still allow for the competitive sourcing of textile inputs for clothing production. ROO should be made less restrictive, that is, requiring single transformation or a simple value added rule. Despite the importance of a regional textile sector to increase competitiveness and value added in the region, restrictive ROO have not proven to be the most successful instrument to encourage the creation of a competitive textile sector.

Regional transport and logistics

With regard to infrastructure the main challenge for intraregional trade is transport infrastructure and logistics. Major weaknesses of transport and logistics in SSA include high port costs and processing fees, high dwell time for inbound containers, poor road transport services with long transit times, unreliable service quality, and poor clearance and transit infrastructure with low capacity and quality (Feidieker 2010). Furthermore, lengthy customs procedures increase transportation times and slow down product movements across borders. With regard to internal transport the cost of road transport is particularly high in the region. Road transport costs from Arusha to Dar es Salaam and Port Elizabeth to Maseru are almost as high as shipping costs from China to South Africa (FIAS 2006). Rail transport is generally cheaper but it can take considerably longer to deliver goods via rail than on the road. Moreover, as most trade in SSA is international and not regional, transport is outward-oriented and relies heavily on ports and shipping issues. The lack of sufficient regional transport networks, poor quality, high cost, and common delays impedes regional integration and imposes considerable extra costs that strangle regional and international trade. Investments, ideally via a regional fund, and changes in regulation to improve intraregional transport infrastructure and logistics processes would be central preconditions to increased regional trade in T&C.

The weak link

The weak link in regional production networks and also for quick-response supply to South African retailers is the textile sector—yarn spinning and fabric knitting and weaving. Clothing firms need a large variety of yarns and fabrics and buyers often demand certain types of inputs or nominate mills located in third countries. Thus, it is neither possible nor useful to produce all types of inputs needed by clothing firms in SSA regionally and the elimination of duties on imported inputs is central. There are strong opportunities in cotton-based yarn and fabric production in SSA. However, there are important challenges to developing a competitive textile sector in SSA, which are related to the capital and skill intensiveness of the textile sector, the importance of low-cost and reliable infrastructure (in particular electricity and water), the importance of scale and reliability, and the uncompetitive nature of existing textile mills in SSA (see above for a more detailed discussion on challenges). Due to scale requirements and competitive advantages in different stages of the cotton-textile-clothing value chain, a regional perspective is central to build a competitive textile sector. This is in particular relevant for South Africa, the country that has the most developed and largest textile sector in SSA and would need to play a central role in regional production networks. South Africa's textile sector will not be competitive if the focus is only on the local market and if there is no regional coordination. A dramatic shift in South Africa's policies at the levels of government, associations, and firms away from the traditional protectionist to a regional perspective is a crucial precondition for developing a regional textile sector. Such a shift would include eliminating regional trade barriers, increasing competitiveness, and coordinating with other SSA cotton, textile, and clothing producer countries.

Foreign ownership

As discussed above, with the exception of Mauritius (and South Africa) the large majority of clothing firms in SSA is foreign-owned and part of triangular manufacturing networks. Hence, the decision power within these foreign-owned firms in SSA is limited with regard to buyers, end markets, and input suppliers. With regard to end markets parent companies are generally not interested in entering regional end markets and thus adapting their global strategy and they have no knowledge about the South African market.[46] Furthermore, in general, firms in SSA are only in charge of manufacturing and sales and merchandising departments are located overseas, which makes relationships with South African retailers more difficult. Only a few, more embedded, Taiwan, China-owned firms with more decision-making power in Lesotho and Swaziland have started exporting to the South African market. In Mauritius the majority of firms is locally owned and sales, merchandising departments, and decision powers are located in

Mauritius. In addition, sourcing decisions are generally located in the headquarters of foreign-owned firms and follow a global strategy, meaning that fabrics for all clothing firms are sourced on a global scale by drawing on their own textile mills or sourcing networks based in Asia. Moreover, parent companies and buyers want to consolidate sourcing and prefer locations offering all inputs, including yarn, fabric, and accessories. Due to the location of sourcing decisions it is difficult for firms in SSA to make sourcing decisions at all and to source regionally. Sourcing decisions are also often made by buyers, which nominate textile mills. This reinforces sourcing from Asia because large buyers have established close relationships with fabric mills, in particular in East Asia. Thus, regional input suppliers would need to build up relationships with buyers to be nominated. However, most firms stated that if there are competitive regional suppliers available, parent companies and buyers generally agree to source from those suppliers due to lead time and flexibility advantages. Thus, there seems to be scope and interest in regional sourcing. To realize this potential, coordinated efforts at the associations and the regional level would be important to establish relationships between regional input suppliers, parent companies, and buyers.

Firm set-up

As discussed above, the largest potential for regional clothing suppliers in the South African market is in the quick response, fashion, and short run segment where regional suppliers have a potential competitive advantage compared to Asian suppliers. To use this potential, regional suppliers have to restructure and become capable in supplying short runs of fashionable products with short lead times. There are several challenges to this strategy. First, vertical integration is weak in the clothing sector in SSA. With the exception of Mauritius most firms are not vertically integrated and fabric often has to be imported from third countries, which increases lead times and reduces production flexibility. Thus, a competitive regional textile sector or at least local or regional dyeing and finishing facilities are an important competitive advantage for fast and fashion production. Second, there is only limited contact with South African retailers and limited knowledge on the demands and capabilities on both sides—the retailers and the clothing firms. With regard to foreign-owned firms a further challenge is that sales and merchandising decisions are made at the headquarters overseas.

Besides these two challenges, already discussed above, the third challenge relates to firm setup. Most firms in SSA, in particular Asian-owned firms that are part of triangular manufacturing networks, have a firm setup that is geared to long-run basic products and exporting to the U.S. market. This firm set-up is not competitive in the small run, fashion, and quick response business. South African-owned firms in Lesotho and Swaziland, firms in Mauritius, and some firms in Madagascar (and Kenya if trade barriers should be reduced) are geared to a greater extent to small-run and fashion products. However, closer relationships and alignment with retailers are central for these firms. There are cluster initiatives in Cape Town and Durban that explicitly work with South African suppliers as well as textile mills, design houses, and retailers to restructure and upgrade production to establish quick-response relationships. Such programs could be extended on a regional scale. There are also lessons to be learnt from Mauritius, which has been successful in fast fashion production for some time and has successfully pursued this strategy for exporting to South Africa. Firms focused on long-run and basic production could partly adapt, but it is also not useful that all firms in the region concentrate on the quick response, fast-fashion production. The latter is suitable for the South African market but not necessarily for other export markets. But even in the South African market there are opportunities to engage in more basic and high-volume production, in particular for the largest retailers. Some restructuring would be necessary as the volumes would not be comparable with U.S. volumes, but as the successful export experience of some Taiwan, China-owned firms from Swaziland and Lesotho to South Africa shows, these firms should be able to cope with these differing demands. For this strategy, however, it is important that sales and merchandising functions are located in the region and are adapted to the South African market.

For both types of potential regional suppliers certain capabilities will be demanded as buyers, including South African retailers, have increased direct sourcing. Thus, besides manufacturing, other capabilities such as input sourcing, financing, product developing, design understanding, communication, and merchandising capabilities are demanded from suppliers. This is because buyers generally want to work with FOB or full-package manufacturers and not with CMT firms. Further CMT production is the most vulnerable as labor costs are the largest expense driving sourcing decisions and as the value added from CMT production is comparatively low. Mauritian firms have upgraded and generally offer full-package manufacturing functions to buyers. Other firms in SSA still have to upgrade their capabilities to be able to fulfill these functions and create direct relationships with South African (and other) buyers. Given the current window of opportunity—South African retailers are currently developing and formalizing their sourcing strategies—regional suppliers have to become proactive and approach South African retailers.

Coordination and market information

Coordination and strategic partnerships are central to establishing competitive regional production and sourcing networks. Coordination and partnerships need to develop between different countries in the region on the one hand and between cotton, textile, and clothing sector associations on the other. For instance, in several SSA countries there are strategies and funds to revitalize the cotton sector because of its potential to support poor rural households. However, it seems that these programs are not aligned with initiatives in the T&C sectors. In 2005, the establishment of the African Cotton and Textile Industries Federation (ACTIF)—a regional organization of textile and clothing associations from different SSA countries—was a very positive development in this regard. One initiative by ACTIF, for instance, is the 'Brand Africa-Origin Africa' campaign, which aims to promote a regional value chain from cotton, textile, and clothing to design and help Africa make its mark in the fashion world by showing buyers the scope of its design, fabrics, and factories. The initiative is backed by cotton, textile, and clothing manufacturers in 18 SSA countries. The initiative begins with a fashion show involving designers from Tanzania, Uganda, Kenya, Ethiopia, and cotton and silk fabrics made in East Africa, followed by a larger event in Mauritius in November 2010 that will involve around 20 designers from 18 countries using African fabric in their designs (just-style 2010h). Another positive example is the annual Source Africa Business-to-Business event—an Africa-wide sourcing event. The event brings buyers from around the world—including U.S. and EU buyers, international sourcing houses, and South African retailers—face-to-face with textile, clothing, and trims suppliers. In April 2009 this event (organized by the USAID-funded Southern Africa Global Competitiveness Hub) took place for the sixth time (just-style 2010h). Organizations such as ACTIF and B2B events can have an important role in reducing the lack of knowledge of existing production within SSA countries, which inhibits increased cooperation along the T&C value chain. South African retailers lack knowledge about the availability, capabilities, and competitiveness of clothing firms in the region; clothing producers lack knowledge about regional input suppliers. Information on industries and specific firms in different countries in the region would be central to facilitate links between different actors along the T&C value chain. Furthermore, potential investors require information about capacity and product ranges within the region; this information is also required by overseas buyers that are often in charge of nominating input suppliers.

Conclusions

The clothing sector in SSA LICs has a strategic significance in creating employment and exports and, more generally, in the industrial development process of these countries. In this chapter the development and challenges of SSA LIC clothing exporters in the post-quota and post-crisis world have been assessed, as well as specific opportunities for and the challenges of regional integration. The clothing sector in SSA LICs stands at a crossroad. Along with exceptional growth of the clothing sector in the early 2000s in several SSA countries, since around 2004 the industry has declined drastically in the main SSA clothing exporter countries. This is related to changes in the global environment for clothing trade, the specific type of integration of SSA LICs into global clothing value chains, and to endogenous factors. The implementation of suitable policies is central and urgent for the survival and development of the clothing sector in SSA LICs. Several policy recommendations to address challenges and increase the competitiveness and sustainability of the clothing sector in SSA LICs have been discussed above. The main policy areas include (i) securing preferential market access; (ii) improving productivity, skills, and capabilities at the firm-level and developing from CMT to FOB and full-package suppliers; (iii) increasing backward linkages and reducing lead times; (iv) improving physical and bureaucratic infrastructure, in particular with regard to transport, logistics and customs, electricity and water, and access to finance; (v) diversifying end markets and developing a brand 'Made in SSA'; (vi) increasing local involvement in the industry at the management and/or owner level; and (vii) increasing regional integration. In the conclusions in chapter 6, global and country-specific challenges from the country case studies are brought together and main policy recommendations are identified.

Notes

1. South Africa differs from the other SSA main clothing exporters. The clothing and also textile sector was developed and heavily protected by the apartheid state. The sectors concentrated on production for the domestic market and T&C firms had close relationships with South African retailers. When apartheid rule ended, South Africa joined the WTO and reduced tariff protection. In the late 1990s and early 2000s T&C firms were still competitive due to their relatively modern technology and a depreciating rand, and in addition to supplying the local market expanded exports. Since 2002, however, the sectors have deteriorated due to declining cost competitiveness and productivity, and an appreciating rand. Exports have collapsed and imports, particularly from China, have increased considerably, crowding out production for the local market (Gibbon 2002b, Morris and Einhorn 2008).

2. In Mauritius, the clothing sector was the focal point of the country's industrialization and de-

velopment strategy in the 1970s, 1980s, and 1990s. Between 1982 and 1990, the number of firms in Mauritius' EPZs (which are dominated by clothing investment) increased from 120 to 570, and employment in these firms quadrupled from 20,000 to 80,000 (Gereffi and Memedovic 2003). In the mid-1990s, the upgrading strategies of most Mauritian clothing exporters, in particular the ones exporting to the EU, centered on improving production, product development and design capabilities, and diversifying products and buyers rather than the riskier strategy of moving from OEM to OBM production. From 1997 onward, large-run and basic production started to be delocalized to Madagascar, which allowed Mauritian firms to remain competitive in this type of production for the EU and U.S. market despite increasing costs at home (Gibbon 2003a).

3. Clothing is defined as HS 61 and 62. There are two sources for clothing export data – import statistics of SSA's trading partners as reported in the UN COMTRADE database and export figures reported by SSA countries. Values differ significantly and values reported by SSA's trading partners exceed SSA's exports statistics in some years by a margin of around 25 percent. Although, there are differences in magnitudes both data sources show the same trends. If not otherwise stated, import data from partner countries is reported in this study.

4. Mauritius and Madagascar obtained preferential market access under the Lomé and later Cotonou Agreement; Madagascar later also under the EBA Initiative. South Africa obtained preferential market access only in 2004 under the Trade, Development and Cooperation Arrangement between South Africa and the EU.

5. The TCF derogation is a special rule that applies to lesser developed SSA countries, allowing them duty-free access for clothing made from fabric originating anywhere in the world. This derogation was initially granted until September 2004 but then extended twice to 2007 and 2012.

6. Furthermore, in the case of Lesotho and Swaziland the Duty Credit Certificate (DCC) Scheme of the Southern African Customs Union (SACU) subsidized clothing exporters. The DCC is a rebate of 25 percent on the duty to be paid on imports of T&C products based on the value of goods exported outside of SACU. It was introduced in March 2003 to run until March 2005 but was renewed until March 2007 and then again until March 2009. Many firms in Lesotho and Swaziland said that the DCC scheme was crucial for their survival in the context of the MFA phaseout. Only a minority of these DCCs was actually used for own-account fabric imports; most were sold to South African retailers who used them for clothing imports. However, the regulation changed in 2006 to only allow reselling to other manufacturers, which reduced the price of DCC from around 80 percent to around 50 percent of the face value. In March 2009 a further extension to the scheme was agreed but the traded value of the DCC became worth even less as the DCC could only be used for imported inputs of seven product lines of yarns and fabrics, down from 102 product lines including clothing. In March 2011 the DCC scheme is scheduled to phase out.

7. Including, as part of the SADC EPA group, Mozambique, Botswana, Lesotho, and Swaziland (but not Angola, South Africa, or Namibia) and, as part of the ESA-EPA group, the Seychelles, Zimbabwe, Mauritius, Comoros, Madagascar, and Zambia (but not Djibouti, Eritrea, Ethiopia, Malawi, Sudan, and Somalia). Kenya, Uganda, Tanzania, Burundi, and Rwanda initialed an interim EPA as part of the EAC-EPA group.

8. The United States imposed quotas under the MFA for certain products in Mauritius, Kenya, and Lesotho that were removed under AGOA, however. Mauritius fully utilized most of its quota allocation but Kenya and Lesotho did not. The other SSA countries did not face quota restrictions.

9. Toward the end of the 1990s, Mauritian producers that had exceeded their quotas in the United States and particularly the EU relocated some of their production to Madagascar to take advantage of its unutilized quotas.

10. Quota prices are typically low early in the year and rise as quota is consumed (Gibbon 2003a).

11. Some countries received derogation with regard to ROO. During the late 1980s the Lomé ROO requirements were changed from single to double transformation. Lesotho successfully applied for derogation, which was allowed for a period of four years and was then renewed for another four years (Salm et al. 2002). In 1997 the derogation expired and since then exports to the EU have been marginal.

12. To be eligible for AGOA preferences countries must meet certain criteria: countries must make progress toward market reform and protection of property rights, maintenance of the rule of law,

removal of impediments to U.S. trade and investment, the introduction of policies to reduce poverty, policies to combat corruption, and compliance with international standards covering workers rights (McCormick et al. 2006).

13. AGOA lesser developed countries are not identical to the UN's LDCs, though the two lists are overlapping. In particular, Kenya and Swaziland are lesser developed countries for the purpose of AGOA, but are not LDCs.

14. Preferences were limited to clothing. However, from 2007 onwards a provision was added to AGOA that allows lesser developed countries to export certain textile articles originating entirely in one or more lesser developed countries.

15. In 2010, the African countries eligible for the clothing provision for AGOA are Benin, Botswana, Burkina Faso, Cameroon, Cape Verde, Chad, Ethiopia, Ghana, Kenya, Lesotho, Madagascar, Malawi, Mali, Mauritius, Mozambique, Namibia, Nigeria, Rwanda, Senegal, Sierra Leone, South Africa, Tanzania, Uganda, and Zambia. Madagascar was removed from the list of AGOA beneficiary countries in January 2010, together with Guinea and Niger.

16. The only important clothing manufacturing country that remains excluded from AGOA benefits is Zimbabwe.

17. An exception being Lesotho in the late 1980s and the first half of the 1990s but this was related to its ROO derogation.

18. The TCF provision was extended but in AGOA IV an abundant supply provision was added and certain denim articles were designated as being in abundant supply, which meant that regional supply would need to be used first before imports under the TCF provision were allowed. This provision was however never really implemented due to strong opposition of some buyers and was repealed in October 2008.

19. In Kenya there are some locally Indian/Kenyan-owned and one (non-Indian origin) Kenyan-owned export firm.

20. In Lesotho only one screen-printing firm is owned by a local and in Swaziland one clothing firm is locally owned, but the husband of the owner is from Taiwan, China.

21. To understand investment patterns political factors also have to be taken into account. Investment in Lesotho and Swaziland is highly dominated by Taiwan, China, which can be explained by strong political and diplomatic ties between these countries and Taiwan, China. These countries still accept Taiwan, China as an independent country, which led to incentives from the government for investment in Lesotho and Swaziland. In Mauritius investment in the 1970s and 1980s was dominated by Hong Kong SAR, China, which remained quite dominant until the first half of the 2000s. This can be explained by policies by the Mauritian government, which offered investors from Hong Kong SAR, China Mauritian passports for a certain minimum investment that was high in demand in the context of insecurity due to China's annexation of Hong Kong SAR, China.

22. Another problem in establishing direct relationships with buyers is that buyers generally have no sourcing or buying offices in SSA. In the beginning of the 2000s due to AGOA, buyers such as Levy's, Gap, and Liz Claiborne and sourcing agents such as MAST, Linmark, and Li & Fung had offices in South Africa and several also in Mauritius and Madagascar. However, in the context of the MFA phaseout and in Madagascar even earlier due to the political crisis (Morris and Sedowski 2006b), sourcing offices closed and there is a general trend in concentrating sourcing offices in Asia. This makes it difficult for local or regional firms to establish direct contacts to buyers. But even before the closure most of these offices were not real sourcing offices; they were mostly involved in QA and compliance. Orders were generally channeled through Taiwan, China, Hong Kong SAR, China, and Singapore where buyers have their main sourcing offices (Gibbon 2002b).

23. For Lesotho and Swaziland exports to South Africa are underreported as they involve intra-SACU trade (see below).

24. Differences with regard to the South Africa market are discussed below in the part on regional integration.

25. Related to these different requirements the set up of firms exporting to the United States and the EU is different. Firms that produce for the U.S. market are specialized in long-run basic products. One firm manager said (and many supported this statement) that the firm is only profitable if they produce one style for more than a month. For example, for a firm with 1,000 to 2,000 workers,

which is now the average of Taiwan, China-owned firms in Lesotho and Swaziland, this means that they need very large volumes. These volumes are generally only available in the U.S. mass market. Workers in these firms are mostly specialized in certain production steps and inputs often come in large volumes.

26. In particular data for Madagascar seems to be too low.

27. Minimum wages in both Cambodia and Bangladesh will be increased to US$61 and US$43 per month in October and November 2010 respectively.

28. Unfortunately, there is no consistent up to date productivity data for the clothing sector in SSA LICs available which makes it not possible to compare unit labor costs.

29. However, when exchange rates change in a negative direction for the buyers, price renegotiations are generally demanded and have to be accepted by suppliers.

30. South African import data shows imports from Lesotho and Swaziland accounting for US$14,528 and US$1,670 respectively in 2008. Export data from Swaziland shows significantly higher trade flows of US$45 million for 2007 which accounts for 5 percent of total South African clothing imports. For Lesotho no export data is available. For Botswana, South African import data shows imports accounting for US$11,288 in 2008. Export data from Botswana shows trade flows of US$49 million for 2006 which accounts for 5 percent of total South African clothing imports. Namibia is no important clothing exporter to South Africa even when looking at export data.

31. For the whole region less than 5 percent of SSA clothing exports went to the region and 11 percent of SSA clothing imports were sourced regionally in 2008.

32. These market concentration levels have prevailed since the 1970s. Most of the large retailers have also subsidiaries in other SSA countries that they are planning to extend. Thus, by establishing sourcing relationships with South African retailers there is the potential of a growing regional market if income and consumption levels in other SSA countries increase.

33. Tariffs on six yarns that are not domestically produced in South Africa were eliminated.

34. A relatively unusual feature of the South African clothing retail sector is that of the six leading retailers, two have in-house production facilities; however, they only produce a minimal share (less than 2 percent) of their intake. Two others source an important part of their intake through a self-organized network of CMT firms where the retailers are in charge of design and input sourcing.

35. The exception is one smaller mid-market retailer whose share of locally sourced intake remained quite stable at around 70 percent for the last 30 years. This retailer tries to develop 'fast fashion' production and has had some problems with importing from third countries due to the small volumes and different styles it requires.

36. Some retailers were skeptical about sourcing from Madagascar due to the political instability.

37. The average consumption level in South Africa is considerably lower than in the United States and the EU, which makes the market very price-sensitive. However, fashionability is also important because clothing is often the only way to represent status in low-income households. An important point related to this is that South Africa is one season behind the U.S. and the EU markets, which explains in part the relatively low investment in design by retailers: European and to a lesser extent U.S. designs can be adapted.

38. Although offshore sourcing was earlier concentrated in long-run basic products (currently the case with South African retailers), many buyers in the United States and EU now also source short-run and more fashionable products from overseas. This is related to changes in sourcing strategies and professionalizing sourcing, which can considerably reduce lead times and increase flexibility, but also due to capabilities of suppliers and improved infrastructure.

39. All retailers said that when the global economic crisis started and U.S. and EU orders declined, they were contacted by Asian suppliers but they were not approached by regional suppliers, with the exception of Mauritius.

40. A shortcoming of the trade data analysis is that there is no accurate data for Lesotho and Swaziland as intra-SACU trade is underrepresented.

41. For yarn it has remained stable at 5 percent.

42. Yarn is defined as HS 5204-5207, 5301-5308, 5401-5406, and 5501-5511.

43. Fabric is defined as HS 5208-5212, 5309-531, 5407-5408, and 5512-5516, chapters 56, 57, 58, 59, and 60.

44. The duty on clothing products made from synthetic or synthetic-rich fabrics peaks at 32 percent and the highest duty on clothing made from cotton peaks at around 20 percent. EU duties on clothing made from man-made fibers and cotton are similar.

45. LDCs in SADC include Malawi, Mozambique, Tanzania, and Zambia.

46. Another point here is that South African retailers pay in rand. For South African-owned firms this is an advantage as they can reduce the currency risk which then only affects imports from Asia. However, firms owned and headquartered in Taiwan, China are not interested in receiving their payment in rand. For them the exchange rate risk increases as their headquarters operations as well as most parts of their global operations and most inputs are handled in U.S. dollars. Only wages and local costs, mostly utility costs, are paid in local currencies.

CHAPTER 4

Cambodia's Clothing Exports: From Assembly to Full-Package Supplier?

Introduction

This chapter assesses the development of the clothing sector in Cambodia and its challenges in the post-quota and post-crisis world. Cambodia is a latecomer to clothing exporting as it only became a clothing exporter in the mid-1990s following almost three decades of political and social unrest. Today, Cambodia is very dependent on the clothing sector, which has played the leading role in its development process from the 1990s onwards. The sector developed rapidly into the largest export sector, accounting for almost 80 percent of Cambodia's export revenues and nearly 30 percent of industrial employment. The growth of the sector was driven by foreign direct investment (FDI) as foreign investors were attracted by Multi-Fibre Arrangement (MFA) quota hopping and preferential market access as well as by Cambodia's low labor costs. Hence, foreign ownership, the MFA quota system, and preferential market access, in particular through the United States-Cambodia Bilateral Textile Agreement in which quota increases were linked to improvements in working conditions, have played central roles in the development of Cambodia's clothing sector.

Although expectations regarding the impact of the MFA phaseout on Cambodia's clothing exports were pessimistic, Cambodia increased export value and market share after 2004. However, Cambodia's clothing industry has declined quite drastically since 2008 in terms of production, exports, employment, and number of firms. Direct reasons for this decline are significant changes in the environment for global clothing trade, in particular, the phaseout of the China safeguards at the end of 2008 and the global economic crisis. Besides these 'external' reasons, 'internal' factors are also important in explaining the decline, in particular the specific integration of Cambodia into global clothing value chains based on quota hopping and, to some extent, preferential market access dominated by foreign investments, cut-make-trim (CMT) production, and a disintegrated clothing industry with limited local or regional linkages. This specific integration of Cambodia limits the role the sector can play in promoting export diversification and industrial development. The implementation of suitable policies has therefore become central for the development of the clothing sector as well as for Cambodia's industrial development prospects more generally.

The chapter is structured in the following way. The first part presents an overview of Cambodia's clothing industry focusing on recent developments of Cambodia's clothing exports and the specific way Cambodia has been integrating into global clothing value chains. In the second part, main internal challenges of the clothing sector that are strongly linked to Cambodia's specific integration are discussed, and policy recommendations are pointed out. The third part concludes.

Overview of Cambodia's Clothing Industry

The development of Cambodia's clothing industry can be divided into four periods: developments before 2004, post-MFA, global economic crisis, and post-crisis.

Phase 1: Developments before 2004

Cambodia is a latecomer to clothing exporting as it only became a clothing exporter in the mid-1990s following almost three decades of political and social unrest. Although the origins of the Cambodian clothing industry go back to the French colonial area (1863–1953), the current foundation of the clothing industry was established by foreign investors from Hong Kong SAR, China, Taiwan, China, Malaysia, and Singapore. These investors were attracted by unused quota under the MFA and preferential market access, as well as by the relatively low labor costs stemming from Cambodia's large labor surplus. In contrast to neighboring countries such as Vietnam, Cambodia did not build on earlier import-substituting industrialization in textile and clothing (T&C). Instead, the government shifted directly from a centrally planned market system to a free market economy in the mid-1990s, including the privatization of the few state-owned T&C firms.

The MFA quota system and preferential market access have played central roles in the development of the clothing sector. The clothing industry in Cambodia developed under the MFA, which supported the growth of clothing exports in several low-income countries (LICs) as established clothing exporter countries reached their quota limits and started triangular manufacturing networks in LICs to use their excess quota or quota-free access to the U.S. and the EU markets. When the sector started in Cambodia it faced no quota restrictions to the United States and the EU as it was not part of the MFA system. In 1996 Cambodia as a nonmember of the World Trade Organization (WTO) was granted most favored nation (MFN) status for the U.S. and the EU markets. In 1999 Cambodia received quota- and duty-free access for clothing exports to the EU market subject to double transformation rules of origin (ROO) under the three-and-a-half year EU-Cambodian Textile Agreement and from 2001 onwards under the Everything But Arms (EBA) Initiative for least developed countries (LDCs). However, the major takeoff of the industry resulted from the United States-Cambodia Bilateral Textile Agreement, which was concluded in 1999.

As exports from Cambodia to the United States increased rapidly, negotiations were started between the U.S. and the Cambodian government in 1998 to bring Cambodia under the MFA quota system. U.S. and Cambodian negotiators agreed on the United States-Cambodian Bilateral Trade Agreement on Textile and Apparel for the three-year period from 1999 to 2001 that established fixed quotas for the 12 largest categories of clothing exports from Cambodia to the United States. However, these quotas were the most generous on a per capita basis among all countries given Cambodia's commitment to improve core labor standards. The two governments agreed that if the Cambodian government was able to secure compliance by clothing factories with the country's labor laws and internationally agreed labor standards, then quotas would be increased on an annual basis. The decisions for quota increases were based on a monitoring program—the Garment Sector Working Conditions Improvement Project—conducted by the International Labour Organization (ILO) (see box 4.1). In 2000 and 2001 a 9 percent increase of all quota categories was decided. In 2001, the trade agreement was extended for three

---

Box 4.1. Better Factories Cambodia

Better Factories Cambodia, the ILO monitoring program in Cambodia, is the most comprehensive and systematic monitoring effort governing any country's clothing sector and is a promising attempt to promote compliance with labor standards through trade agreements. It combined positive incentives to comply with labor standards offered under the bilateral textile agreement between the United States and Cambodia with monitoring of compliance by the ILO. All factories in the sector are registered with Better Factories Cambodia. A team of local Khmer-speaking inspectors is engaged in a constant 10-month cycle of monitoring visits, which culminates in factory reports and a publicly available synthesis report. The process is streamlined via a computerized information management system that buyers and suppliers can access. The monitors' checklist (based on Cambodian labor law and the ILO core labor standards[a]) covers over 480 items. Better Factories Cambodia can be seen as a model program and the new ILO-IFC Better Work program is taking this experience to other countries and eventually also other sectors.

The program is based on two policy innovations (Polaski 2009): (i) the creation of a trade agreement that provides positive market access incentives as rewards for improved labor conditions, and (ii) the inauguration of a new monitoring role in the private sector by an international organization. Before this program, linking trade and labor rights generally involved creating disincentives: for example, preferential market access could be reduced if labor laws were not enforced. Cambodia, however, was guaranteed a baseline quota that could be extended annually based on progress of working conditions in the previous period. Because the arrangement was repeated each year it created the potential for continuous improvements. The United States-Cambodia agreement with its requirement for reliable, timely, and credible information about actual factory conditions pushed the ILO to move beyond its traditional scope of action in the public sphere and to monitor the private sector through on-site inspections of factories.

There were two shortcomings in the arrangement, which were subsequently addressed (Polaski 2009). First, the ILO monitoring program provided for voluntary participation by factories, but the quota bonus was awarded to the whole country based on the overall performance of the clothing sector. The information would be incomplete and probably not representative as there existed a free rider problem. The Cambodian government established a regulation that limited the availability of export licenses to the United States to those firms participating in the monitoring program, which resulted in full participation and a complete monitoring of the sector. In 2006 this regulation was adapted to also include subcontracting firms as in some cases monitoring was circumvented by using subcontractors. Second, the ILO monitoring program required reports on working conditions but there was no decision about the form of the reports, in particular if aggregate or individual firm information should be reported. The reporting was divided into two stages. A first report published aggregate results for all firms inspected. These synthesis reports give an overview of problems in the sector without naming individual firms. After a grace period during which factories can remedy any problems found, the factories are re-inspected. If problems have not been remedied then they are reported for each factory by name in a subsequent report. This system secures a high level of transparency.

Source: Better Factories Cambodia (2010), Miller et al. (2008), and Polaski (2009).
a. The member states of the ILO, currently 183 countries, agreed that all workers have certain fundamental rights, regardless of the level of development of countries. These include the right to freedom of association and collective bargaining, freedom from forced labor, restriction on employment of children and eliminations of the worst forms of child labor, and freedom from discrimination in employment (ILO 1998).

additional years from 2002 to 2004. Across the board quota increases of 9 percent, 12 percent, and 18 percent were awarded for those years (Polaski 2009). The United States-Cambodia Textile Agreement and the ILO monitoring program were central for the initial growth of the clothing sector in Cambodia. They granted generous and increased quotas that secured exports to the U.S. market and gave exposure to Cambodia so that consumers, buyers, and manufacturers got to know Cambodia as a clothing exporter country.

The government of Cambodia generally supported the development of the sector. The government approved the establishment of 100 percent foreign-owned firms in Cambodia in 1994, has improved the business environment, and has provided favorable polices for foreign investors. These policies include duty-free imports for export sectors, the provision of tax holidays and incentives, the introduction of laws to establish export processing zones (EPZs), one-stop services to simplify investment procedures, and the negotiation of bilateral investment agreements with various countries to protect foreign investors (Natsuda et al. 2009). The government also prepared a sector strategy for the clothing sector in 2005, which has not however been implemented. However, besides FDI-friendly policies, state capacity for proactive policies to support the clothing sector and increase competitiveness and upgrading has been rather weak, in particular compared to competitor countries such as China and Vietnam.

The following section shows the significant development of the clothing sector in Cambodia in terms of exports, number of firms, and employment.

Exports

Clothing exports have increased significantly since the mid-1990s.[1] Import data from Cambodia's trading partners shows an increase from US$63 million in 1995 to US$2,434 million in 2004 up to a peak of US$4,037 million in 2008 (see table 4.1). Between 2000 and 2008 clothing exports grew with an annual average growth rate of nearly 20 percent. The share of Cambodia in global clothing exports increased from 0.33 percent in 1998 to 1.21 percent in 2008. Looking at Cambodia's clothing export data as reported by the Ministry of Commerce, export values are lower, accounting for US$1,158 million in 2001, US$1,983 million in 2004, and reaching a peak of US$2,960 million in 2008 (see table 4.2). The Ministry of Commerce also reports data for 2009 where exports declined to US$2,344 million (see below on the impact of the global economic crisis). With regard to export markets, in 2008 over 60 percent of exports went to the United States and 25 percent to the EU (see table 4.3).

Table 4.1. Cambodia's Clothing Exports

	1995	1998	2001	2004	2005	2006	2007	2008
Total exports (US$ million)	63	579	1,430	2,434	2,696	3,324	3,764	4,037
Growth rate (%)	—	101	18	24	11	23	13	7
Global share (%)	0.04	0.33	0.73	0.97	1.00	1.15	1.19	1.21
Woven (US$ million)	30	240	689	1,108	1,106	1,128	1,155	1,127
(%)	48	41	48	46	41	34	31	28
Knit (US$ million)	33	338	741	1,326	1,591	2,196	2,609	2,910
(%)	52	58	52	54	59	66	69	72

Source: UN COMTRADE.
Note: Imports reported by partner countries. Values in million US$.

Table 4.2. Cambodia's Clothing Exports (as reported by Cambodia)

	2001	2002	2003	2004	2005	2006	2007	2008	2009
Total exports (US$ million)	1,158	1,344	1,610	1,983	2,190	2,652	2,866	2,981	2,419
Growth rate (%)		16.1	19.8	23.2	10.4	21.1	8.1	4.0	19.0
U.S. exports (US$ million)	829	960	1,123	1,272	1,565	1,906	1,999	1,988	1,508
(%)	71.6	71.4	69.8	64.2	71.4	71.9	69.8	66.7	62.3
EU exports (US$ million)	309	356	408	580	491	571	632	659	578
(%)	26.7	26.5	25.3	29.3	22.4	21.5	22.0	22.1	23.9
Canada exports (US$ million)	6	7	58	97	92	116	154	199	195
(%)	0.5	0.5	3.6	4.9	4.2	4.4	5.4	6.7	8.1
Other markets (US$ million)	13	21	21	34	43	58	81	156	138
(%)	1.2	1.6	1.3	1.7	1.9	2.2	2.8	5.2	5.7

Source: Cambodian Ministry of Commerce.
Note: Values in million US$.

Table 4.3. Cambodia's Main Clothing Export Markets

Country	2000		2004		2006		2008	
	Value (US$ 1,000)	Share (%)	Value (US$ 1,000)	Share (%)	Value (US$ 1,000)	Share (%)	Value (US$ 1,000)	Share (%)
United States	854,180	70.4	1,507,837	61.9	2,266,087	68.2	2,502,741	62.0
EU-15	271,876	22.4	725,706	29.8	781,106	23.5	985,651	24.4
Canada	10,704	0.9	104,431	4.3	127,878	3.8	245,604	6.1
Poland	672	0.1	2,952	0.1	6,970	0.2	47,916	1.2
Mexico	—	—	3,426	0.1	13,864	0.4	31,820	0.8
Russian Federation	—	—	—	—	7,803	0.2	24,174	0.6
Singapore	61,015	5.0	36,924	1.5	37,206	1.1	23,030	0.6
Switzerland	2,881	0.2	14,509	0.6	14,626	0.4	21,957	0.5
Japan	1,731	0.1	9,554	0.4	13,638	0.4	18,804	0.5
Turkey	559	0.0	2,426	0.1	6,443	0.2	18,679	0.5
Norway	3,736	0.3	6,724	0.3	8,395	0.3	14,760	0.4

Source: UN COMTRADE.
Note: Values in 1,000 US$.

Number of firms and employment

The number of clothing factories increased from around 20 in 1995 to a peak of nearly 300 in 2007[2] (see table 4.4). This number only accounts for firms exporting directly and thus having an export license and being members of the Garment Manufacturing Association in Cambodia (GMAC). Altogether there are around 500 firms also including small firms producing for the local market and subcontractors of exporting firms. The industry is highly concentrated in Phnom Penh; some firms are also located near the port of Sihanoukville. Most clothing firms are not located in EPZs as locations outside EPZs offer the same incentives, including duty-free imports, tax holidays, and other financial incentives; comparable infrastructure; and the geographical availability of workers. In terms of factory size, just over one quarter of factories employ less than 500 workers, most factories employ between 500 and 2,000 workers.

Table 4.4. Number of Firms and Employment in Cambodia's Clothing Industry

	2000	2002	2004	2005	2006	2007	2008	2009
Nr. of firms								
registered	216	248	300	351	398	432	455	487
operating	190	188	219	247	290	292	284	243
Employment								
registered	171,506	226,484	300,043	328,466	379,293	414,789	407,927	405,249
operating	162,412	210,440	269,846	283,906	334,063	353,017	324,871	281,855

Source: GMAC, end of year data.

In 1995 the clothing sector employed around 19,000 workers; at its peak in 2007 it employed over 350,000 workers (see table 4.4). Around 90 percent of the workers are women, over 60 percent are below the age of 24, 47 percent have only elementary school education or less, and most workers come from rural areas (Hatsukano 2005). It is estimated that besides these direct jobs also 242,000 indirect jobs have been created through the clothing sector: 113,000 in the services sector, including transportation and trade; 37,000 in nonclothing manufacturing, in particular in construction; and 92,000 jobs in the agriculture sector (EIC 2007, cited in Natsuda et al. 2009).

Phase 2: Post-MFA

Competition among clothing exporters has intensified since 2005 when the MFA phased out. Expectations on the impact of the MFA phaseout on Cambodia's clothing exports were pessimistic. Cambodia was however able to increase its export value and market share after 2004. Looking at import data by Cambodia's trading partners, total clothing exports increased to US$2,696 million in 2005, which accounts for an 11 percent increase over 2004 (see table 4.1). The share of Cambodia in global clothing exports increased from 0.97 percent in 2004 to 1 percent in 2005 and 1.15 percent in 2006. This increase was based on knit exports, which increased by nearly 20 percent in 2005 while woven exports stagnated, as well as on U.S. exports. U.S. exports increased by 20 percent in 2005 (with woven exports increasing by 6 percent and knit exports by 36 percent; see table 4.5). Cambodian exports to the EU, however, fell by 8 percent from 2004 to 2005 (with woven exports decreasing by 26 percent and knit exports by 3 percent; see table 4.6). Looking at Cambodia's export data, total export increased by 10 percent in 2005. U.S. exports increased by nearly 25 percent; EU exports decreased by 15 percent (see table 4.2).

Table 4.5. Cambodia's Clothing Exports to the United States

	1996	1998	2001	2004	2005	2006	2007	2008	2009
Total exports (US$ million)	2	358	921	1,417	1,703	2,131	2,421	2,369	1,866
Growth rate (%)	—	265	15	15	20	25	14	-2	-21
U.S. share (%)	0.0	0.7	1.6	2.1	2.4	2.9	3.2	3.2	2.9
Woven (US$ million)	2	170	517	776	827	834	837	786	585
(%)	95	47	56	55	49	39	35	33	31
Knit (US$ million)	0	189	404	640	875	1,297	1,584	1,584	1,281
(%)	5	53	44	45	51	61	65	67	69

Source: USITC.
Note: Values in million US$.

Table 4.6. Cambodia's Clothing Exports to the EU-15

	1995	1998	2001	2004	2005	2006	2007	2008	2009
Total exports (€ million)	43	151	395	517	475	552	524	554	535
Growth rate (%)	—	7	40	23	-8	16	-5	6	-3
EU-15 share (%)	0.1	0.2	0.5	0.6	0.5	0.6	0.5	0.5	0.5
Woven (€ million)	19	44	114	134	99	99	83	83	70
(%)	44	29	29	26	21	18	16	15	13
Knit (€ million)	24	107	281	383	376	453	442	471	465
(%)	56	71	71	74	79	82	84	85	87

Source: EUROSTAT.
Note: Value in million euro.

The number of operating firms increased from 219 in 2004 to 247 in 2005 and total employment from around 270,000 to nearly 280,000 in 2005 (see table 4.4). However, although employment has increased, there has been considerable employment adjustment within the industry. As buyers have consolidated their suppliers between and within countries and have sourced from fewer but larger factories, generally smaller factories closed in Cambodia and the remaining factories have increased in size. The number of factories in Cambodia employing more than 5,000 workers more than doubled between 2004 and 2005 (Natsuda et al. 2009).

When the MFA phased out at the end of 2004, the United States-Cambodia Textile Trade Agreement, which was based on the quota system, also ended. But the Cambodian government and clothing firms decided to continue the ILO monitoring program for three more years and together with the ILO developed a long-term plan to make the monitoring program eventually self-sustaining. The focus shifted from the U.S. Department of Labor to the Cambodian government, manufacturers, and buyers, and the project expanded to include capacity-building and training programs for government officials, managers, and workers (Polaski 2009). However, one of the main incentives of the program was lost at the end of 2004 when the MFA phased out—access to higher quotas for improvements in working conditions. Since then the primary incentive for buyers has been labor compliance and the associated 'reputation risk insurance' as the ILO monitoring program has higher credibility than buyers' own codes of conduct (CoC).

This export growth after the MFA phaseout and the end of the United States-Cambodia Bilateral Textile Agreement has to be viewed in the context of the re-imposition of quotas on certain categories of clothing imports from China to the United States and the EU between 2005 and 2008. For the United States, over 40 percent of Cambodia's exports occur in categories in which the United States imposed safeguards on clothing exports from China. Furthermore, Vietnam, a main competitor of Cambodia, continued to be subject to quotas after 2004 as it only became a WTO member in January 2007.

Phase 3: Global Economic Crisis

Due to the global economic crisis global demand for clothing products sharply declined in 2008 and 2009. The crisis has affected many countries around the world. Cambodia's clothing sector has been one of the hardest hit in the region. GMAC reported that the slowdown in orders started in the second half of 2008 and continued in 2009. Looking at import data by Cambodia's trading partners, total clothing exports increased by 7 percent in 2008, which is considerable lower than growth rates in previous years (see table 4.1). Clothing exports to the United States fell by 2 percent in 2008 and 21 percent in 2009 and clothing exports to the EU increased by 6 percent in 2008 and declined by 3 percent in 2009 (see tables 4.6 and 4.7). Looking at Cambodia's export data, total export increased by 4 percent in 2008 and decreased by 19 percent in 2009. Exports to the United States decreased by 2 percent in 2008 and 26 percent in 2009; exports to the EU increased by 4 percent in 2008 and decreased by 13 percent in 2009.

Not only have orders decreased but prices have been affected considerably, in particular in the second half of 2009. All firms interviewed reported that the pressure on prices from buyers has increased due to the crisis and that they had to reduce prices on average by 5 to 10 percent (which, however, varies significantly from product to product). Unit value analysis for U.S. and EU-15 exports of Cambodia shows that unit values have generally declined for woven and knit products since 2000.[3] For the United States, unit prices for knit and woven products (where volumes are reported in dozens[4]) declined in 2008 and 2009, as well as post-MFA in 2005 and 2006. For the EU, unit values of knit and woven exports declined in 2008; however, unit values of woven exports increased in 2009.[5] Data from Cambodia's Ministry of Economy and Finance shows that unit prices of Cambodia's total clothing exports declined by 10 percent in the first half of 2010 compared to the previous years—to the United States by 11 percent and to the EU by 8 percent (Seiha 2010). Figure 4.1 shows a decline in unit prices since 2004, in particular for exports to the United States. Besides prices, lead times also have been reduced

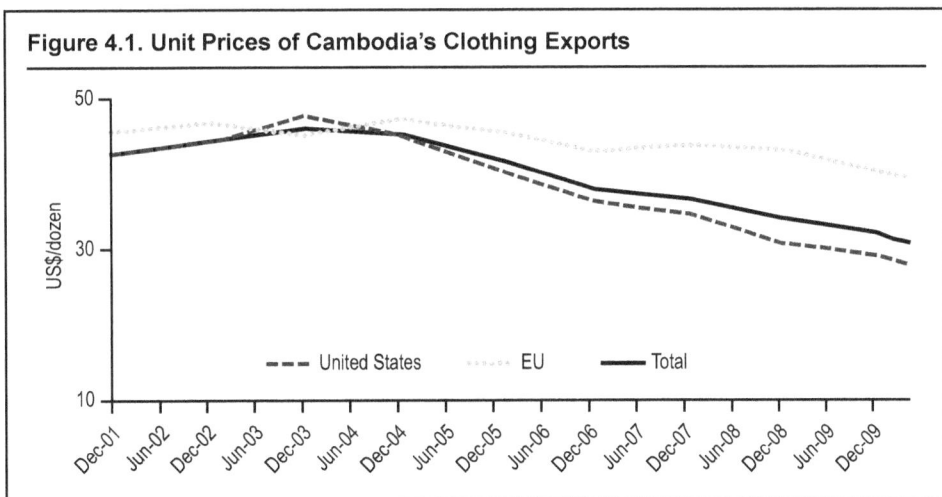

Figure 4.1. Unit Prices of Cambodia's Clothing Exports

Source: MEF; Seiha 2010.
Note: Export price in US$/dozen.

and contract time has been shortened, leading to increased flexibility on the buyers' side but limited planning possibilities on the suppliers' side. The crisis also led to financing problems as access to credit from banks has become more difficult and prices have increased, and as credit lines from suppliers have decreased, in particular from textile mills. Generally, buyers have not adapted their credit line demands to support their suppliers, with a few exceptions.

The reduction in exports is mirrored by a rise of factory closures. While 292 factories were operating in 2007, in 2008 the number decreased to 284 and in 2009 to 243 (see table 4.4). Beginning in November 2008, a wave of factory closures ended a trend of relatively steady growth. Within a year's time, the number of operating factories dropped from a peak of 313 in October 2008 to a low of 241 in November 2009, with most of the remaining factories running at only 60–70 percent of their capacity (Better Factories Cambodia 2010). Altogether around 70 factories have closed down since the start of the global economic crisis in 2008. Total employment declined from 353,000 in 2007 to 325,000 in 2008 and 282,000 end of 2009 (see table 4.4). Around 75,500 workers lost their jobs since the start of the global economic crisis in 2008, which represents 20 percent of the workforce in the sector. In addition to job losses, wages declined due to cuts in regular working hours (including work suspensions and mandatory leave) and reduced overtime. Furthermore, duration of contracts was shortened and payments were delayed (Better Factories Cambodia 2010). Job losses, decreasing job security, and reduced wages have contributed to an increase in the number of strikes. In 2008 there were 30 percent more strikes reported than in 2007 (from 80 in 2007 to 105 in 2008). This number, however, decreased to 58 in 2009, which can be largely explained by factory closures.

The export decline in 2009 can be explained by three main factors: (i) the reduction of orders due to the global economic crisis, (ii) the phaseout of the China safeguards at the end of 2008, and (iii) increased competitiveness of Cambodia's main competitor countries Vietnam and Bangladesh. The China safeguards shielded Cambodia from direct competition with China after the MFA phaseout until the end of 2008 but the impact should not be overstated as China is not a direct competitor of Cambodia. In the 2000s China moved up the value chain and started to export higher-value clothing products. However, this has partially changed due to the global economic crisis as China has again moved to more basic clothing exports. This has increased competition in the basics market segment. Nevertheless, Vietnam and Bangladesh are the main direct competitors of Cambodia. In 2005 Cambodia's clothing sector still had a competitive advantage but this has changed since then due to several factors. First, Vietnam and Bangladesh are not that focused on the U.S. market, which has been particularly affected by the crisis as they export to the EU to a larger extent than Cambodia. Second, antidumping safeguards phased out for Vietnam and the country became member of the WTO in January 2007, receiving more favorable market access to the U.S. and the EU markets. Third, Vietnam and even more Bangladesh are highly competitive in the low-end basics market segment due to their low costs structure. However, both countries have also upgraded and an increasing share of firms in those countries offers more than CMT capabilities and is in charge of input sourcing and pattern making. Further, backward linkages have increased in both countries. Fourth, besides generally decreased orders in the context of the global economic crisis, buyers changed the composition of sourcing countries shifting orders to the lowest cost and most competitive sourcing countries, including China, Bangladesh, and Vietnam. Fifth, the majority of firms in Bangladesh and to a lesser extent in Vietnam are locally owned, which increases upgrading possibilities and the potential for local linkages and spillovers due to more decision-making power located locally (see below). In contrast, in Cambodia the large majority of clothing factories are foreign owned and part of triangular manufacturing networks. With increasing job losses in the company's home bases, in particular China, orders for CMT factories in Cambodia have decreased as orders have been shifted from marginal to core suppliers.

Phase 4: Post-crisis?

Developments with regard to exports, number of firms, and employment draw a rather gloomy picture of the clothing sector in Cambodia. However, data from the first half of 2010 suggest that the industry has hit the bottom. Employment and the number of firms seem to have stabilized and in January 2010, for the first time since December 2008, clothing exports increased (by 7.3 percent) compared to the same month of the previous year. In the first half of 2010 exports increased by 10.3 percent compared to the previous year. However, the global environment for clothing trade has changed post-crisis. Earlier trends have been accelerated in the aftermath of the global economic crisis, including the increased importance of lead times and flexibility, demands for higher manufacturing skills and broader capabilities and services from suppliers, and generally supply chain rationalization strategies of global buyers (see chapter 2). Price decreases demanded in the crisis context by buyers will very likely become permanent. Competition in the low-value segment, where Cambodia is concentrated, has further increased as some more advanced countries, in particular China, which moved up to higher-value products in the 2000s have moved again to lower-end production in the context of the global economic crisis. It is not clear how fast China will move into higher value-added products again in the post-crisis environment. In addition, import structures may change post-crisis as the way out of the global economic crisis may be driven by developing countries. Although the United States and EU-15 markets will still be the major import markets, at least for some time, other markets will gain in importance. In particular, clothing imports will increase in importance in fast-growing emerging countries such as China, India, Brazil, and the Russian Federation. In this context also regional end markets may become central as substitutes for reduced exports to developed countries' end markets.

The discussion above shows that after exceptional growth of Cambodia's clothing exports from the mid-1990s to 2007, exports have declined in 2008 and 2009, which has had a large impact on production, number of firms, and employment. The development of Cambodia's clothing sector has been based on quota hopping, at least partly preferential market access, and mostly Asian investment and CMT production, and has been characterized by limited local involvement and linkages. This specific integration into global clothing value chains has increased vulnerability as evidenced by the decline of the sector in the context of the global economic crisis and it limits the role the sector can play in promoting export diversification and industrial development. Cambodia's clothing sector faces critical challenges that have to be addressed to increase competitiveness and sustainability, particularly in light of changes in industry dynamics and heightened competition.

Main Challenges of Cambodia's Clothing Exporters

In this part main internal challenges of the clothing sector in Cambodia are discussed. They are strongly linked to Cambodia's specific integration into global clothing value chains. In addition, some policy recommendations are pointed out.

End Market and Product Concentration

A major challenge for Cambodia's clothing exports is the lack of diversification in markets and products. Cambodia's clothing exports are highly concentrated with regard to end markets, which has been realized in the global economic crisis where demand in Cambodia's major export market—the United States—has declined dramatically. In 2008 a total 86 percent of clothing exports went to United States (62 percent)[6] and the EU-15 (24 percent; see table 4.3). The only other important end market is Canada with 6 percent of exports. The concentration towards the United States and the EU-15, however, has decreased; those two markets accounted for 93 percent in 2000. Within the U.S. and the EU-15 markets Cambodia's clothing exports mostly go to large buyers. It is estimated that the largest buyer—GAP—sources one third of Cambodia's total exports (USAID 2005) and the largest 15 buyers over 50 percent (Natsuda et al. 2009). Table 4.7 shows the top 20 buyers in Cambodia based on volume of production.

Table 4.7. Top 20 Buyers in Cambodia, 2008

Position	Buyer	Position	Buyer
1	GAP	11	Matalan
2	H&M	12	Blue Star
3	Levi Strauss	13	Nike
4	Adidas	14	PVH
5	Target	15	C&A
6	Sears Holdings	16	Wal-Mart
7	Children's Place	16	Kohl's
8	Charles Komar	18	MGT
9	William Carter	19	American Marketing
10	VF Jeanswear	20	JC Penney

Source: Miller et al. (2008).

This high concentration to the United States (and to a lesser extent the EU-15 market) can be explained by several factors. First, due to the Bilateral United States-Cambodia Textile and Apparel Agreement, Cambodia had favorable quota access to the U.S. market. Access to the EU-15 market has also been on a preferential basis since 1999—even more as it has been quota- and duty-free—but it has been subject to double transformation ROO, which has been difficult to fulfill for Cambodia's clothing exporters[7] (see below). The exception in this regard is sweaters, which can fulfill EU ROO and account for an important share of EU exports. Second, transnational producers based in Hong Kong SAR, China, Taiwan, China, and the Republic of Korea, which are the main investors in Cambodia's clothing sector, have concentrated on the U.S. market and have well-established relationships with U.S. buyers. Third, end markets are very different and demand different capabilities. Orders from U.S. mass-market retailers are large and price is the most important criteria; quality and lead time are also central but not as much as price. EU orders are generally smaller, demand more variation, and have different standards with regard to quality, fashion and design content, and lead times. Lead times and quality are generally more important sourcing criteria. The Japanese market is again different from the U.S. and the EU markets as quality, design, and lead times are even more important criteria and as orders are smaller and involve more variation. Thus, increasing exports to the EU and to Japan would diversify end markets and products, because different types of products and related capabilities are demanded from buyers selling in the EU or the Japanese market.

Besides these constraining factors, export market diversification is critical to increase growth and reduce volatility of clothing exports. GMAC wants to maintain competitiveness in the U.S. market but also expand in the EU market and diversify to different European countries, because exports currently are concentrated in Germany, the United Kingdom, France, and Spain. Japan is particularly interesting as it has a large clothing market of US$24 billion and is the third-largest clothing importer after the EU and the United States. The Japanese GSP includes duty-free access for almost all of Cambodia's industrial products, including clothing requiring two-stage ROO for knit and one-stage ROO for woven (ADB 2004). Up to now it has depended heavily on Chinese clothing imports, which account for more than 80 percent of its total clothing imports, but Japan has the objective to diversify its import countries within the context of the 'China plus 1' strategy. Bangladesh will probably become the main 'plus 1' country but there could also be a role for Cambodia. Other high-potential export markets are Norway, Australia, and New Zealand, where Cambodia enjoys preferential market access, as well as emerging markets such as Mexico, Brazil, Argentina, Turkey, the Middle East (in particular the United Arab Emirates), Russia, China, India, and regional markets (see below on regional integration).

GMAC has promoted Cambodia's clothing sector in China and Japan but these efforts have to be intensified and extended to more markets. The association could support breaking into new markets by negotiating favorable market access, marketing and promotional initiatives, local and international exhibitions to attract foreign buyers, image building, and possibly the establishment of a 'Made in Cambodia' brand at the association level. This is not only important with regard to new markets but also for enhancing Cambodia's reputation in existing markets. Information on different markets and buyers will also be required by exporters, which could be provided at the association level.

Clothing exports are also highly concentrated in a few products. The top five product categories accounted for 53 percent of total U.S. clothing exports in 2008 and for 67 percent in the EU market; the top 10 product categories accounted for 67 percent and 77 percent respectively (see table 4.8 and 4.9). Furthermore, the top export product categories to the United States and EU are overlapping; 7 of the top 10 products appear in the United States and the EU list. Cambodia's clothing exports are concentrated in high-volume, low value-added cotton products, which are supplied into the low and medium market segment in the United States and to a lesser extent the EU. Around 70 percent of Cambodia's clothing exports are knitted clothing products, 30 percent are woven ones. From 1995 to 2003 knit and woven exports accounted for similar values. Woven exports, however, have stagnated since 2004 whereas knit exports continued to increase (see table 4.1). The United States is the largest end market for woven and knit

Table 4.8. Top Export Products to the United States, 2008

HS	Description	Value (in million US$)	Share (%)
611020	Sweaters, pullovers, sweatshirts	462	19.5
620462	Women's or girls' trousers	311	13.1
620342	Men's or boys' trousers	203	8.6
610462	Women's or girls' trousers	155	6.5
610910	T-shirts, singlets, tank tops	114	4.8
611030	Sweaters, pullovers, sweatshirts	97	4.1
610510	Men's or boys' shirts	78	3.3
610610	Women's or girls' blouses and shirts	78	3.3
611420	Garments nesoi	60	2.5
610220	Women's or girls' overcoats	37	1.6
	Total U.S. exports	2,369	

Source: USITC.

Table 4.9. Top Export Products to the EU-15, 2008

HS	Description	Value (in million US$)	Share (%)
611020	Sweaters, pullovers, sweatshirts	173	31.2%
611030	Sweaters, pullovers, sweatshirts	123	22.1%
610910	T-shirts, singlets, tank tops	40	7.2%
620342	Men's or boys' trousers	20	3.5%
611011	Sweaters, pullovers, sweatshirts	16	2.8%
610990	T-shirts, singlets, tank tops	13	2.3%
620463	Women's or girls' trousers	12	2.2%
610462	Women's or girls' trousers	11	2.0%
620462	Women's or girls' trousers	10	1.8%
610220	Women's or girls' overcoats	10	1.8%
	Total EU-15 exports	554	

Source: EUROSTAT.

products but particularly for woven, where U.S. exports accounted for nearly 75 percent of woven exports in 2008 (U.S. exports accounted for nearly 60 percent of knits). Exports to the EU have generally higher unit value than to the United States. In a comparison with competitor countries, Cambodia's unit values of total exports to the EU were lower than in Sri Lanka, India, and Vietnam but higher than in China, Bangladesh, and Pakistan in 2005 (see table 4.10; Tewari 2008).

Table 4.10. Unit Values of EU Clothing Exports, 2005

Country	Unit values (euro/kg)
Turkey	18.87
Sri Lanka	15.46
India	15.36
Vietnam	13.39
Cambodia	13.38
China	11.01
Bangladesh	7.80
Pakistan	7.53

Source: COMEXT data, adapted from Tewari (2008).

Cambodia has currently a competitive advantage in basic clothing products. However, a part of the production needs to diversify and upgrade to higher-value products due to the following reasons. First, profit margins and value addition is higher in higher-value products and when more production steps are conducted besides CMT, such as input sourcing and design (see below). Risk is also lower if export products are more diversified. Second, Cambodia's main competitiveness factor is low labor costs. In the course of the economic and social development process of Cambodia wages will increase (also related to labor disputes, see below). Thus, the clothing industry in Cambodia should not only rely on basic production in which labor costs need to be competitive. Third, as discussed above, export market diversification may be related to product diversification as other end markets such as the EU and Japan demand different (and in this case higher) quality, fashion, and design standards. There are few comparable markets to the United States with regard to order size.

The main challenges to upgrading into higher-value products are quality, lead times, and missing design and technical skills (see below). Since market research and R&D is necessary to diversify and upgrade export products, a research center built on public-private partnership could be established. Its role would be to gather and disseminate information to local manufacturers on the latest developments in products, markets, and buyers.

Foreign Ownership

The clothing sector in Cambodia is dominated by FDI; almost 95 percent of the factories are foreign owned. In 2008, the main owner nationalities were Taiwan, China (25 percent, 86 factories), Hong Kong SAR, China (19 percent, 68 factories), and China (18 percent, 65 factories) followed by Korea (10 percent), Malaysia (5 percent), and Singapore (4 percent, see figure 4.2). Firms from 'greater China' (including Taiwan, China, Hong Kong SAR, China, and China) accounted for over 60 percent of all clothing factories in Cambodia.[8] Overall Chinese investment, including Hong Kong SAR, China, accounted for 59 percent of approved investment in the clothing sector in the period 2000 to 2005; Taiwan, China investment accounted for 23 percent (Natsuda et al. 2009). Only 7 percent

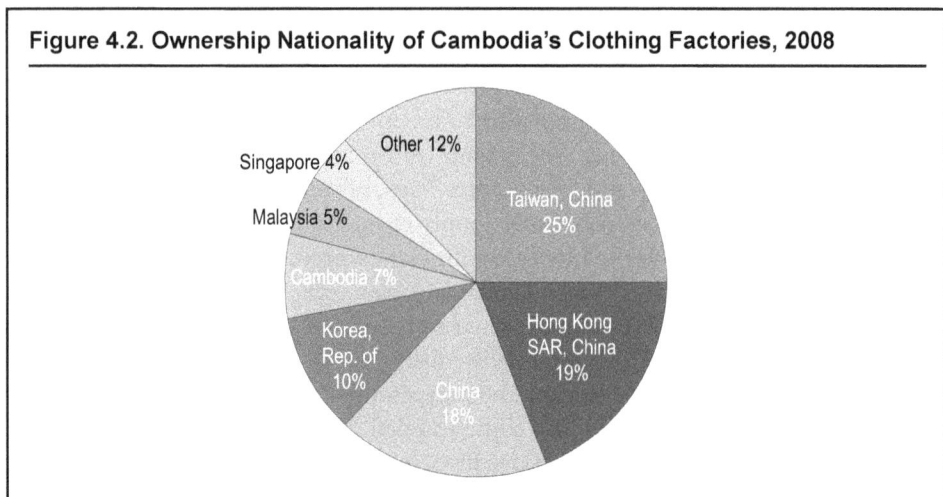

Figure 4.2. Ownership Nationality of Cambodia's Clothing Factories, 2008

Source: GMAC.

of clothing firms are owned by Cambodians and those are mostly smaller firms (around 3 percent of employment is accounted for by Cambodian-owned firms) and generally work on a subcontracting basis for larger foreign-owned firms. This is similar to Sub-Saharan Africa LIC clothing exporters (see above) but different from regional competitor countries such as Vietnam or even more Bangladesh, where local ownership is more significant or even dominant (see below).

Ownership structures are important as they determine how supplier firms are linked to international production and distribution networks (Natsuda et al. 2009). Factories in Cambodia are largely integrated into triangular manufacturing networks where global buyers source from transnational producers located in Taiwan, China, Hong Kong SAR, China, Korea, China, Malaysia, or Singapore that organize transnational manufacturing networks. Thus, factories in Cambodia are integrated into global clothing production networks through their foreign parent companies. Production, export, and management decisions are mostly made at the headquarters of the parent companies.[9] Unlike locally owned factories, those foreign-owned firms in Cambodia have limited leverage and autonomy in terms of strategic decision making and in attracting orders, because negotiations with buyers are generally located at the headquarters of the parent companies (Natsuda et al. 2009). The parent companies are generally in charge of input sourcing, product development and design, logistics, merchandising, and marketing, and have the direct relationships with buyers. Thus, transnational producers are able to leverage the skills and expertise of their home offices for value-adding activities. This strategy reduces the need for capacity building, investment, and upgrading in Cambodia. Consequently, this maintains the role of Cambodia as a CMT producer (see below, Nathan Associates 2007). Foreign-owned firms also tend to be more mobile than locally owned ones as they do not have the same urge to make firms survive as they are not embedded in the specific location and can shift orders to clothing factories in other locations and/or locate to other countries. Investments in clothing factories depreciate within three to five years and firms can be closed within a week. Thus, the viability of the industry hinges not only on the performance of factories located in Cambodia but on whether they continue to serve the business strategies of foreign owners (Nathan Associates 2007).

Export clothing factories have existed in Cambodia for more than 15 years and still there has been very limited local initiative. Thus, a central challenge is to increase local involvement in the industry at the management and/or owner level. This will help to embed the sector; foster local skills, linkages, and spillovers; and make it more sustainable. The limited local involvement in Cambodia can be explained by the late entry of Cambodia into clothing exporting. For instance, when Bangladesh entered the clothing export business in the 1970s and 1980s, entry barriers were still relatively low in the sector and smaller local firms could enter supply chains of global buyers. Furthermore, market access was guaranteed as those countries had excess quota (see below). This, however, has changed in the 1990s and 2000s and even more in the context of the MFA phaseout and the global economic crisis when entry barriers and capabilities demanded from supplier firms increased, substantially raising the bar for local firms wanting to start as clothing exporters. Financial and human resource requirements at the firm level became higher, as broader capabilities and also relationships to buyers and input suppliers became more important. But besides time, institutional factors are also central, in particular the existence of a local entrepreneurial class and government support. There are no explicit programs in Cambodia to support local skills, linkages, and spillovers. Nor are there programs to support the establishment of locally owned firms that take into account their specific challenges, including no access to finance through headquarters, no established relationship with buyers and input suppliers, and skill gaps. Another problem is that the local Cambodian elite with funds to invest has not invested in the clothing sector but has acted more like rentiers—investing in land, cars, houses, and/or financial markets—and has often no relation to productive investment. A central challenge therefore is how to bring the local elite to invest in productive activities, including T&C. Investment promotion activities targeted at local investors and potential foreign joint venture partners could be implemented. Such activities would need to also include small- and medium-size investments as currently the investment promotion code involves high minimum levels of investment that discourage smaller and often local investments.

Concentration in CMT Production

Besides a concentration in basic products Cambodia's clothing sector is also concentrated in only a few production steps. Most factories in Cambodia are involved in CMT production. Thus, the factory is supplied with inputs by its buyers or the parent company and is only in charge of cutting, or even only making and trimming, and then exports the final product. According to a survey in 2006, 139 out of 164 clothing firms (87 percent) were only engaged in CMT production (Yamagata 2006). The ADB (2004) estimates that over 70 percent of clothing exports were based on CMT in 2004. GMAC supports these figures and states that 60 percent of the factories (typically subsidiaries of companies overseas) are only involved in CMT production, 25 percent in free on board (FOB), and 15 percent in subcontracting arrangements. In contrast to CMT, FOB firms are in charge of input sourcing and purchase fabric, trims, and other inputs on their own. FOB firms may also be involved in sample-making and negotiations with buyers. These are significant distinctions because the financing of input and export costs requires financial resources and input sourcing capabilities and the development of samples requires competencies and management skills beyond cutting and sewing (Nathan Associates 2007). Other areas to increase functions and capabilities besides input sourcing and sample making are design understanding or contribution, merchandising, marketing, and the relationship with buyers. However, most of these functions—in particular, merchandising, marketing, and the direct relationship with buyers—are conducted at the headquarters of the parent companies overseas. Foreign ownership and the specific integration of Cambodia in the global clothing value chain through triangular manufacturing networks limits the possibility for taking over more functions with higher value added as these functions are assumed by the headquarters on a regional or global basis. In contrast to locally owned firms, the question of what foreign owners decide to produce in Cambodia is not only related to local capabilities but also to their choice of what and how to produce in their global production network (Natsuda et al. 2009).

However, in certain areas (particularly sampling/pattern making and input sourcing) there seems to be scope for factories located in Cambodia. An important factor, particularly for developing from CMT to FOB firms, is access to low-cost finance. The high borrowing costs in Cambodia are a critical constraint to developing FOB capabilities. Most Cambodian FOB suppliers use internal funds (that is, operating cash flow) or foreign sources of finance. Greater access to low-cost finance is crucial to increase FOB capabilities. But access to finance is only one of several demands of FOB firms; other demands include competencies in the areas of selling, fabric sourcing, pattern making, product development, design understanding, and the capacity to manage greater risk (Nathan Associates 2007). The lack of local skills is a central challenge to upgrading into these functions (see below).

Lack of Backward Linkages and Long Lead Times

Access to raw materials, in particular yarn and fabrics, is crucial for clothing exporters. Cambodia is a net exporter of clothing but a net importer of textiles. The clothing industry depends almost entirely on imported yarn, fabrics, and accessories. Over 90 percent of inputs are imported and there is very minimal mill capacity. The domestic material content is largely limited to cardboard cartons, hangers, and poly bags. Cambodia's fabric imports in 2008 were 25 percent of the country's total merchandise imports (Natsuda et al. 2009). According to GMAC, Cambodia's clothing industry imported around US$1 billion in raw materials in 2008. In 2008, 41 percent of textile imports came from China, 30 percent from Hong Kong SAR, China, 9 percent from Korea, 6 percent from Malaysia, and 5 percent from Thailand (see table 4.11). Only 16 percent of textile imports are sourced from the region, mainly from Malaysia, Thailand, and Vietnam (see below on regional integration).

Table 4.11. Cambodia Textile Imports: Top 10 Importers in 2008

	2000		2004		2006		2008	
Country/economy	Value (US$ million)	Share (%)	Value (US$ million)	Share (%)	Value (US$ million)	Share (%)	Value (US$ million)	Share (%)
China	76	19.3	280	35.2	429	38.3	541	41.4
Hong Kong SAR, China	201	51.1	302	38.0	347	31.0	390	29.8
Korea, Rep. of	38	9.5	51	6.3	90	8.0	114	8.7
Malaysia	24	6.1	34	4.3	54	4.8	75	5.8
Thailand	13	3.3	45	5.7	74	6.6	67	5.1
Vietnam	—	—	22	2.8	30	2.7	43	3.3
Pakistan	—	—	10	1.2	14	1.2	24	1.8
Indonesia	10	2.5	15	1.8	17	1.5	14	1.0
Singapore	21	5.3	19	2.3	36	3.2	10	0.8
Luxembourg	—	—	—	—	5	0.4	8	0.6
India	1	0.3	3	0.4	7	0.6	8	0.6
World	394		795		1,118		1,308	

Source: UN COMTRADE.
Note: Values in million US$.

Becoming a competitive yarns and fabrics producer, in particular in the woven segment, is challenging. First, Cambodia lacks local fiber production in cotton and menmade fibers. Second, investments in the textile sector are more capital-intensive than investments in the clothing sector, in particular in woven. The difficult access to and high cost of finance in Cambodia is not supportive for such types of investments. Third, investments in the textile sector rely even more on infrastructure than in the clothing sector, in particular electricity and water. The electricity-intensity of knitting and weaving and even more of spinning is much higher than of sewing. GMAC stated that potential investors said they would invest in textile mills if electricity costs went down to below 10 cents per kilowatt from a level of around 20 cents today. Furthermore, fabrics need to be dyed and washed, which requires secure availability of water. Fourth, the textile sector is more knowledge and skill-intensive than the clothing sectors. The availability of labor with appropriate technical, design/fashion, and management skills is limited in Cambodia and there is a limited supply of formal training facilities (see below). Fifth, some regional competitors such as China are highly competitive in fabrics production with regard to price, quality, lead times, and availability and it will be difficult to match those countries. Thus, even though lead times and production flexibility would be improved by locally producing yarns and fabrics, this may not be the most cost effective means of production.

Although these challenges have to be taken seriously, backward integration will be central to increase competitiveness with regard to lead times, production flexibility, and costs (that is, transport, port, and customs clearance) as well as to increase domestic value added and local linkages and spillovers. Moreover, preferential market access to the EU requires a two-stage transformation. The biggest advantage of local input production is lead times. For individual firms it is too costly to maintain an inventory of fabrics and more importantly production needs to be in accordance with the specification of buyers. Thus, fabrics can generally be only ordered after buyers have placed the orders. Lead times for input sourcing are, at the minimum, reduced by the shipping time when sourced locally, which on average accounts for 30 days from East Asia (from the mill to the factory). But due to closer relationships with local textile mills or even vertical integration, the time reduction is probably even higher. This is a crucial saving of time and money in a context where lead times become increasingly important in buyers' sourcing decisions and it is particularly important for Cambodia, which has long lead times compared with competitor countries. For woven clothing items, firms in China are able to deliver clothing faster (40 to 60 days) than all other Asian countries. India is second (50 to 70 days), and Sri Lanka and Vietnam offer lead times comparable with Malaysia, Indonesia, and Thailand (60 to 90 days). Cambodia (80 to 110 days) lags significantly. Bangladesh needs even 90-120 days in woven. For knit clothing Bangladesh has integrated operations and Vietnam goes in the same direction. Cambodia has nearly no integrated operations in woven or knit. China, Malaysia, and Thailand have the same lead time for knit clothing, 50 to 60 days. Sri Lanka and Vietnam offer the same lead time as Indonesia—60 to 70 days. India has also 60 to 70 days. Bangladesh has lead times of 60 to 80 days in knits and Cambodia is last with 80 to 110 days (see table 4.12; Rasiah 2009). Thus, among competing countries in Asia, Cambodia's lead times are relatively

Table 4.12. Lead Times in Days for Woven and Knit Clothing, 2008

Country	Woven	Knit
China	40-60	50-60
India	50-70	60-70
Thailand	60-90	50-60
Malaysia	60-90	50-60
Sri Lanka	60-90	60-70
Vietnam	60-90	60-70
Indonesia	60-90	60-70
Bangladesh	90-120	60-80
Cambodia	80-110	80-110

Source: Gherzi Textile Organization, cited in Rasiah (2009).

long. Firms interviewed stated that lead time is one of the main challenges in fulfilling buyers' demands. Furthermore, due to these comparatively long lead times, upgrading in higher-value and fashion products is limited.

It would not make sense to produce all types of fabrics in Cambodia but certain basic fabrics that are broadly used could be produced locally, where scale economies would be substantial due to the importance of the clothing sector. Mills could be established close to the border with Vietnam and operated in collaboration with Vietnam, to use the lower electricity costs of Vietnam and to be able to supply clothing firms in both countries. Since a competitive local textile sector contributes to the competitiveness of the clothing sector by reducing costs and lead times and increasing flexibility, a favorable environment for textile investment should be ensured. Policies could involve long-term loans at reduced interest rates for textile investments; the attraction of FDI specifically to the textile sector; the development of more efficient infrastructure—in particular for electricity and water, which are central for a competitive textile sector; and greater emphasis on skill development in areas relevant for textile production.

The largest lead time reduction would clearly occur through vertical integration or local sourcing. But increasing the local supply of yarn and fabric enough to fill the large gap between demand and supply is challenging and not attainable in the short run. There are, however, other options to reduce lead times. First, improvements in efficiency and productivity at the factory level—in particular with regard to decision-making processes, production structures, and supply chain management—can importantly contribute to reducing lead times. Second, improvements in trade facilitation—in particular in the transport infrastructure, logistics, and customs facilities—can also reduce lead times. Third, as an alternative to establishing competitive local yarn and fabric mills at the scale necessary for supplying inputs to the clothing sector, more focus could be put on fabric-processing and the capacity of the dyeing and finishing industry could be increased. This would enable firms to stock up fabric of the most common constructions in greige form in advance of orders and then dye and finish the fabric once the order and the design is received, which would reduce lead times and increase local value added. However, a close relationship with buyers would be necessary as the type of fabric would need to be known in advance as only the color and design could be adapted closer to production. Fourth, ideally, this could be combined with establishing a central bonded warehouse (CBW). A CBW could stock up T&C inputs such as fabric in finished and greige form of the most common constructions, accessories, dyes and chemicals, yarn, T&C machinery, and spare parts in amounts determined by expected demand. Manufacturers can then purchase these inputs duty-free from the CBW directly as export orders are received (World Bank 2005a). In this case, manufacturers may save on shipping time as they can immediately source the inputs when they receive the order. A CBW also requires a close relationship with buyers, as they generally stipulate the exact fabric they need and often also nominate fabric mills. This information would be needed in advance. A CBW could be organized by the industry association to share the costs and reap economies of scale. Fifth and most important, increased regional sourcing could play a central role in reducing input costs and lead times. Only 16 percent of total textile imports were sourced from Association of Southeast Asian Nations (ASEAN) member countries in 2008, a number that has remained quite stable since 2000 (see below on regional integration).

Low Productivity and Lack of Skills

Low wages of workers in Cambodia are generally accompanied by low productivity, which erodes part of the benefits of low-cost labor. Despite the relatively long existence of a clothing export sector, adequate productivity improvement has been lacking. However, there are large differences within the industry in Cambodia. Some (generally larger) firms have high productivity levels and are world-class clothing producers, while others are lagging. Factory-level productivity depends on a host of factors, including labor costs; production methods; worker, management, and technical skills; and capital and technology. Factors external of factories are also central for productivity such as low-cost, quality, and reliable inputs and infrastructure and logistics (see below).

Absolute labor costs are comparatively low in Cambodia and there is a large supply of workers. The base minimum wage of a production worker in Cambodia is US$50 per month[10] which is US$1.92 per day if 26 days are worked each month (8 hours of work per day, 6 days per week) leading to an average hourly wage of US$0.24. Labor costs, including legally mandated benefits, often diverge significantly from base wages. Including all benefits and average overtime the average wage accounts for US$77 per month, US$2.67 per day, or US$0.33 per hour (Nathan Associates 2007). With regard to average labor costs per hour, Cambodia ranks second after Bangladesh in a comparison with regional competitor countries in 2008 (see table 4.13). However, productivity is comparatively low. Cambodia's labor productivity is estimated to be 65 percent of China's while Bangladesh and Vietnam were at 75 and 95 percent respectively (Natsuda et al. 2009). A World Bank study in 2004 concluded that firms and workers in Cambodia are generally less productive than in China, India, Pakistan, and Bangladesh and that Cambodia's low

Table 4.13. Average Clothing Manufacturing Labor Costs (Including Social Charges) in 2008

Countries	Labor cost (US$/hour)	Countries	Labor cost (US$/hour)
Asian competitors		U.S. regional suppliers	
Bangladesh	0.22	Mexico	2.54
Cambodia	0.33	Honduras	1.72–1.82
Pakistan	0.37	Dominican Republic	1.55–1.95
Vietnam	0.38	Nicaragua	0.97–1.03
Sri Lanka	0.43	Haiti	0.49–0.55
Indonesia	0.44	EU regional suppliers	
India	0.51	Turkey	2.44
China 3	0.55–0.80	Morocco	2.24
China 2	0.86–0.94	Russian Federation	1.97
China 1	1.08	Tunisia	1.68
Malaysia	1.18	Bulgaria	1.53
Thailand	1.29–1.36	Jordan	1.01
		Egypt	0.83

Source: Jassin-O'Rourke Group, LLC (2008).
Notes: Values in US$ per hour, including social charges. Costs are average costs and there might be important differences within countries. China 1, 2, and 3 refer to different regions within Mainland China.

labor costs do not wholly compensate for the low productivity of its workers (World Bank 2004). A study of Nathan Associates in 2007 concluded with regard to Vietnam that the difference in wages does not compensate for the higher productivity of labor in Vietnam.[11]

The relatively low productivity is related in part to a lack of worker skills but, more importantly, to a lack of skills at the manager and supervisor level. Managers and supervisors have a crucial role in defining factory productivity levels, labor relations, and potential for upgrading. The vast majority of managers and supervisors are foreigners in Cambodia's clothing firms. Cambodians have advanced but primarily in human resources and compliance management, office functions, and maintenance. Other management positions are still generally held by foreigners. These managers have brought experience, which was critical for the rapid establishment of the clothing sector in Cambodia. However, they may now pose a challenge to upgrading and productivity improvements due to their limited training and skills in production processes or industrial engineering, outdated and unsuitable management practices, and communication barriers with regard to language and culture (Nathan Associates 2007). Another problem is that the transmission of knowledge to local workers is also slowed by language difficulties: the little learning possible probably does not take place. This affects Cambodian workers' perceptions of their opportunities in the workforce as they see little potential to improve wages on the basis of development in skills.

With regard to workers, there seems to be a lack of skilled sewing operators. There is high demand for skilled sewing operators but, due to limited supply, most firms hire unskilled workers and train them within the firm. Firms' representatives and GMAC state that training schools along the lines of vocational training institutions would be very useful. However, coordination between the government, GMAC, firms, and (in certain areas) buyers is crucial in the development of vocational training institutions to develop skills directly needed in the private sector. Besides specific skills for the clothing sector, the quality of the basic education system, which is below that of regional competitors, is a concern of firms in the clothing sector. The secondary school enrollment rate in Cambodia is the lowest of major Asian clothing exporter countries and accounted for 29 percent in 2005 (WDI 2007). Thus, besides specific training institutions for the clothing sector the basic education systems should be improved.

The skill gap is particularly high in the area of technical and design/fashion as well as in middle-management skills. Middle-management and technical and engineering jobs are widely held by foreigners, who are expensive compared to local hires. Around 5,000 Chinese clothing technicians and supervisors are dispatched to clothing factories in Cambodia through Chinese human resource agencies (Natsuda et al. 2009). According to a survey of 164 clothing factories, 30 percent of top managers were from mainland China, 21 percent from Taiwan, China, 15 percent from Hong Kong SAR, China, and only 8 percent from Cambodia in 2006 (Yamagata 2006). Eighty percent of middle managers are foreigners, but firms want to localize their management to reduce costs. Besides reduced costs local managers would also reduce problems with cultural barriers between management and workers. Potentially, this could make the sector more sustainable and increase linkages and spillovers to the local economy. The design and fashion capacity in Cambodia is also very limited. Buyers increasingly are demanding design capabilities or at least a design understanding and value added can be significantly increased in the production process (if also some design steps are provided by suppliers)

Therefore building up design capabilities is crucial. Furthermore, a lack of a design and fashion perspective limits upgrading possibilities to higher-value and fashion products as well as export market diversification. However, before starting with design capabilities, sample and pattern making skills should be strengthened.

There is only a limited supply of training institutes in Cambodia. The most important ones are the Cambodia Garment Training Center (CGTC), which is funded by Agence Française de Développement (AFD) and run by GMAC and offers training in basic sewing skills; and the Garment Industry Productivity Center (GIPC, renamed to Cambodia Skills Development Center (CASDEC)), which was funded by United States Agency for International Development (USAID) but is now largely financially self-sufficient and offers training in technical and industrial engineering, especially targeting middle management. GIPC/CASDEC also works directly with firms offering assistance for production management, including workflow, planning, controls, and supervision. There are several other training schools in discussion. It is central that the government works together with GMAC and the clothing factories to develop vocational training centers as well as training for pattern making, technical and product development, design, and middle-management skills that meet the demand of the private sector. Besides skill development, capital investment will be central to increase productivity. China and India have recently scaled up investment in T&C to upgrade technology supported by government investment funds. The Indian government has provided various incentives for investments in the T&C sector under the 'technology upgradation fund scheme' (TUDS). A similar 'upgrading fund' is needed in Cambodia to support investment in new machinery, technology, and skills.

Leveraging Better Factories Cambodia

Labor, and more recently environmental, compliance have become central in sourcing policies of global buyers. Under pressure from compliance-conscious consumers and civil society organizations, buyers have taken compliance seriously and most have developed CoC in the second half of the 1990s. These codes generally include labor and increasingly environmental standards that often constitute a precondition for firms to enter sourcing networks. Due to the bilateral United States-Cambodia textile agreement and the related ILO monitoring program, which has after the phaseout of the MFA and the United States-Cambodia trade agreement developed to Better Factories Cambodia, Cambodia is known for good labor compliance in the clothing sector. The Foreign Investment Advisory Service (FIAS) conducted a survey on sourcing criteria with the 15 largest U.S. and EU buyers accounting for 45 percent of Cambodia's clothing exports in 2004 (FIAS 2004). The survey showed that Cambodia was rated the highest on 'level of labor standards' and 'protecting the rights of workers to organize unions' among Asian clothing exporting countries including China, Vietnam, Thailand, and Bangladesh. It was also found that 47 percent of buyers considered ILO standards as either critical or of major importance, another 40 percent considered them to be moderately important (FIAS 2004). The good compliance record of Cambodia and the importance of compliance in buyers' sourcing decisions are very promising. However, two issues have to be taken into account.

First, as discussed above at the end of 2004, as the United States-Cambodia Textile Trade Agreements phased out the Cambodian government and clothing firms decided to continue the ILO monitoring program. However, one of the main incentives of the program was lost—access to higher quotas for improvements in working conditions. The 'reputation risk assurance' constitutes the key incentive for global buyers since the MFA phaseout. Although compliance with core labor standards has become a precondition for entering buyers' sourcing networks, it is only one criterion in buyers' sourcing decisions and arguable not the most important one. As can be seen in the context of the global economic crisis, even buyers that have supported the ILO monitoring program have reduced orders and shifted to the most competitive countries. Thus, the focus in Cambodia on working conditions should be connected to advances in other important areas such as productivity at the firm level, skill development, upgrading of capabilities and infrastructure, local involvement at the managers' and owners' level, local linkages and spillovers, backward integration, and end market diversification. For Cambodia's clothing sector to increase competitiveness it will be critical that labor compliance is complemented by addressing other central challenges. The Better Factories Cambodia program has put in place institutional structures in Cambodia that facilitate collaboration between the government, industry associations, firms, and trade unions and workers. These structures could be used for these broader policies to complement monitoring and labor compliance.

Second, although Cambodia has a positive image with regard to labor compliance, there are some serious issues with regard to industrial relations. In recent years, strikes have increased, which can be attributed to several factors. One factor is that in the context of the global economic crisis, orders have decreased and several firms had to close, reduce their workforce, or reduce working time of their workers. Job losses, decreasing job security, and reduced wages have contributed to an increase in the number of strikes. Most strikes involved claims for higher wages, lay-off compensation, payments for entitlements, non-discrimination against union members, and rehiring of retrenched workers. Another reason for more strikes is that although labor rights and working conditions have improved importantly, in certain areas improvements have been limited. As Miller et al. (2008) conclude social audits have the propensity to impact on child labor, forced labor, and health and safety but tend to have a more limited impact on freedom of association and collective bargaining, discrimination, living wages, and working hours. Low wages and excessive working hours have prevailed in Cambodia as well as problems with establishing collective bargaining, all of which have contributed to the high number of strikes. There have been protests demanding higher minimum wages and a planned nationwide strike organized by the local Free Trade Union (FTU), which lead to an agreement between the government, employers, and five large pro-government unions in July 2010 to increase the minimum wage from US$50 to US$61 per month in October 2010. The FTU demanded however a minimum wage of US$70. A final factor underlying strikes is that labor unions are strongly linked to political parties, which politicizes labor disputes in Cambodia. It is common that several unions exist in one factory. There exist five to six umbrella unions for the clothing sector but in many factories there are more than six unions.

Hence, Better Factories Cambodia has had an important role in the development of the clothing sector in Cambodia but it could be extended in certain areas. Labor compliance needs to be connected to productivity improvements, skill development, upgrading of the industry, infrastructure development, and local involvement. Furthermore, the program should not only involve monitoring but should be extended to more hands on support (a change already in progress), including training, capacity building, and technical assistance. Also, information on the sourcing practices of global buyers and their relationship with supplier firms should be made publicly available along with data on noncompliant suppliers. This information can be used to confront buyers with the impact of their buying practices on factories' and workers' capacity to improve labor compliance (Miller et al. 2009). Finally, the program should be extended to environmental compliance, which is already planned.

Referring to the last point above, up to now environmental compliance has not been an important topic in Cambodia. Recently, however, pressures from buyers and also from the media and from communities have increased. Environmental compliance is particularly relevant in the textile sector in the dyeing and washing segment where water treatment is a central concern. Thus, with the development of backward linkages environmental compliance will become more relevant. In the area of environmental compliance strategic government intervention is central to develop central facilities as well as to support firms with credit programs for their investments in compliant facilities. GMAC, Better Factories Cambodia, and IFC are planning a new line of services to help Cambodian clothing factories make production more efficient and greener by reducing emissions and improving energy efficiency (Better Factories Cambodia 2010).

Inadequate Physical and Bureaucratic Infrastructure

Overcoming infrastructure constraints is a priority in sustaining and increasing competitiveness in the clothing sector in Cambodia. Cambodia's infrastructure has improved significantly since 1994, but there are still major bottlenecks, in particular in the area of power and logistics. In general the quality of Cambodia' infrastructure is poor and within the group of its regional main competitor countries it is only comparable to Bangladesh. By far the biggest concern is the high costs of electricity. According to Cambodia's Investment Climate Assessment in 2009 (IFC 2009), Cambodia ranked near the bottom among regional competitors on all electricity costs indicators. The cost of electricity in Cambodia is estimated to be more than twice that of regional and global competitors (Nathan Associates 2007). In Cambodia electricity costs amount to 19–22 U.S. cents per kilowatt-hour compared to costs in Vietnam of around 7–8 cents per kilowatt-hour. Also, connecting to the grid is expensive and electricity from the grid is unreliable. Therefore, most medium and large factories have their own power generators to protect themselves from electricity cutoffs, but that is a major investment and expensive. As a result many factories cannot justify additional costs for accessing the grid and maintaining backup generators and remain independent from the grid (Nathan Associates 2007). Although electricity costs are important for competitiveness in the clothing industry, the latter has far lower electricity intensity levels than the textile industry. Therefore, the high cost of electricity is a critical obstacle to industry upgrading and backward integration.

Transport infrastructure between the port in Sihanoukville and Phnom Penh where most clothing factories are located has improved. However, transport is concentrated on the road as the railway infrastructure is poorly developed. The railway between Sihanoukville and Phnom Penh is under construction and eventually could provide cheaper transport options. Logistics costs are generally high, including port, import, and export charges. Customs clearance is an expensive and lengthy process, and increases costs and lead times. Although the average time required to clear a shipment declined to 4.3 days for exports and 5.1 days for imports (IFC 2009), further progress is necessary. For instance, in Singapore it takes some hours or even only 25 minutes to clear a shipment.

GMAC demands clearing in one day, which would be a realistic target. With regard to the business environment, despite improved procedures, starting a business and enforcing contracts is still comparatively costly and takes a long time in Cambodia. Corruption also increases costs, for example in the areas of import and export procedures, documents, customs inspection and clearance, starting a business, and getting access to the grid.

Access to and costs of finance are important concerns but affect clothing firms differently. The majority of foreign-owned firms does not rely on Cambodian banks for financing but is able to access finance through their headquarters (however, during the global economic crisis some of their headquarters also struggled with access to finance). For local and smaller firms and, in particular startups, access to finance is a critical challenge as banks are risk averse and generally have high collateral requirements. Costs are relatively high too due to high interest rates. To establish a locally owned industry, access to achievable finance through specific finance mechanisms for investment and working capital will be central. Access to finance also will be central for productivity improvements and to upgrade production and products. As discussed above an 'upgrading fund' could be established to facilitate access and reduce costs of finance for investments into productivity improvements and upgrading.

Limited Regional Integration

Regional sourcing and production networks could play a central role in increasing competitiveness by reducing input costs and lead times as well as by offering more services by leveraging regional strengths. Moreover, regional end markets could be central in the context of end market diversification. Increased integration and coordination with regard to backward and forward linkages within ASEAN could increase the competitiveness of the whole region thanks to complementary competitive advantages of the Southeast Asian main T&C exporter countries. ASEAN member countries offer a wide range of products and services along the T&C value chain including fibers, fabrics, clothing, machinery, design, and logistics. Some countries have cost-competitive clothing industries while others excel in yarn production and fabric-dyeing and finishing. Still others specialize in logistics, design, and marketing (Nathan Associates 2006). For instance, Cambodia and the Lao People's Democratic Republic are the only LDCs in ASEAN that enjoy market access privileges and—together with Vietnam—have concentrated in clothing production. Thailand and Indonesia have an important textile sector that could supply inputs to clothing sectors in the region. Malaysia has long experience in T&C production and has highly skilled workers and managers, including in design and fashion skills. These different strengths of the countries in the region could be leveraged and economies of scale, vertical integration, and horizontal specialization could be promoted.

Intraregional trade has grown in recent years within ASEAN, but T&C trade among ASEAN countries is still limited. In Cambodia, textile imports from ASEAN member countries accounted for 16 percent of total textile imports in 2008. This figure has remained quite stable, accounting for 17 percent in 2000. Most regional textile imports come from Malaysia (6 percent), Thailand (5 percent), and Vietnam (3 percent). With regard to end markets, in Cambodia less than 1 percent of total clothing exports go to ASEAN member countries, a share that has decreased from 5 percent in 2000 (see table 4.14). These exports only go to one country, Singapore. Thus, intraregional trade is concentrated in textiles and input sourcing; the region is only to a very limited extent used as an end market for clothing products.

Table 4.14. Cambodia's Textile Imports from and Clothing Exports to ASEAN

	2000		2004		2006		2008	
	Value (US$ million)	Share (%)	Value (US$ million)	Share (%)	Value (US$ million)	Share (%)	Value (US$ million)	Share (%)
Textile imports								
ASEAN	68	17.3	134	16.9	211	18.9	210	16.0
Indonesia	10	2.5	15	1.8	17	1.5	14	1.0
Malaysia	24	6.1	34	4.3	54	4.8	75	5.8
Singapore	21	5.3	19	2.3	36	3.2	10	0.8
Thailand	13	3.3	45	5.7	74	6.6	67	5.1
Vietnam	0	0.1	22	2.8	30	2.7	43	3.3
World	394		795		1,118		1,308	
Clothing exports								
ASEAN	61	5.0	37	1.5	37	1.1	23	0.6
Singapore	61	5.0	37	1.5	37	1.1	23	0.6
World	1,214		2,434		3,324		4,037	

Source: UN COMTRADE.
Note: Values in million US$.

There are important challenges to intraregional trade and investment (Tewari 2008). First, with regard to regional input sourcing, East Asian imports are still dominant in Southeast Asia's main clothing exporter countries, including Cambodia, despite the presence of important Southeast Asian textile producers. Cambodia's clothing sector has a strong relation to East Asian textile producers due to foreign ownership, triangular manufacturing networks, and concentration in CMT, which gives clothing firms located in Cambodia limited decision-making power with regard to input suppliers. Sourcing decisions are generally located in the headquarters and follow a global strategy: fabrics for all clothing firms are bought on a global scale by drawing on owners' own textile mills or their sourcing networks based in Asia. Most clothing factories are owned or managed by ethnic Chinese and have strong business relationships, investment, and cultural ties with Chinese fabric suppliers. Sourcing decisions are also often made by buyers who nominate certain yarn, fabrics, and trim suppliers. This reinforces sourcing from Asia because large buyers have established close relationships with fabric mills, in particular in East Asia. In this context, it may be difficult for regional fabric suppliers to establish relationships with factory owners. Second, Southeast Asian countries have a limited product variety of yarn and fabrics and other inputs. This is problematic as buyers prefer to bundle input sourcing and to use a 'one stop shop' for all their input needs, including yarn, fabric, accessories, trims, and textile machinery. Furthermore, despite the proximity of regional countries, they are often not cost-competitive. Third, with regard to using the region as an end market, most regional exporters seem to be focused on global rather than regional markets. Exporting to regional markets will require different skills, as volumes and demands differ compared to the U.S. and the EU markets.

Reducing intraregional trade barriers is a precondition for increased intraregional trade and investment. ASEAN aspires to become a single market and production base by 2020. In 2004 ASEAN member countries signed the Vientiane Action Program (VAP), which calls for the accelerated integration by 2010 of 11 ASEAN priority sectors, including T&C. Under the Common Effective Preferential Tariff (CEPT) scheme of the ASEAN Free Trade Area (AFTA), which predated the VAP, ASEAN countries have to apply a preferential tariff rate and are required to reduce tariffs on T&C products to 5 percent or less. But progress has been uneven. While the six original members of ASEAN (Brunei Darussalam, Indonesia, Malaysia, the Philippines, Thailand, and Singapore) have reduced their tariffs on intra-ASEAN T&C trade, the remaining members (Cambodia, Lao PDR, Myanmar, and Vietnam) have longer time frames to meet their AFTA commitments. VAT requires the elimination of all tariffs. Although most ASEAN countries have promised to eliminate all but a handful of tariffs on T&C products by 2010, Cambodia, the Philippines, and Vietnam have exempted a significant number of tariff lines from elimination (Nathan Associates 2006). Moreover, many clothing producers in the region operate under special tax regimes such as EPZs and bonded warehouses. These regulations would need to be standardized to facilitate intraregional trade. Improvements in intraregional transport, logistics, and customs facilities for regional sourcing are also central to reduce costs and lead times in regional trade.

Intraregional trade can be encouraged through elimination of tariffs, trade facilitation, and customs improvements—but it must also be actively promoted. The ASEAN Competitiveness Enhancement (ACE) Project has the objectives to enhance competitiveness and integration of ASEAN's T&C and tourism supply chains. In the T&C sectors the objectives are to enhance and promote ASEAN's image and reputation in the global market as a reliable, full-package provider of quality T&C; to further integrate ASEAN's T&C sectors; and to enhance the competitiveness, quality, and innovation of ASEAN's T&C sector through reduced lead times and improved product capabilities. Thus, the objectives include increasing regional production networks and sourcing and outsourcing relationships between firms in different ASEAN countries. Key work areas include facilitating partnerships between ASEAN textile mills and clothing factories to create cross-border virtual vertical factories offering full services to global buyers, as well as to enable intra-ASEAN trade in T&C by allowing suppliers to showcase their products and virtually network on a B2B Website. There is also collaboration between training centers in different ASEAN countries. ACE is financed by USAID and works closely with the ASEAN Federation of Textile Industries (AFTEX), which is a group of ASEAN member countries' T&C associations. AFTEX meets regularly to discuss policies and to implement ASEAN-wide projects with the objectives of advocating a common position in international trade policy, promoting intra-ASEAN trade, and promoting ASEAN T&C products to the global market. AFTEX has also been involved in negotiating free trade agreements and organizing trade fairs. Such programs are very useful for increasing intraregional trade and regional integration. However, they could be extended from input sourcing and trade in textiles and other inputs to trade in end products as the region also could be used as an end-market to diversify export markets.

Conclusions

The clothing sector in Cambodia has a strategic significance in creating employment and exports and in the process of industrial development of the country more generally. In this chapter the development and challenges of the clothing sector in Cambodia in the post-quota and post-crisis world have been assessed. Besides exceptional growth of

Cambodia's clothing sector from the mid-1990s onwards, Cambodia's clothing industry has declined quite drastically since 2008 in terms of production, exports, employment, and number of firms. Data from the first half of 2010 suggest that the industry has hit the bottom and that the number of firms and employment is stabilizing and exports are increasing again. However, the global environment for clothing trade has changed significantly, which is related to changes in buyers' sourcing policies and the MFA phase-out. This trend has been accelerated by the global economic crisis. Cambodia has an important role in global clothing trade, but to remain and even increase its role, Cambodia's clothing sector has to respond to this new environment. Several policy recommendations to address challenges and increase the competitiveness and sustainability of Cambodia's clothing sector have been discussed above. Main policy areas include (i) improving productivity, skills, and capabilities at the firm level and developing from CMT to FOB and full-package supplier; (ii) increasing backward linkages and reducing lead times; (iii) improving physical and bureaucratic infrastructure, particularly with regard to transport, logistics and customs, electricity, and access to finance; (iv) diversifying end markets; (v) increasing local involvement in the industry at the management and owner level; and (vi) increasing regional integration. In the conclusions in chapter 6, global and country-specific challenges from the country case studies are brought together and main policy recommendations are identified.

Notes

1. There are two sources for clothing export data—import statistics of Cambodia's trading partners as reported in the UN COMTRADE database, and export figures reported by the Cambodian Ministry of Commerce. The values differ significantly and values reported by Cambodia's trading partners exceed Cambodia's exports statistics by a margin of around 25 percent. Although there are differences in magnitudes, both data sources show the same trends.

2. The Garment Manufacturing Association in Cambodia (GMAC) reports the number of officially registered firms and effectively operating firms; the difference being temporarily closed firms and firms in closure. The numbers reported in this chapter refer to effectively operating firms.

3. It has to be taken into account that this is an aggregate analysis, which masks product specific variations.

4. USITC reports unit prices (customs value/unit of quantity) for different categories of volumes—dozens, dozen pairs, and numbers. However, due to limited data availability we can only analyze unit values for products reported in dozens.

5. Eurostat reports volume data in net kilograms.

6. The Cambodian currency is pegged to the U.S. dollar and the country is dollarized.

7. The EU allows for regional cumulation in the context of the Association of Southeast Asian Nations (ASEAN) if countries meet a certain value added criterion. A product of a country in a regional group that is then processed in another country in that group will be considered as the product of the country where the final processing took place. However, the value added in the final processing has to be higher than the highest customs value of the products used originating in any other countries of the group. When this condition is not satisfied the product has the origin of the country of the regional group that accounts for the highest customs value within the regional group. As the local value added of clothing products is quite low in Cambodia, benefits from this regional cumulation rule have been limited to certain types of products, in particular sweaters where local value added is higher. Furthermore, regional sourcing is very limited, accounting only for 16 percent of textile imports in 2008 (see below on regional integration).

8. At GMAC meetings there are generally nine nationalities present, including Taiwan, China; Hong Kong SAR, China; China; Korea; Malaysia; Singapore; the United Kingdom; Indonesia; and Bangladesh.

9. There are differences, however, between certain nationalities. Hong Kong SAR, China investors tend to have more functions located in Cambodia such as input sourcing and merchandising and in some cases even relationships to buyers. In contrast, Taiwan, China and (mainland) China factories fulfill most functions—besides the direct manufacturing activities—in their headquarters outside of Cambodia.

10. The minimum wage will be increased to US$61 per month in October 2010 due to protests and a planned nationwide strike in July 2010.

11. Unfortunately, there is no consistent up to date productivity data for Cambodia's clothing sector available, which makes it impossible to compare unit labor costs.

CHAPTER 5

Bangladesh's Clothing Exports: From Lowest Cost to Broader Capabilities?

Introduction

This chapter assesses the development of the clothing sector in Bangladesh and its challenges in the post-quota and post-crisis world. Bangladesh's clothing export sector started in the late 1970s and early 1980s when manufacturers from the Republic of Korea and other East Asian countries started to invest in and source from Bangladesh, motivated by Multi-Fibre Arrangement (MFA) quota hopping and by access to Bangladesh's abundant supply of low-cost labor. During the 1980s the sector transformed into a sound industry and a period of rapid export growth started. Clothing became the main export product of Bangladesh in the late 1980s and comprises nearly 80 percent of total exports today. Foreign investment, the MFA quota system, and preferential market access to the EU as well as specific government support policies and local entrepreneurs have played central roles in the development of Bangladesh's clothing sector.

Although expectations on the impact of the MFA phaseout on Bangladesh clothing exports were rather gloomy, Bangladesh was able to increase export value and market share after 2004. In addition, during the global economic crisis Bangladesh has been one of the few winners by increasing market shares in both U.S. and EU-15 markets. Bangladesh's main competitive advantage is low labor costs—the lowest of main clothing exporter countries. Moreover, besides low costs, Bangladesh has other competitive strengths, including a comparatively long experience in the sector, local ownership, increasing backward linkages, and increasing capabilities in addition to cut-make-trim (CMT). However, despite continued growth in the sector and important competitive strengths, the clothing sector faces challenges that have to be addressed to sustain or accelerate growth, and to promote export diversification and industrial development more generally.

The chapter is structured in the following way. The first part introduces Bangladesh's clothing industry, focusing on recent developments of Bangladesh's clothing exports and the specific way that Bangladesh has been integrating into global clothing value chains. In the second part, main internal challenges of the clothing sector are discussed and policy recommendations are pointed out. The third part concludes.

Overview of Bangladesh's Clothing Industry

The development of Bangladesh's clothing industry can be divided into four periods: developments before 2004, post-MFA, global economic crisis, and post-crisis.

Phase 1: Developments before 2004

Bangladesh has a long experience in textile and in made-to-order clothing production, mostly for the domestic market. However, a readymade clothing industry for the domestic market only developed more recently. Two of the first exporters, Reaz Garments (which was the first firm to export to France in 1977) and Jewel Garments, developed from this domestic-oriented readymade clothing industry. The clothing export sector only started on a large scale in the late 1970s and early 1980s when manufacturers from Korea, Taiwan, China, and other East Asian countries started to invest in and source from Bangladesh motivated by MFA quota hopping and by access to Bangladesh's abundant supply of low-cost labor. Quddus and Rashid (2000) identify the breakthrough of the clothing export industry in 1978 when the Bangladeshi entrepreneur Quader of the company Desh was invited by the chairman of Daewoo, then a large clothing manufacturer from (quota-restricted) Korea, to collaborate in the production and export of clothing. As part of this collaboration Daewoo provided free training to 130 Desh supervisors and managers at its plants in Korea in 1979, which provided important initial transfer of technology and skills. In 1980 Desh's new factory started to operate, constructed with support from Daewoo, and was the largest in Asia outside Korea at that time.[1] In the mid-1980s the sector developed into a sound industry and a period of rapid export growth started. Clothing became the main export product of Bangladesh in the late 1980s and comprises nearly 80 percent of total exports today. Foreign investment, the MFA quota system, and preferential market access to the EU as well as specific government support policies and local entrepreneurs have played central roles in the development of Bangladesh's clothing sector.

MFA quota system: The clothing industry in Bangladesh developed under the MFA, which supported the growth of clothing exports in several low-income countries (LICs) as established clothing exporter countries reached their quota limits and started triangular manufacturing networks in LICs to use their unfilled quota. Bangladesh faced no quota restrictions for clothing and textile exports to the EU, Norway, and Canada (only since 2003) and none for textile exports to the United States. For clothing exports to the United States, Bangladesh had faced quota restrictions for 30 product categories since 1985. Quotas were imposed in 1985 after a triple digit growth rate during the previous five years, with exports to the United States rising to US$150 million (1 percent of the U.S. market). However, in export tax equivalents the quotas amounted to 7.6 in 2003, which is low compared to India (20), China (36), and Pakistan (10.3; Mlachila/Yang 2004). Thus, the nonexistence of quotas for the EU market and the relatively less restrictive quotas for the U.S. market under the MFA ensured markets for Bangladesh's clothing exports. Until the mid-1990s Bangladesh was a clear winner of the MFA quota system but this started to change in the second half of the 1990s where Bangladesh reached the U.S. quota limit in some product categories.

EU GSP: Another important factor was preferential market access to the EU for least developed countries (LDCs) under the Generalized System of Preferences (GSP) scheme since the early 1980s, which contributed to the growth of exports to the EU and made the EU the largest export destination of Bangladeshi clothing products. Although exports to the EU were lower than those to the United States throughout the 1980s, the picture changed in the 1990s and by 2000 exports to the EU accounted for over 50 percent of total clothing exports. Preferential market access to the EU, however, requires the fulfillment of double transformation rules of origin (ROO), which could not be fulfilled by all clothing exports, in particular woven products (see below). As a result the EU has particularly developed to a major importer of knitwear from Bangladesh.

Specific government policies to support the clothing sector: Besides a general 'anti-export' bias in Bangladesh's economy until the early 1990s, specific policies that secured access to imported raw materials and supported export-oriented activities had a central role in the start and growth of the export clothing sector. Two policies were particularly important both of which were put in place in 1980: the bonded warehouse and back-to-back letter of credit (L/C) facilities. An early support mechanism was the duty drawback facility. However, this involved upfront payment of duties on imported inputs as well as value-added tax on local inputs that tied up funds of manufacturers besides involving cumbersome procedures for reimbursement. To relieve clothing manufacturers of these difficulties, the government introduced the system of bonded warehouse in 1980. The bonded warehouse facility eliminated the duty-payment requirement and also substantially reduced bureaucratic hassles and delays (World Bank 2005b). A second important policy support mechanism was the introduction of back-to-back L/C facilities. Through the use of this facility, exporters are able to open L/C in a local bank for the import of inputs against the export orders placed in their favor by the final clothing importers (master L/C). The cost of the imported items along with interest and other charges would be deducted by the local bank from the proceeds of the sales of the final output. Hence, the manufacturer was spared the financial involvement in the purchase of the imported inputs and the financial outlay requirement for clothing manufacturing was reduced to wages and other operating costs (World Bank 2005b). A third relevant policy in the 1980s was cash incentives through which clothing manufactures received direct financial support.

The following section shows the significant development of the clothing sector in Bangladesh in terms of exports, number of firms, and employment, and also highlights the shift in ownership structure.

Exports

Exports have increased significantly since the mid-1980s.[2] Import data from Bangladesh's trading partners shows an increase from US$2,544 million in 1995 to US$7,945 million in 2004 up to a peak of 13,325 million in 2008 (see table 5.1). There was, however, a slowdown in clothing exports growth in the early 2000s and a 1 percent decline in 2002. The share of Bangladesh in global clothing exports increased from 1.7 percent in 1995 to 4 percent in 2008. The overall export figures mask a significant change in the composition of Bangladesh's clothing exports. In the 1980s Bangladesh only produced woven clothing products but from the early 1990s exports of knit clothing products, principally sweaters and T-shirts, started and experienced fast growth. In 1991 the share of knitted clothing was 15 percent in total clothing exports, in 2005 knit exports reached 50 percent, and in 2008 they were higher than woven exports, reaching 55 percent (see table 5.1). Looking at Bangladesh's clothing export data, export values are lower accounting for US$1,969 million in 1995, US$6,231 million in 2004, and US$9.323 million in 2007 (see table 5.2). With regard to export markets, nearly 60 percent of exports went to the EU-15 and another 27 percent to the United States in 2008 (see table 5.3).

Table 5.1. Bangladesh's Clothing Exports

	1995	1998	2001	2004	2005	2006	2007	2008
Total exports (US$ million)	2,544	3,704	5,032	7,945	8,026	10,414	11,175	13,425
Growth rate (%)	—	10.6	3.5	25.3	1.0	29.8	7.3	20.1
Global share (%)	1.7	2.1	2.6	3.2	3.0	3.6	3.5	4.0
Woven (US$ million)	1,762	2,394	2,968	4,035	3,991	5,050	5,220	5,994
Share (%)	69	65	59	51	50	48	47	45
Knit (US$ million)	782	1,310	2,064	3,911	4,035	5,364	5,955	7,431
Share (%)	31	35	41	49	50	52	53	55

Source: UN COMTRADE.
Notes: Imports reported by partner countries. Values in million US$.

Table 5.2. Bangladesh's Clothing Exports (as reported by Bangladesh)

	1995	1998	2001	2004	2005	2006	2007
Total exports (US$ million)	1,969	3,784	4,039	6,231	6,846	8,252	9,323
Growth rate (%)	—	40.8	-2.0	23.6	9.9	20.5	13.0
Global share (%)	1.4	2.3	2.3	2.5	2.6	2.8	2.8
Woven (US$ million)	1,563	2,820	2,758	3,224	3,499	4,180	4,589
Share (%)	79	75	68	52	51	51	49
Knit (US$ million)	406	964	1,282	3,007	3,347	4,072	4,735
Share (%)	21	25	32	48	49	49	51

Source: UN COMTRADE.
Notes: Exports reported by Bangladesh. Values in million US$.

Table 5.3. Bangladesh's Main Clothing Export Markets

Country	2000		2004		2006		2008	
	Value US$ million)	Share (%)	Value US$ million)	Share (%)	Value US$ million)	Share (%)	Value US$ million)	Share (%)
EU-15	2,481	51.0	5,052	63.6	6,276	60.3	7,822	58.3
United States	2,088	42.9	2,003	25.2	3,005	28.9	3,562	26.5
Canada	101	2.1	343	4.3	428	4.1	530	3.9
Turkey	—	—	—	—	79	0.8	339	2.5
Poland	4	0.1	—	—	68	0.7	224	1.7
Mexico	7	0.1	24	0.3	51	0.5	123	0.9
Switzerland	36	0.7	56	0.7	78	0.7	106	0.8
Czech Rep.	6	0.1	27	0.3	55	0.5	89	0.7
Russian Federation	—	—	—	—	—	—	86	0.6
Norway	27	0.6	52	0.7	62	0.6	84	0.6

Source: UN COMTRADE.
Note: Values in million US$.

Number of firms and employment

The number of clothing firms increased from around 130 in 1983 to around 5,500 in 2009, including around 2,000 in the knitwear segment, 3,500 in the woven segment, and some involved in both segments (BGMEA, BKMEA). Altogether there are over 6,000 firms registered with the Bangladesh Garment Manufacturers and Exporters Association (BGMEA) and the Bangladesh Knitwear Manufacturers and Exporters Associations (BKMEA), but some are registered with both associations. Additionally, there are sub-contractors that don't export directly and are thus not members of the associations. The industry is highly concentrated: in 2005 the top 500 firms exported nearly 75 percent of total clothing exports; the top 650, more than 80 percent (World Bank 2005b). The industry is also geographically concentrated around Dhaka where around 75 percent of the firms are located; most of the rest are located in Chittagong and smaller parts in Gazipur and Narayanganj. Most clothing firms are located outside of export processing zones (EPZs).[3] In 2005 1 percent of clothing firms operated in EPZs and around 65 percent of those had foreign ownership (World Bank 2005b, see below). Mostly large factories and foreign-owned firms are located in EPZs in the clothing sector because of restrictions on foreign investment outside of EPZs until 2005. In addition, EPZs provide better access to and reliability of infrastructure, especially power, as EPZs have their own power plant; a 'one stop shop' for all infrastructure and regulatory requirements; easy access to land; incentives such as a ten-year tax holiday (compared to seven to eight years outside of EPZs); and higher security. Some local firms also prefer EPZs due to the above-mentioned advantages. The disadvantage of locating in EPZs is that production costs, in particular labor costs, are higher. In contrast to other sectors, benefits such as duty-free imports are available to all clothing firms and not restricted to those located in EPZs.

Employment in the clothing sector grew from 0.2 million in 1986 to over 3 million in 2010 (just-style 2010d), comprising 40 percent of manufacturing sector employment. Indirect employment is estimated at around 10 million. In the 1990s more than 90 percent of workers in the sector were women, mostly young, uneducated, unmarried, and from rural areas, but this share has decreased to below 80 percent. The changing female intensity of employment is related to changes in the composition of clothing exports (Ahmed 2009a). The woven segment employs mostly women workers and the knit segment (and even more the sweater segment) mostly men. Only 33 percent of workers in the knit segment were women in the early 2000s (Bakht et al. 2002) compared to around 90 percent in woven. This can be explained by different capital-intensity and skill requirements: (i) the production process in knit clothing is more capital intensive and as production processes become more mechanized the gender profile tends to shift towards men; (ii) a larger proportion of knitwear firms are vertically integrated and are also involved in fabric-knitting, which is more capital and skill intensive than sewing; and (iii) the fabric-knitting section is often operated in an overnight shift and women were not allowed to work between 10pm and 6am according to Bangladesh labor law (Bakht et al. 2002). However, this law changed and according to current labor law (from 2006) women are allowed to work between 10pm and 6am if they give their permission.

Ownership structure

While foreign direct investment (FDI) played a central role in establishing the clothing industry in Bangladesh, the industry is now dominated by locally owned firms. Of the estimated 4,303 firms end of 2006, only 83 were wholly or partially foreign-owned (see table 5.4). Until 2005 FDI was restricted to EPZs and within EPZs it was conditional upon associated investment in backward-linkage industries (spinning and/or weaving/ knitting, dyeing, and finishing). The revised industrial policy in 2005 removed these restrictions but there is no evidence of any significant FDI outside of the EPZs since the removal (IMF 2008). Aggregate FDI in the textile and clothing (T&C) sector in EPZs from 1983 to 2006 is estimated at around US$500 million, which accounts for around 75 percent of total aggregated investment in T&C factories in EPZs (see table 5.5). Despite the dominance of FDI in EPZs, the vast majority of employment in the clothing sector is in locally owned firms located outside EPZs. The average number of employees in these factories was around 500 in 2006. The average number of employees in firms with FDI was substantially higher, reaching around 1,150 (IMF 2008).

Table 5.4. Ownership and Employment in Bangladesh's Clothing Sector

	1997	2002	2006
Locally owned factories	2,503	3,618	4,220
Employees in locally owned factories	1,300,000	1,800,000	2,200,000
Average employees per locally owned factory	519	498	521
Employment in EPZ clothing factories	—	—	122,098
Employment in wholly and partially foreign owned firms	—	—	95,559
Number of wholly or partially owned foreign firms in EPZs	—	—	83

Source: BGMEA, BEPZA, adapted from IMF (2008).

Table 5.5. Textile and Clothing Investment in EPZs, Cumulative for 1983–2006 (US$ million)

Investor	Woven clothing and accessories	Knitwear	Textiles	Total
100% foreign owned	247.2	65.6	168.6	481.5
Joint venture	50.5	5.9	18.6	75
100% domestically owned	54.1	12	42	108.1
Total	351.8	83.6	229.2	664.6

Source: BEPZA, adapted from IMF (2008).

Compared to other LICs, the involvement of locals in the clothing industry at the owners and management level is high in Bangladesh. Local entrepreneurs have played an important role in the development of the clothing sector, which makes the sector more embedded and increases the potential for local linkages and spillovers. Before the growth of the clothing sector there had not existed a significant number of local export entrepreneurs and export activity was generally limited to the jute sector. There is also no long tradition of a local, domestically oriented entrepreneurial class. However, due to markets guaranteed by quotas and after the first investment from and collaboration with Korean and other East Asian firms, the clothing sector established the reputation of being a sector where profits could be made easily and without high risks, because the investment to start a clothing factory was relatively low in the 1980s and 1990s. To start a small factory with around 100 workers required an investment of around US$2,000 in the mid-1980s. The situation is very different today, as firms need to be large to be profitable and to fulfill the demands of buyers. Specific government policies such as the bonded warehouse, back-to-back L/C, and cash incentive facilities were also central to facilitate local involvement in the sector.

Phase 2: Post-MFA

Competition among clothing exporters has intensified since 2005 when the MFA phased out. Expectations on the impact of the MFA phaseout on Bangladesh's clothing exports were pessimistic. However, Bangladesh's clothing exports have experienced robust growth after 2004. Export values increased and market share remained stable between 2004 and 2005 and increased again afterwards. Bangladesh is among six countries (other than China) that managed to capture significant market share in the U.S. and/or EU markets after the MFA phaseout. The other countries are Cambodia (United States), India (EU and United States), Indonesia (United States), the Philippines (United States) and Vietnam (EU and United States; IMF 2008).

Looking at import data by Bangladesh's trading partners, total clothing exports increased to US$8,000 million in 2005, which accounts for a 1 percent increase to 2004 (see table 5.1). The share of Bangladesh in global clothing exports decreased from 3.2 percent to 3 percent in 2005 but then increased again to 3.6 percent in 2006. This increase was based on knit exports as woven exports declined by 1 percent while knit exports increased by 3 percent in 2005; the increase was also based on U.S. exports. U.S. exports increased by 21 percent in 2005 (with woven exports increasing by 22 percent and knit exports by 18 percent, see table 5.6). Bangladesh exports to the EU, however, fell by 5 percent from 2004 to 2005 (with woven exports decreasing by 13 percent and knit exports increasing by 1 percent, see table 5.7). Looking at Bangladesh's export data, total export increased by 10 percent in 2005 (see table 5.2).

Table 5.6. Bangladesh's Clothing Exports to the United States

	1996	1998	2001	2004	2005	2006	2007	2008	2009
Total exports (US$ million)	1,018	1,498	1,929	1,871	2,268	2,808	2,995	3,353	3,345
Growth rate (%)	—	13	-1	6	21	24	7	12	0
U.S. share (%)	2.7	3.0	3.3	2.8	3.2	3.8	4.0	4.6	5.2
Woven (US$ million)	795	1,168	1,449	1,372	1,681	2,075	2,178	2,412	2,497
Share (%)	78	78	75	73	74	74	73	72	75
Knit (US$ million)	223	330	480	499	587	733	817	941	848
Share (%)	22	22	25	27	26	26	27	28	25

Source: USITC.
Note: Values in million US$.

Table 5.7. Bangladesh's Clothing Exports to the EU-15

	1995	1998	2001	2004	2005	2006	2007	2008	2009
Total exports (€ million)	967	1,635	2,794	3,689	3,509	4,556	4,344	4,667	5,016
Growth rate (%)	—	12	9	20	-5	30	-5	7	7
EU-15 share (%)	1.9	2.5	3.5	4.3	3.9	4.7	4.3	4.5	5.1
Woven (€ million)	605	868	1,325	1,522	1,328	1,678	1,499	1,513	1,662
Share (%)	63	53	47	41	38	37	35	32	33
Knit (€ million)	362	767	1,469	2,167	2,181	2,878	2,845	3,154	3,354
Share (%)	37	47	53	59	62	63	65	68	67

Source: EUROSTAT.
Note: Values in million euro.

The United States and the EU established safeguard quotas against imports from China in 2005, which phased out in 2008. The impact of the safeguards phaseout has to be assessed together with the global economic crisis, which started in 2008 and had important impacts on global clothing exports. However, the positive development of clothing exports in Bangladesh after the MFA phaseout cannot solely be explained by the China safeguards.

Phase 3: Global Economic Crisis

Due to the global economic crisis, global demand for clothing products sharply declined in 2008 and 2009. The crisis has affected many countries around the world. However, Bangladesh has been relatively resilient to the crisis and could increase its share in global clothing exports. Looking at import data by Bangladesh's trading partners, total clothing exports increased by 20 percent in 2008 and Bangladesh's share in global clothing trade increased from 3.5 to 4 percent between 2007 and 2008 (see table 5.1). Clothing exports to the United States increased by 12 percent in 2008 and stagnated in 2009 (see table 5.6). Clothing exports to the EU increased by 7 percent in 2008 and 2009 (see table 5.7). Imports to the United States from Bangladesh's competitor countries such as Vietnam, India, and Sri Lanka decreased by 2.9 percent, 7.4 percent, and 17.5 percent respectively in 2009. Imports from China, however, increased by 2.5 percent in 2009. Bangladesh's export data is only reported until 2007 in the UN COMTRADE database. However, looking at Bangladesh's monthly export data from BGMEA, after showing resilience to the global economic crisis until summer 2009, clothing exports turned negative in the second half of 2009 and declined by 6.7 percent compared to the same period in 2008. Nevertheless, data for the whole year 2009 shows that clothing exports increased by 15.4 percent.

Although export values have not been significantly affected by the global economic crisis, prices have been affected considerably, in particular in the second half of 2009. All firms reported that the pressure on prices from buyers has increased due to the crisis and that they had to reduce prices on average by 5 to 10 percent (which varies however from product to product: BKMEA reported price decreases of 5 to 7 percent and BGMEA price decreases of up to 20 percent). Table 5.8 shows unit values of Bangladesh's clothing exports calculated from Bangladesh's export data. Unit values for woven and knit products declined in 2009, as well as in general over the whole period 2004 to 2009.[4] Besides prices, lead times also have been reduced and contract time has been shortened. Thus, the main effects of the crisis in Bangladesh are increased pressures on prices and lead times.

Table 5.8. Unit Values of Bangladesh's Clothing Exports

	FY04	FY05	FY06	FY07	FY08	FY09
Woven	3,538	3,598	4,084	4,658	5,167	5,919
Volume	91	92	109	133	147	170
Unit Value	3.26	3.25	3.13	2.92	2.93	2.91
Knit	2,148	2,820	3,817	4,554	5,533	6,429
Volume	91	120	165	200	242	291
Unit Value	1.96	1.96	1.93	1.90	1.91	1.84

Source: Bangladesh Bank, adapted from Arnold 2010.
Notes: Values in million US$; volumes in million dozens; unit values in US$/unit.

Several factors explain the resilience of Bangladesh's clothing exports to the global economic crisis. First, the so called 'Wal-Mart effect' describes how consumers increase the purchase of low-end products during a recession as they substitute more expensive products with cheaper ones offered by discounters such as Wal-Mart. Wal-Mart is the largest buyer of clothing from Bangladesh. While the retail sector has suffered considerably during the crisis, sales by Wal-Mart increased in 2008 and 2009. Second, The 'China effect' describes how buyers have shifted orders from China to Bangladesh as Bangladesh has become the world's lowest-cost producer. China had lost some of its competitive edge in the basic clothing market due to the appreciation of its currency, rising labor costs, and labor shortages. However, China has increased support to its clothing sector in the context of the crisis and has shifted again to lower value products, which increases competition in this market segment. Third, interviewees stated that Bangladeshi firms could better respond to decreased prices in the context of the crisis than firms in other countries due to the comparatively high profits of clothing factories in Bangladesh before the crisis, which made it possible to offer lower prices by squeezing the profit margin. Furthermore, wages were squeezed. Other sources state that suppliers were willing to reduce margins to be able to reinforce relationships with buyers during the crisis. Moreover, the Bangladesh taka did not appreciate during the crisis, which had an important impact on sustaining Bangladesh's competitive export position. Fourth, the large share of local ownership in Bangladesh compared to other LICs has also played a role as orders have been generally moved away from foreign-owned, marginal producers in triangular manufacturing networks of transnational producers during the crisis and concentrated in core firms (see above on Sub-Saharan Africa (SSA) and Cambodia).

Phase 4: Post-Crisis?

The global environment for clothing trade has changed post-crisis. Earlier trends such as increased importance of lead times and flexibility, the demand for high manufacturing, and other capabilities and services from suppliers, plus general supply-chain rationalization sourcing policies, have been accelerated in the context of the global economic crisis (see chapter 2). Price decreases demanded in the crisis context by buyers will very likely become permanent. Competition in the low-value segment has further increased as some more advanced countries, in particular China, which already moved up to higher value products in the 2000s before the crisis, have moved again to lower-end production. It is not clear how fast China will move into higher value-added products again in the post-crisis environment. China's exports in the top 10 export categories of Bangladesh had increased in 2008 and 2009, before they subsequently declined. In addition, import structures may change post-crisis as the way out of the global economic crisis may be driven by developing countries. Although the U.S. and EU will remain the major import markets, at least for some time, other markets will gain in importance. In particular, clothing imports will increase in importance in fast-growing emerging countries such as China, India, Brazil, and the Russian Federation. In this context, also regional end markets may become central to substitute for reduced exports to developed countries' end markets. Bangladesh's clothing sector has important competitive strengths but faces also challenges that have to be addressed to increase competitiveness, in particular in light of these changes in industry dynamics and increased competition.

Main Challenges of Bangladesh's Clothing Exporters

In this part, main internal challenges of the clothing sector in Bangladesh are discussed. Furthermore, some policy recommendations are pointed out.

End-Market and Product Concentration

A major challenge for Bangladesh's clothing exporters is the lack of diversification in markets and products. The EU-15 and the United States together comprise of 85 percent of Bangladesh's total clothing exports with the EU-15 accounting for 58 percent and the United States for 27 percent (see table 5.3). Woven products mainly go to the U.S. market and knit products mainly to the EU. In the United States 72 percent of exports account for woven products (which accounts for an important part of denim products) while in the EU only 33 percent of exports are woven products (see table 5.6 and 5.7). The only other important end markets are Canada (3.9 percent), Turkey (2.5 percent), and Poland (1.7 percent). The concentration towards the United States and the EU, however, has decreased; those two markets accounted for 94 percent in 2000. BGMEA reports that in 2009 Bangladesh exported clothing products worth US$240 million to Turkey, US$82 million to Mexico, US$49 millions to Australia, US$43 million to South Africa, and US$40 million to Brazil. Exports to Japan more than doubled to US$74 million (World Bank 2010). But despite these promising developments there is much more potential for end-market diversification. Within the EU, including Central and Eastern Europe (CEE) countries, exports could be diversified from their current concentration toward the United Kingdom, France, Germany, and Spain. Exports to Canada, Japan, Turkey, Mexico, Switzerland, Russia, Norway, Australia, New Zealand, South Africa, and Brazil, which are quite marginal today, could be further promoted. New high-potential export markets are Argentina, the Middle East (in particular the United Arab Emirates), China, and especially regional markets—most importantly India (see below on regional integration).

Japan is a particularly interesting market as it is the third-largest clothing importer after the EU and the United States. The Japanese GSP includes duty-free access for almost all of Bangladesh's industrial products, including clothing requiring two-stage ROO for knit and one-stage ROO for woven (ADB 2004). Up to now, Japan has depended heavily on Chinese clothing imports, which account for more than 80 percent of its total clothing imports, but Japan has the objective to diversify its import markets within the context of the 'China plus 1' strategy. Bangladesh is very well-situated to become the 'plus 1' country, which would lead to a significant increase of exports to the US$24 billion clothing market of Japan where Bangladesh today only accounts for US$72 million (2 percent). Uniqlo, the largest Japanese clothing retailer (US$2 billion annual sales), is interested in a joint venture in Bangladesh. The Japanese market, however, is different from the U.S. and EU markets as quality, design, and lead times are more important criteria and as orders are smaller and involve more variations. Thus, increasing exports to Japan would diversify both end-markets and products, as different types of products and related capabilities are demanded in the Japanese market.

There have been efforts in recent years to enter into new markets and BGMEA and BKMEA sent missions to South Africa and Brazil; also, missions were invited from Japan. Furthermore, clothing exporters receive small cash incentives for exports to new destinations (outside of the EU, the United States, and Canada) in the period 2009 to 2012. These efforts have to be intensified and extended to more markets. Negotiating favorable market access, marketing and promotional initiatives, local and international exhibitions to attract foreign buyers, as well as image building at the association level could support breaking into new markets. This is not only important with regard to new markets but also for enhancing Bangladesh's reputation in existing markets. Information on different markets and buyers will be also required by exporters, which could be provided at the association level.

Also, clothing exports are highly concentrated in a few products. The top five product categories accounted for 58 percent of total U.S. clothing exports in 2008 and for 69 percent in the EU-15 market; the top 10 product categories for 70 percent and 83 percent respectively (see tables 5.9 and 5.10). Furthermore, the top export product categories to the United States and EU are overlapping—5 of the top 10 products appear in both the U.S. and the EU lists. The product concentration of Bangladesh's clothing exports is much higher than of competitor countries such as China and India. For knitwear, t-shirts, cotton shirts, and sweaters dominate. For woven clothing, pullovers and trousers are the leading products. Bangladesh is concentrated in the production of high-volume, low value-added basic products that are supplied into the low and medium market segment in the EU and the United States. The unit price of these products is very low, in general lower than the world average. Unit-value analysis shows that unit values of clothing exports from China and also India and Sri Lanka are considerably higher for most products than from Bangladesh. In the case of EU exports a comparison with competitor countries shows that only Pakistan has lower unit values; Sri Lanka, India, Vietnam, Cambodia, and China account for higher unit values (see table 4.10 in chapter 4; Tewari 2008). This is related to Bangladesh being cost competitive but also to being concentrated in basic products, while these other countries export higher-value products. Knit products where exports are concentrated in the EU market are generally in a higher-value segment than woven products, which are concentrated in the U.S. market. Clothing production in Bangladesh is also concentrated in cotton-based products and there is only limited export of clothing products based on man-made fibers.

Table 5.9. Top Export Products to the United States, 2008

HS	Description	Value (in million US$)	Share (%)
620342	Men's or boys' trousers	817	24.4
620462	Women's or girls' trousers	447	13.3
620520	Men's or boys' shirts	336	10.0
611020	Sweaters, pullovers, sweatshirts	201	6.0
610910	T-shirts, singlets, tank tops	136	4.1
610821	Women's or girls' briefs and panties	101	3.0
611030	Sweaters, pullovers, sweatshirts	88	2.6
620343	Men's or boys' trousers	84	2.5
620920	Babies' garments	76	2.3
620630	Women's or girls' blouses and shirts	68	2.0
	Total U.S. exports	3,353	

Source: USITC.

Table 5.10. Top Export Products to the EU-15, 2008

HS	Description	Value (in million euro)	Share (%)
610910	T-shirts, singlets, tank tops	1,269	27.2
611020	Sweaters, pullovers, sweatshirts	626	13.4
620342	Men's or boys' trousers	571	12.2
611020	Sweaters, pullovers, sweatshirts	449	9.6
620462	Women's or girls' trousers	295	6.3
610510	Men's or boys' shirts	219	4.7
620520	Men's or boys' shirts	198	4.2
610610	Women's or girls' blouses and shirts	89	1.9
620530	Men's or boys' shirts	78	1.7
610462	Women's or girls' trousers	77	1.7
	Total EU-15 exports	4,667	

Source: EUROSTAT.

Production of basic clothing products is Bangladesh's current competitive advantage. Future growth in clothing exports in Bangladesh will probably come from an increasing market share in basic clothing products for the EU and the United States. However, complementing the growth in production of basics, there is potential growth for higher value products. This is supported by the following reasons. First, profit margins and value added is higher in higher-value products and if more production steps are conducted besides CMT such as input sourcing and design. Risk is also lower if export products are more diversified. Second, in basic products the main competitiveness factor is labor costs, which drive sourcing decisions. This is currently favorable for Bangladesh, but may change because during the process of economic and social development of Bangladesh, wages will increase (also related to labor disputes and compliance issues; see below). Thus, the clothing industry in Bangladesh should not only rely on basic production in which labor costs are the central competitiveness factors. Third, as discussed above, export market diversification may be related to product diversification as other end markets such as Japan demand other (and in this case higher-quality) fashion and design standards. There are few comparable markets to the EU and in particular the United States with regard to large orders of basic products.

Many of the new buyers over the past few years in Bangladesh have come from the medium market segment (for example, Marks & Spencer and Marshall Fields) as they have faced downward pressures on prices (Arnold 2010). These firms require higher-quality, smaller order sizes, more frequent style changes, and shorter lead times. In addition, firms such as H&M, Zara, and Mango have started sourcing fashion basics from Bangladesh, which requires even more production flexibility and shorter lead times. The main challenges to upgrading into higher-value products and to extend production for those medium and fast-fashion buyers are quality, lead times, and missing design and technical skills (see below). However, there has been important upgrading in Bangladesh's clothing sector. Ten years ago most firms were CMT firms and they received all inputs (mostly fabrics and accessories) from buyers, just performed the cutting and sewing and then exported the final products. Today, the majority of firms are in charge of input sourcing. Although most buyers nominate yarn and fabric mills, factories are generally in charge of ordering and financing these inputs. Since market research and development (R&D) is necessary to diversify and upgrade export products, a research center built on a public-private partnership could be established. Its role would be to gather and disseminate information to local manufacturers on the latest developments in products, markets, and buyers.

Lack of Backward Linkages and Long Lead Times

Access to raw materials, in particular yarn and fabrics, is crucial for clothing exporters. Bangladesh is a net exporter of clothing but a net importer of textiles. The domestic textile industry cannot fulfill the growing demand for inputs needed in the clothing industry. There are three types of clothing firms in Bangladesh (Ahmed 2009a): (i) integrated manufacturing where factories import cotton and are involved in spinning, weaving or knitting, and sewing; (ii) factories importing yarn and being involved in weaving or knitting and sewing; and (iii) factories importing fabrics and being involved in sewing. Although all cotton is imported, there is an important difference between knits and wovens with regard to yarn and fabrics imports. Most knit firms belong to the first two categories while woven firms belong to the last category. The dominant form in the knit segment is integrated fabric and sewing factories and independent spinning mills (BKMEA). While 75 percent of fabrics used in woven are imported, the import share for fabrics used in knit is only 20 percent; most yarn for knitting (70 percent) is also sourced locally (BGMEA, BKMEA, World Bank 2005a). Both knit and woven fabric mills are nearly exclusively involved in cotton-based fabrics; the production of man-made fabrics is very limited in Bangladesh. For instance, about 90 percent of the yarn used for clothing is cotton (either 100 percent or blends). As a result of backward linkages in knit, the value of cotton imports has increased more rapidly than the imports of textiles (Arnold 2010). Most accessories (such as thread and zippers) and extra services such as printing, embroidery, washing, and dyeing are locally sourced today, in contrast to a decade ago when the majority of accessories were imported (World Bank 2005a). Compared to other LICs such as Cambodia and Vietnam, backward linkages are more developed. With regard to imports, more than half of imported textile inputs come from China (55 percent), followed by India (15 percent), Hong Kong SAR, China (9 percent), Pakistan (8 percent), Thailand (3 percent), and Korea (3 percent, see table 5.11).

Table 5.11. Bangladesh's Textile Imports: Top 10 Importers in 2008

Country	2000 Value (US$ million)	2000 Share (%)	2004 Value (US$ million)	2004 Share (%)	2006 Value (US$ million)	2006 Share (%)	2008 Value (US$ million)	2008 Share (%)
China	453	30.3	912	42.4	1,406	50.0	1,952	54.7
India	212	14.2	258	12.0	315	11.2	539	15.1
Hong Kong SAR, China	306	20.4	330	15.3	400	14.2	329	9.2
Pakistan	—	—	140	6.5	205	7.3	281	7.9
Thailand	52	3.4	98	4.5	114	4.1	119	3.3
Korea, Rep. of	283	18.9	187	8.7	130	4.6	109	3.0
Indonesia	81	5.4	78	3.6	81	2.9	65	1.8
Malaysia	30	2.0	44	2.1	46	1.6	47	1.3
Japan	28	1.9	32	1.5	32	1.1	29	0.8
United States	9	0.6	—	—	—	—	20	0.6
Vietnam	5	0.3	11	0.5	12	0.4	16	0.4
World	1,495		2,151		2,813		3,566	

Source: UN COMTRADE.
Notes: Imports reported by partner countries. Value in million US$.

The different situation with regard to knit and woven fabric mills can be explained by different investment requirements. A knit fabric mill, including a dyeing and finishing unit of a viable minimum economic size, requires an investment of at least US$3.5 million whereas the investment required for a similar factory in woven fabric amounts to at least US$35 million (Ahmed 2009a, World Bank 2005b). The cash incentive granted in 1994 for exports of clothing made from locally produced yarn and fabric encouraged investments in spinning and composite knitting mills (World Bank 2005b). Other incentives, which encouraged investment in knit mills, included low (subsidized) interest rates and government support in terms of investment in land development, power, and infrastructure. Due to the larger costs of investments in woven mills a similar development did not happen in the woven segment. However, more recently investment in woven textiles has also increased, in particular through FDI and in integrated spinning and weaving mills, but the remaining demand and supply gap is still large.

Becoming a competitive yarns and fabrics producer, in particular in the woven segment, is challenging. First, Bangladesh lacks local cotton and man-made fiber production. Second, investments in the textile sector are more capital intensive than investments in the clothing sector, in particular in woven. The high cost of finance in Bangladesh is not supportive for such types of investments. Third, investments in the textile sector rely even more on infrastructure than the clothing sector, in particular electricity and water. The electricity-intensity of knitting and weaving and even more spinning is much higher than that of sewing. Furthermore, fabrics need to be dyed and washed, which requires secure availability of water. The current power crisis is a central constraint for extending the textile sector in Bangladesh (see below). Fourth, some regional countries such as India and Pakistan and even more China are highly competitive in fabrics production with regard to price, quality, lead times, and availability and it will be difficult to match those countries. There are varying perceptions about the competitiveness of the local textile sector but there seem to be challenges in the area of price and quality. Thus, even though lead times and production flexibility would be enhanced by producing yarns and fabrics locally, this may not be the most cost effective means of production.

Although these challenges have to be taken seriously, further backward integration, including woven fabrics, will be central to increase competitiveness with regard to lead times, production flexibility, and costs (including transport, port, and customs clearance) as well as to increase domestic value added and local linkages and spillovers. Furthermore, preferential market access to the EU requires two-stage transformations.[5] The biggest advantage of local input production is lead times. For individual firms it is too costly to maintain an inventory of fabrics and, more importantly, production needs to be in accordance with the specification of buyers with regard to the type and color of fabrics. Thus, generally fabrics may be only ordered after the buyers have placed the orders, thereby increasing the total production time by several weeks. For knitwear, inputs, including local yarn, are normally available within days either locally or from India. For woven products, the majority of inputs are imported, mostly from China, India, Hong Kong SAR, China, Pakistan, and Thailand. Procurement and delivery from Asian mills outside Bangladesh typically requires three to six weeks (Arnold 2010). This is a crucial difference in a context where time has become increasingly important in buyers' sourcing decisions. Currently, Bangladesh has long lead times compared to competitor countries. In Bangladesh lead times for clothing products vary on average between 60 to

80 days for knit and 90 to 120 days for woven (see table 4.11 for a comparison with Asian competitor countries in chapter 4). Firms interviewed stated that lead time is one of the main challenges in fulfilling buyers' demands. Furthermore, due to these comparatively long lead times upgrading in more value and fashion products is limited. The market segments that Bangladesh currently serves still allows for relatively long lead times. Lead time, however, will become much more critical as Bangladesh moves into higher value-added clothing and fashion products (IMF 2008). Also, buyers interviewed stated the lack of local yarns and fabrics as a constraint as they prefer vertically integrated firms followed by firms able to source locally. For instance, Wal-Mart, the largest buyer of clothing from Bangladesh, is investigating the option for an investment in a mega mill in Bangladesh to reduce costs and improve lead times, which would be the first investment of Wal-Mart in the production segment in the T&C sector.[6]

Vertical integration or local sourcing would yield the largest lead-time reductions. Hence, a favorable environment for textile investment should be ensured. Policies could involve long-term loans at reduced interest rates for textile investments; the attraction of FDI specifically to the textile sector; the development of more efficient infrastructure, in particular for electricity and water, which are central for a competitive textile sector; and greater emphasis on skill development in areas relevant for textile production. But increasing local supply of yarn and fabric to fill the large remaining gap between demand and supply in woven is challenging and not attainable in the short run. There are, however, complementary options to reduce lead times. First, improvements in efficiency and productivity at the factory level, in particular with regard to the decision-making process, production structures, and supply chain management, can significantly contribute to reducing lead times. Second, improvements in trade facilitation, in particular in the transport infrastructure, logistics, and customs facilities, can also reduce lead times. Third, as an alternative to establishing competitive local yarn and fabric mills at the scale necessary for supplying inputs to the clothing sector, focus instead could be put on fabric processing and the capacity of the dyeing and finishing industry. This would make it possible to stock up fabric of the most common constructions in greige form in advance of orders and then dye and finish the fabric once the order and the design is received, which would reduce lead times and increase local value added. However, a close relationship with buyers would be necessary because the type of fabric would need to be known in advance, and only the color and design could be adapted closer to production. Fourth, ideally, the focus on fabric processing could be combined with establishing a central bonded warehouse (CBW). A CBW could stock up T&C inputs such as fabric in finished and greige form of the most common constructions, accessories, dyes and chemicals, yarn, T&C machinery, and spare parts in amounts determined by expected demand.[7] Manufacturers can then purchase these inputs duty-free from the CBW directly as export orders are received (World Bank 2005a). In this case, manufacturers may save on shipping time as they immediately source the inputs when they receive the order. For a CBW, a close relationship with buyers also would be necessary as buyers generally stipulate the exact fabric they need and often also nominate fabric mills. This information would be needed in advance, which requires a regular and close relationship between buyers and supplier firm. A CBW could be organized by the industry associations to share the costs and reap economies of scale. Fifth, and most important, increased regional sourcing could play a central role in reducing input costs and lead times. Regional sourcing has increased in importance; 23 percent of textile imports were sourced from SAARC member countries in 2008, which increased from 14 percent in 2000. India was the second-largest textile importer in 2008, accounting for 15 percent; China dominated with 55 percent of total textile imports; Hong Kong SAR, China was third with nearly 10 percent (see table 5.10 and below on regional integration).

Low Productivity and Lack of Skills

Bangladesh's main competitive advantage is the availability of low-cost labor. The low wage of workers in Bangladesh, however, is accompanied by low productivity, which erodes part of the benefits of low-cost labor. Despite the long existence of a clothing export sector, adequate productivity improvements have been lacking. However, there are large differences within the industry: some firms (generally larger and often foreign owned and EPZ-located) have high productivity levels and are world-class clothing producers, whereas others are lagging considerably (World Bank 2005b). Factory-level productivity depends on a host of factors, including labor costs; production methods; skills of workers, superiors, and management; and capital and technology. Factors external of factories are also central for productivity such as low-cost, high-quality, reliable inputs and infrastructure and logistics (see below).

Absolute labor costs are very low in Bangladesh and there is a large supply of workers. Bangladesh had the lowest labor costs per hour in a comparison with competitor countries in 2008 (see table 4.13 in chapter 4). Average labor costs per hour are more than twice as high in India and about four times as high in China. The minimum wage is Tk 1,662 (US$24). However, the minimum wage will increase to Tk 3,000 (US$43) in November 2010, an increase of 80 percent, as a reaction to widespread labor unrest (see below; just-style 2010c). The increased wage is still among the lowest in the world. However, a central problem in Bangladesh is that productivity is comparatively low. Average annual value addition per worker in Bangladesh was estimated at US$2,500 compared to nearly US$7,000 for a group of similar Chinese factories in 2005 (World Bank 2005a). But even after adjusting for productivity differences across countries, Bangladesh's clothing industry retains a significant per unit labor cost advantage (World Bank 2005b).[8] Buyers who source from a variety of countries consistently rank Bangladesh as their lowest-cost source of supply.

A critical reason for the relatively low productivity is the lack of skilled workers, supervisors, and managers. With regard to workers, the skill gap is estimated at 25 percent at the operator level,[9] which translates into more than 500,000 missing skilled operators (BGMEA). Clothing firms traditionally have recruited mostly young female workers from rural areas as helpers with very little or no formal education or vocational training, who after a period of three to six months have picked up skills and became machine operators. This is still a common practice among Bangladesh's clothing firms. A small group of firms has started to provide more systematic and organized in-firm training, in particular foreign-owned firms in EPZs. Employers, however, are reluctant to provide in-firm training for operators due to high worker turnover of on average 10 to 20 percent. The industry associations could play a key role in promoting in-firm training and providing capacity building to their members. BGMEA and BKMEA could raise awareness among their members about the productivity-improving benefits of skill training, provide training for trainers, and make it mandatory for their members to provide in-firm training (Elmer 2010).

Besides in-firm training, there exists a limited number of out-of-firm skill training programs for line operators at the public and private sector level, often with support from donors, in particular IFC, EU, GTZ, UNIDO, ILO, and the World Bank.[10] The actual number of people trained out-of-firm, however, is insufficient to cover the skill gap (Elmer 2010). The industry associations BGMEA and BKMEA are the most important private actors providing skill training. Public programs are largely based on the vocational training system. A problem with the vocational training system is that programs often have low quality and do not provide the skills needed by the labor market. This is related to limited cooperation between the public and the private sector. Coordination between government, associations, and firms and in certain areas also with buyers is central in the development of a system of out-of-firm training programs to ensure the market relevance of the skills developed. BGMEA has developed a training model that has already been tested in some locations (for example, Rangpur) but has not been scaled up. This model involves clothing firms, associations, and the government. The government provides the necessary facilities including land, buildings, and dormitories; the associations in consolidation with the firms provide the machines and equipment, develop and provide the training courses, and finance the training; and the firms guarantee to hire the graduates of these training courses. A consolidated program along these lines would be very useful to improve skills of sewing operators. However, besides specific skills for the clothing sector, the quality of the basic education system, which is far below that of regional competitors (with the exception of Cambodia), is a concern of firms in the clothing sector. Thus, besides specific training institutions, the basic education system needs to be improved.

The skill gap is particularly high in the area of middle management and technical and design/fashion skills such as pattern masters, product developers, designers, textile engineers, production managers, or merchandising and marketing professionals. These skills are critical for diversification of production and upgrading to higher-value products and activities. No specific estimates are available for the skill gap in these professions. However, the Ministry of Labor estimates that around 17,000 foreigners work in the clothing industry in Bangladesh to cover part of that gap (Elmer 2010). Workers in middle management used to be promoted from the shop floor, but firms have started to hire more external candidates. External recruitment was led by foreign firms, which were the first ones to open product development, merchandising, and marketing departments, which required new sets of skills. However, as more functions were demanded also in larger local firms, the latter have recruited more external candidates. The design and fashion capacity in Bangladesh is very limited. As buyers increasingly demand design capabilities or at least design understanding, and value added can be significantly increased in the production process if also some design steps are provided by suppliers, the building up of design capabilities is crucial. Furthermore, the lack of a design and fashion perspective limits upgrading possibilities to higher-value and fashion products as well as export market diversification. Technically skilled and engineering jobs, in particular in textile engineering, are widely held by foreigners who are expensive compared to locals (earning up to US$300 plus housing). The 17,000 expatriates in Bangladesh's clothing sector are mostly technically experienced workers from Sri Lanka, India, Pakistan, the Philippines, China, Taiwan, China, Korea, and Turkey (BGMEA).

The skill gap at these higher skill levels is not sufficiently addressed by the public and private sector and coordination, again, is limited. There is only a very limited supply of training programs for middle management, technical, and design/fashion skills in Bangladesh. A successful example is the BGMEA Institute of Fashion and Technology (BIFT), which started in 2000 and aims to create market-oriented skills for young people, middle-management professionals, and fashion designers. It offers courses including certificates, a diploma, and a BA and MA in apparel merchandising and fashion design by collaborating with the London College of Fashion, Nottingham Trent University, and Niederrhein University. BKMEA established a 'Productivity Improvement Program' (PIP) in 2007 with the objective to accomplish overall productivity improvements within the existing manufacturing system without major capital investments. The approach is to implement lean production systems to eliminate waste and increase competitiveness in terms of cost, quality, and lead time. Such a program could also be developed for the woven segment by BGMEA. Also, there should be more capital investment and government support to increase worker productivity at the association level. China and India have recently scaled up investment in T&C to upgrade technology supported by government investment funds. The Indian government has provided various incentives for investments in the T&C sector under the 'technology upgradation fund scheme' (TUDS). A similar 'upgrading fund' is needed in Bangladesh to support investment in new machinery, technology, and skills.

Bad Record in Labor and Environmental Compliance

Bangladesh has a bad record with regard to labor and environmental compliance in the clothing sector and in the past many exporters have neglected compliance with international and domestic labor and environmental standards. This is problematic as labor and increasingly environmental compliance have become central in sourcing policies of global buyers and often constitute a precondition for firms to enter sourcing networks. The existing situation with regard to compliance may also affect attempts to gain duty-free access to the U.S. market. Thus, improving compliance is a central challenge in Bangladesh's clothing sector. As low costs, in particular labor costs, are a major source of competitiveness of the clothing industry in Bangladesh, the increased concern about compliance has exposed firms in Bangladesh to the challenge of how to achieve a balance between price competition on the one hand and labor and environmental standards on the other hand (Ahmed 2005; Ahmed/Peerlings 2009).

With regard to labor compliance, wages and working conditions have long been a source of concern, as can be seen in frequent strikes and labor unrest. Labor unrest accelerated during the last months. Most recently protests centered on a manufacturing zone in Ashulia close to Dhaka, where owners were forced to shut all 250 clothing factories after workers clashed with security forces. These protests mark an escalation in clothing-industry violence in Bangladesh that has been festering for years (just-style 2010d). The most common labor issues in Bangladesh's clothing sector are low wages, lack of appointment letters, long working hours, lack of holidays, late payment, no maternity leave, and no dormitories for workers. Government investigations found 30 percent of factories are noncompliant. In addition, over 90 percent of the factories claiming to be compliant have one or more sweatshop conditions, including delays in promotion and pay rises after training entry level workers, irregular or reduced pay, low overtime benefits, long working hours, poor working conditions, absence of paid leave and medical facilities, absence of maternity benefits, absence of occupational safety and protection, absence of conveyance and housing, and neglect of trade unionism and labor laws (just-style 2010d). Increased labor unrest is also related to a change from female to more male employment as male workers are generally better organized.

A main issue with regard to labor compliance is low wages. Although Bangladesh has had a minimum wage since 1994, there is no mechanism that adjusts it to inflation and other macroeconomic changes and there had been no change until October 2006. Responding to labor unrest the government announced a minimum wage increase from Tk 930 in 1994 to Tk 1,662 in 2006 (US$24),[11] but this still falls short of living wage estimates, in particular in a context of persistently high inflation driven by food prices.[12] Unskilled workers in the clothing sector receive even less—Tk 800 (US$11.5) a month. Protestors have been calling for minimum wages to be raised to Tk 5,000 (US$72) a month to enable workers to keep pace of expenses (which was reduced from initial demands of Tk 6,200, or US$89). Also a group of global buyers sent a letter to the Bangladeshi Prime Minister in February 2010 stating that 'swift action' was needed to tackle the problem, motivated by fears that sweatshop allegations could taint their reputations as socially responsible companies. In July 2010 the Bangladesh Ministry of Labor and Employment agreed to increase the minimum wage to Tk 3,000 (US$43) per month[13] as of October 31, 2010, which accounts for an increase of 80 percent (just-style 2010c). This was based on recommendations of the Minimum Wage Board, which includes representatives from the government, the industry, and workers.[14] It is estimated that this wage increase will add 7 percent to production costs of clothing producers (just-style 2010c). However, the new wage falls short of the US$75 per month that workers are demanding and it remains to be seen whether it will be enough to end labor unrest. Trade unions and campaigners expressed disappointment at the scale of the proposed increase. Clothing buyers from retailers including Wal-Mart, Tesco, H&M, Zara, Carrefour, Gap, Metro, J.C. Penney, Marks & Spencer, Kohl's, Levi Strauss, and Tommy Hilfiger agreed in principle to support the wage increase but it remains to be seen whether they are prepared to cover part of the wage increase by paying suppliers more.

Several other steps have been taken to address working conditions in Bangladesh, which have lead to improvements in labor compliance since the 1990s. BGMEA and BK-MEA have taken initiatives to monitor workers' rights in factories but on a very limited scale. Twenty counselors work for BGMEA, which is very limited for an industry with more than 5,500 firms. A more comprehensive program financed by the World Bank and IFC started in the EPZs in 2005 and has led to significant progress in monitoring and enforcing labor standards in EPZ firms. Sixty counselors are appointed by BEPZA to work in the eight EPZs and prepare monthly reports on compliance for every factory. The counselors work in teams of two and each team is responsible for around 10 factories, which they visit on a daily or weekly basis. They provide orientation to management with respect to compliance, raise awareness among workers, support the establishing of workers' associations, monitor social compliance, and arbitrate between workers and management in cases of disputes. Earlier workers' representation and welfare committees have been replaced by workers' associations that have more rights, including direct election and right to discuss broader issues such as collective bargaining in the areas of wages, working hours, and policy of appointment.[15] This program has worked effectively in the EPZ context for several reasons (Ahmed 2009b, c; Ahmed/Peerlings 2009).

First, there is a feeling of community inside EPZs and due to co-location there is a positive peer pressure on compliance. Second, EPZs have a central zone administration that acts as a regulatory authority, and the zone management has a variety of tools available to monitor and enforce compliance. For instance, compliance can be part of leasing agreements and access to services can be conditional on compliance. Third, traveling distances are short in the EPZ context and the logistics of conducting inspections are hence simplified. Fourth, shared facilities, including health care facilities, training facilities, dormitories, and recreation facilities, can be created within the zone.

A question is how this limited program can be extended to the whole sector in Bangladesh. The Department of Labor has very limited resources to hire an adequate number of inspectors and has fewer enforcement options than EPZ authorities. But, as in Cambodia, the government and the associations could only give export licenses to firms that are part of the compliance and monitoring program. The government could further work together with the International Labour Organization (ILO) in their newly established 'Better Works' program. Buyers should also be involved in compliance programs. Many buyers in the clothing sector have developed their own codes of conduct (CoC), but suppliers are often not supported in fulfilling the CoC of buyers and there seems to be generally limited coordination between the sourcing and the corporate social responsibility (CSR) departments of buyers. With regard to the minimum wage increase, which will become effective in November 2010, it will be seen if buyers are prepared to take over part of the increase in their prices paid to suppliers. The president of BGMEA stated: "After an 80 percent revision of wages with an associated 10-20 percent increase in production costs, we are waiting for increased prices from the buyers who petitioned the Prime Minister to force us to double the wages" (just-style 2010g).

Environmental compliance has up to now not been an important topic in Bangladesh. Recently however, pressures from buyers and also from the media and from communities have increased and within the EPZs there is discussion to extend the labor compliance program to environmental compliance. Environmental compliance is particularity relevant in the textile sector, especially in the dyeing and washing segment where effluent water treatment is a central concern. Thus, with the development of backward linkages, environmental compliance will become more relevant. In the area of environmental compliance strategic government intervention is key to developing central facilities such as effluent treatment facilities as well as supporting firms with credit programs for their investments in compliant facilities. Buyers could also play an instrumental role in supporting environmental upgrading.

Inadequate Physical and Bureaucratic Infrastructure

Overcoming infrastructure constraints in the area of power, transport, and logistics is a priority in sustaining and increasing competitiveness in the clothing sector in Bangladesh. Currently, by far the biggest concern is the lack of reliable power supply. Recent power outages due to low gas pressure have made it difficult for manufacturers to produce efficiently and deliver goods on time. As a consequence most large and medium-sized factories maintain their own generators, which are relatively costly—2.5 times the price of getting power from the grid (World Bank 2005a). But generators are also affected by the gas shortage. Power is highly dependent on gas due to the natural gas endowment of Bangladesh and the lower price of gas (by around 30 percent) compared to alternative energy sources. Many firms have gas-based power facilities. The situation used to be better in EPZs, where electricity availability was secured, but recent power outfalls have also affected firms in EPZs. Gas pressure has declined in EPZs since September 2009 and the situation has further deteriorated in recent months. The EPZ's spinning, dyeing, finishing, and composite knit factories have been most affected because of their electricity-intensive production process, which requires 24-hour uninterrupted gas supply for full production. The Bangladesh Textile Mill Association (BTMA) claims that irregular gas supply has caused a 50 percent decline in textile production and BKMEA states that orders can no longer be fulfilled due to gas shortage. Some factories in EPZs are converting their machineries to operate by furnace oil or diesel, but this increases production costs considerably. Power outages have also caused delays in production schedules. In 2009, Bangladeshi factories on average had to air-freight 3,100 metric tons of clothing a month to the EU (about 7.5 percent of their total EU exports). By February 2010, the volume air-freighted to the EU had increased to 8,600 tons, which accounts for nearly a fifth of the country's monthly total. This has critical impacts on prices. Sea-freighting a t-shirt from Bangladesh to Europe costs around two U.S. cents a shirt. Air-freighting it averages 60 to 65 cents (Flanagan 2010b). If the energy crisis is not resolved quickly, the viability of the industry is endangered.

After power, transport and logistics are the second most important infrastructure challenges. Bangladesh ranks 87 in the Logistics Performance Index while its South Asian competitors India and Pakistan rank 39 and 68 respectively. There are only two ports (Chittagong and Mongla) in Bangladesh and the clothing sector only uses the port in Chittagong. Facilities have improved but the port still lacks modern equipment and handling time could be further reduced (see Arnold 2010 for a detailed discussion). Bangladesh has no deep sea port, which means that the mother vessels stop in Singapore, Malaysia, or Sri Lanka and transfer cargo to or from feeder vessels (with capacity ranging from 500 to 1,200 TEU) that go to or come from Chittagong. The setup of a deep-sea port in Bangladesh would reduce shipping times by three to four days. However, the set-up of a deep-sea port would require large investments and it is not certain that mother vessels would regularly approach a deep-sea port in Bangladesh. If regularity of ships is not secured, the feeder system could be preferable as it allows for more frequent ship transports given the smaller cargo. The capacity of the feeder vessels could be increased, which would not require investment in a new port, but port facilities in Chittagong could be extended. The road between Dhaka (where the majority of clothing firms are located) and Chittagong largely has only two lanes and is not designated for articulated trucks. Although it should only take six hours to drive between Dhaka and Chittagong, it generally takes much longer due to heavy traffic. The container unit train operation between Dhaka and Chittagong could ease transport constraints between Dhaka and Chittagong. However, the low frequency of train operations and limited capacity, the longer transit time compared with trucks, and the inefficient management of Bangladesh Railways make this alternative currently unviable. Customs and clearance time has improved: two years ago it amounted to four days, whereas now it takes around three days. This is however still much longer than for instance in Singapore where customs clearance only takes several hours or even only 25 minutes (BGMEA, BKMEA). A clearance time of one day would be a feasible objective for Bangladesh.

Access to finance for investment and working capital does not seem to be a major concern for clothing firms in contrast to cost of finance. In 2010 the interest rate was limited to a maximum of 13 percent, but this is still considerably higher than interest rates in competitor countries (even when inflation is taken into account) such as China, India, Sri Lanka, Malaysia, Thailand, and Vietnam. Also, for smaller firms and in particular start-ups, access to finance is a problem as banks are risk averse and demand high collateral. In particular, to increase productivity and upgrade capabilities and products, access to finance will be central. As discussed above, an 'upgrading fund' could be established to facilitate access to and reduce costs of finance for investments into productivity improvements, upgrading, and skills. The development away from CMT towards full-package suppliers in Bangladesh's clothing sector will further require secure sources of finance.

Limited Regional Integration

In an area of growing regional integration worldwide, South Asia is among the regions least integrated. Despite a multitude of regional cooperation and trade agreements under various stages of implementation,[16] the potential for regional trade and investment still remains largely unused. Intra-SAARC trade accounted for only 5 percent of the region's total trade in 2005 versus ASEAN's 25–30 percent and EU's over 60 percent of intraregional trade flows (Tewari 2008). T&C is the largest manufacturing sector, a major employer and a leading export sector in all South Asian countries, in particular in Bangladesh, Sri Lanka, Pakistan, and India, but regional trade is limited.

Regional sourcing and production networks could play a central role in increasing competitiveness by reducing input costs and lead times as well as offering more services by leveraging regional strengths. Also, regional end markets could be central in the context of end-market diversification. Increased integration and coordination with regard to backward and forward linkages could increase the competitiveness of the whole region due to the complementarily in competitive advantages of the South Asian main T&C exporter countries. India, Pakistan, Sri Lanka, and Bangladesh have all large T&C industries, but there are important differences in the structure of their exports. Sri Lanka and Bangladesh exports are dominated by the clothing sector, accounting for 95 percent and 97 percent of the countries' T&C exports respectively, and both countries are net importers of yarn and fabric. By contrast Pakistan's exports are dominated by textiles, which comprise around two thirds of its exports. India is in the middle with roughly half of its exports coming from textiles and half from clothing. India and Pakistan have both a large raw material base in cotton and both produce cotton yarn and fabrics. Furthermore, within clothing exports there are important differences. India and Sri Lanka tend to export higher-value products whereas Bangladesh is concentrated in large volumes of relatively low-value products. Pakistan's main exports are cotton made-ups (bed linen and home furnishing), yarn and fabric, and some basic men's wear. India and Sri Lanka's unit values of clothing exports are significantly higher than those of Bangladesh and Pakistan, in particular for the EU (see table 4.10 in chapter 4; Tewari 2008). India has a skilled workforce and has developed significant design capabilities. Sri Lanka is well positioned in the middle market in certain types of products, in particular lingerie, and has established some design capabilities. These different strengths of the countries in the region could be leveraged and economies of scale, vertical integration, and horizontal specialization could be promoted. The region could develop into a global T&C hub offering expertise from design to manufacturing, all production steps along the chain, and different types of products (UNDP 2006).

Intraregional trade in T&C has grown in recent years. Exports to and from India dominate this increase in absolute terms, but Bangladesh (and also Sri Lanka) have seen relatively large increases (although from a very low base). India's textile exports to Bangladesh doubled between 2001 and 2006 but Bangladesh increased its textile exports to India by 83 times; to Pakistan textile exports increased fourfold and textile exports to Sri Lanka doubled. Similarly Bangladesh increased clothing exports to India tenfold, doubled its clothing exports to Pakistan, and increased clothing exports to Sri Lanka by 66 percent (Tewari 2008). The bulk of increased regional trade, however, comes from textiles. Less than 1 percent of total clothing exports from South Asia was exported to other South Asian countries but more than 6 percent of the region's textile exports went to the region. Thus, there is more regional trading with regard to input sourcing and the region is used only to a very limited extent as an end market for clothing products. For Bangladesh regional textile imports accounted for 23 percent of total textile imports in 2008, up from 14 percent in 2000. India is the largest regional textile supplier, accounting for 15 percent of total textile imports followed by Pakistan with 8 percent (see table 5.12). With regard to end markets the region is marginal, accounting for only 0.04 percent of Bangladesh's total clothing exports. Bangladesh clothing exports have a duty-free export quota of eight million pieces in India, which was established in the context of the free trade agreements between Bangladesh and India. However, Bangladesh has not used the whole quota. In 2009 only half of the quota was used, which is related to the existence of nontariff barriers, including high specific duties (see below). In textile exports (which only account for 3 percent of Bangladesh's total T&C exports) the region accounted for 22 percent in 2008.

Table 5.12. Bangladesh's Textile Imports from and Clothing and Textile Exports to SAARC

	2000		2004		2006		2008	
	Value	Share (%)	Value	Share (%)	Value	Share (%)	Value	Share (%)
Textile imports (in million US$, reported by partner countries)								
SAARC	212	14.2	401	18.6	526	18.7	827	23.2
India	212	14.2	258	12.0	315	11.2	539	15.1
Pakistan	—	—	140	6.5	205	7.3	281	7.9
Sri Lanka	—	—	4	0.2	7	0.2	7	0.2
World	1,495		2,151		2,813		3,566	
Clothing exports (in 1,000 US$)								
SAARC	1,322	0.0	1,383	0.0	1,471	0.0	5,201	0.0
India	1	0.0	1,334	0.0	1,183	0.0	4,093	0.0
Pakistan	—	—	42	0.0	267	0.0	359	0.0
Sri Lanka	—	—	8	—	21	—	275	0.0
World	4,861,533		7,945,280		10,414,400		13,425,400	
Textile exports (in 1,000 US$)								
SAARC	25,933	10.3	52,163	14.5	100,355	24.1	99,943	22.0
World	251,066		359,256		416,541		454,202	
Share of T&C (%)	5.2		4.5		4.0		3.4	

Source: UN COMTRADE.

Intraregional investment also has become more important in recent years, in particular in the textile sector, as investment from India in Bangladesh particularly has increased. But besides the textile sector, there is also growing interest among Indian, Sri Lankan, and Pakistani firms to invest in Bangladesh's clothing sector. There are increasing numbers of inquiries about joint ventures in Bangladesh by South Asian T&C producers to set up clothing facilities. For instance, large Sri Lankan firms visited Bangladesh to screen investment and sourcing opportunities (BGMEA, BKMEA).

However, there are important challenges to intraregional trade and investment and to the development of the region as a global T&C hub (Tewari 2008). First, with regard to regional input sourcing East Asian imports are still dominant in South Asia's main clothing exporter countries, accounting for nearly 70 percent of total textile imports in Bangladesh. Bangladesh (and also Sri Lanka) have a long experience of sourcing from East Asia. This is because the development of their clothing sectors is related to quota hopping investment and sourcing from East Asian manufactures. Buyers have reinforced these relationships as they generally nominate supplier firms for their orders and have long-standing relationships with East Asian suppliers. This is particularly the case for CMT firms, which are not involved in input sourcing. But also, when suppliers are in charge of input sourcing, buyers tend to nominate suppliers. Thus, the decision-making power of suppliers about input suppliers is limited. However, as lead times are central in buyers' sourcing decisions, they generally are interested in competitive regional suppliers to reduce lead times and increase flexibility. Thus, there seems to be scope to increase regional sourcing from the buyers' side but regional input suppliers have to establish relationships with buyers to be nominated.

Second, South Asian countries have a limited product variety of yarn and fabrics due to a strong concentration in cotton-based inputs. This is problematic as buyers prefer to bundle input sourcing and to use a 'one stop shop' for all their input needs, including yarn, fabric, accessories, trims, and textile machinery. Furthermore, despite the proximity of regional countries they are often not cost-competitive.

Third, with regard to using the region as an end market, most regional exporters seem to be focused on global rather than regional markets. A reason for limited intraregional clothing trade is that the consumption of readymade clothing has been low in South Asia due to the preference for made-to-order clothing (Tewari 2008). However, as domestic markets for readymade clothing and organized retail are rising in South Asia, the potential is increasing for intraregional trade in clothing. Tewari (2010) states that the growth of the domestic market and organized retail in India is fuelling demand for more efficient supply chains and proximate production networks, which supports greater intraregional trade and investment. But exporting to regional markets will require different skills as volumes and demands differ compared to the U.S. and the EU markets and intraregional marketing and distribution networks would be necessary to increase regional sales of end products.

The most important challenge to increased intraregional trade and investment with regard to input sourcing and end markets are intraregional trade barriers. Despite regional integration efforts most countries still restrict T&C imports from the region through high tariffs, specific duties, and nontariff barriers. The implementation of SAFTA started in July 2006 with the objective to reduce tariffs between 0 and 5 percent by 2015 for India, Sri Lanka, and Pakistan and by 2018 for Bangladesh and the other member countries. However, most T&C products are placed on the sensitive list of each country, which exempts them from tariff reduction. Bangladesh, India, and Pakistan included most T&C products on their sensitive list whereas Sri Lanka has a relatively short sensitive list for T&C products (UNDP 2006). In particular, textiles and textiles articles account for very high tariffs on the sensitive list. India's tariff lines for textiles and textiles articles are among the highest, accounting on average for 34.2 percent. Nepal is the highest with 37 percent, Bangladesh is next with 31.6 percent, and then Pakistan with 24 percent (Taneja and Sawhney 2007, cited in Tewari 2008). These countries should follow Sri Lanka, which has an average tariff rate of 1.9 percent for textiles and textile products. Another challenge is India's specific duties on T&C imports. Before the final removal of the T&C import ban in India, India's T&C industries lobbied for specific duties on a large number of fabrics and clothing products in 2000. These compound duties use the ad valorem duty rate to calculate a specific duty that is imposed generally on low-value products for which domestic demand is high and where other developing countries are competitive.

The elimination of intraregional trade barriers, which include tariffs, specific duties, and nontariff barriers, is a precondition for increased regional integration in the T&C sectors. Furthermore, improvements in intraregional transport, logistics, and customs facilities are central to reduce costs and lead times in regional trade. Besides these central measures, intraregional trade must also be actively promoted. The ASEAN Competitiveness Enhancement (ACE) Project is a good example in this regard (see chapter 4). A similar program could be developed for the SAARC region.

Conclusions

The clothing sector in Bangladesh has a strategic significance in creating employment and exports and in the industrial development process of the country more generally. In this chapter the development and challenges of the clothing sector in Bangladesh in the post-quota and post-crisis world have been assessed. The development with regard to exports, number of firms, and employment yields a positive picture of the clothing sector in Bangladesh. However, the global environment for clothing trade has changed significantly, which is related to changes in buyers' sourcing policies and the MFA phaseout, and has been accelerated by the global economic crisis. Bangladesh has an important role in global clothing trade, but to maintain or improve its position the Bangladeshi clothing sector has to respond to this new environment. Several policy recommendations to address challenges and increase the competitiveness and sustainability of Bangladesh's clothing sector have been discussed above. The main policy areas include (i) solving the power crisis and improving physical and bureaucratic infrastructure in other areas such as transport, logistics, and customs; (ii) improving productivity, skills, and capabilities at the firm level and developing further from CMT to FOB and full-package supplier; (iii) increasing further backward linkages and reducing lead times; (iv) improving labor compliance; (v) diversifying end markets; and (vi) increasing regional integration. In the conclusions in chapter 6 global and country-specific challenges from the country case studies are brought together and main policy recommendations are identified.

Notes

1. Desh cancelled the collaboration with Daewoo in 1981 after only 18 months following the military coup in Korea and a change in the management at Daewoo.

2. There are two sources for clothing export data—import statistics of Bangladesh's trading partners and export statistics of Bangladesh. The values differ significantly and values reported by Bangladesh's trading partners exceed Bangladesh's exports statistics by a margin of around 20 percent. Although there are differences in magnitudes, both data sources show the same trends.

3. There are eight EPZs operating in Bangladesh, and two public ones and one private one are under construction.

4. Note that this is an aggregate analysis, which masks product specific variations.

5. Currently only around half of the clothing exports to the EU use GSP facilities; the rest is traded on a MFN basis. The utilization rate varies between knit and woven clothing accounting for around 90 percent for knit exports and only for 16 percent for woven exports. This has contributed to the very rapid growth of Bangladesh's exports of knitwear to the EU and to the less dynamic development of woven exports. The EU offered a change in the ROO requirements with regard to regional cumulation in the context of the South Asian Association for Regional Cooperation (SAARC) in 1995 and 2001. The EU GSP allowed SAARC member countries the possibility for regional cumulation, which involved the eligibility of a special ROO treatment if countries meet a certain value added criterion. Bangladesh, however, rejected this regional cumulation provision due to protest from the BKMEA and the Bangladesh Textile Mill Association (BTMA).

6. The investment was however delayed due to the power crisis (see below).

7. If the products would not be sold in the domestic market, then they could be re-exported, because in a CBW they have not legally entered the country and thus no tariffs and custom procedures are necessary.

8. Unfortunately, there is no consistent up-to-date productivity data for Bangladesh's clothing sector available, which makes it impossible to compare unit labor costs.

9. The estimates of the operator skills gap range from 20–30 percent. The BGMEA's official estimate is 25 percent (Elmer 2010).

10. The World Bank funds a US$79 million training project aimed at improving the skill set and employability of workers in Bangladesh. The Skills and Training Enhancement Project (STEP) started in 2010 is designed to strengthen public and private training institutions in the country, and improve in particular the abilities of workers in Bangladesh's clothing industry.

11. EPZs are under a different labor law since 1982, which is known as Instructions 1 and 2. In the EPZ the minimum wage for workers in the clothing sector accounts for US$30 but the average wage paid is generally higher.

12. Rises in living costs since 2006 account for 200 percent for food and 100–200 percent for house rents, transportation, and other basic expenses. The Asia Floor Wage campaign estimates a realistic living wage for a family in Bangladesh at just over Tk 10,000 per month (just-style 2010d).

13. This minimum wage refers to the lowest entry-level grade-7 worker. The new pay structure has 7 grades. The minimum pay of the highest grade-1 has been raised to Tk 9,300 (US$133) per month from the current Tk 5,140 (US$74). The wage of an apprentice worker has been increased to Tk 2,500 (US$36) from Tk 1,200 (US$17) per month (just-style 2010f).

14. However, factory owners, represented by the BGMEA, only agreed to the minimum wage rise if it was under-pinned by a series of benefits to support their businesses, including a 120-day delay in implementation of the new wages, the withdrawal of their advance income tax and value-added tax (VAT), reduced charges for utility and port services, lower bank interest rates, and the creation of a US$70 million fund to build dormitories for workers (just-style 2010f).

15. A problem, however, is that these workers' associations lack some trade union rights and are not connected to an outside union. Thus, they do not fulfill the core labor standards of the International Labour Organization (ILO).

16. Such agreements include the South Asian Association for Regional Cooperation (SAARC); the South Asian Preferential Trading Agreement (SAPTA); the Bay of Bengal Initiative for Multi-Sectoral Economic Cooperation (BIMSTEC) involving Bangladesh, India, Myanmar, Sri Lanka, Thailand, Nepal, and Bhutan; and since 2004 the South Asian Free Trade Area (SAFTA).

CHAPTER 6

Conclusions: How to Compete in the Post-Quota and Post-Crisis World?

This chapter presents main conclusions with regard to global and country-specific dynamics and challenges, and what they mean for entry into and upgrading within global clothing value chains and for using the sector as a springboard for export diversification and industrial development in low-income countries (LICs). Besides country differences, LIC clothing exporters face common internal challenges in the post-quota and post-crisis world. These common internal challenges as well as main policy recommendations for LICs to address these challenges are further identified in this chapter.

Global Dynamics: Consolidation, Increased Entry Barriers, and Heightened Competition

The main arguments for the clothing sector as a springboard for export diversification and industrial development in LICs are that (i) entry barriers are low and LICs with large supplies of unskilled labor can quickly participate in clothing manufacturing, and (ii) clothing manufacturing can be a launching pad for upgrading into higher value added and more skill- and technology-intensive activities within and across sectors. But are these assumptions with regard to entry and upgrading still valid for the clothing sector and LICs today? As discussed in chapter 2, the environment for global clothing trade has recently changed significantly driven by (i) changes in the regulatory system, in particular the phaseout of the Multi-Fibre Arrangement (MFA); (ii) the global economic crisis; and (iii) changes in the strategies of global buyers and their sourcing policies. These developments have lead to global consolidation whereby leading clothing supplier countries and firms have strengthened their position in the clothing value chain (Gereffi and Frederick 2010). At the country level, low-cost Asian clothing exporter countries such as China, Bangladesh, India, and Vietnam are increasing their market share in the United States and the EU. This has happened primarily at the expense of regional supplier countries (for example, Mexico and Central American and Caribbean suppliers to the United States as well as North African and Central and Eastern Europe (CEE) suppliers to the EU), Sub-Saharan Africa (SSA) clothing suppliers, and smaller LICs in different regions. At the firm level the increasing adoption of 'supply chain rationalization' sourcing strategies has benefited larger and more capable suppliers at the expense of smaller and marginal suppliers in all countries.

Global consolidation has critical implications for possibilities to enter and upgrade within global clothing value chains and questions previous assumptions that see clothing exporting as an easy avenue to entry and upgrading. Global consolidation has increased entry barriers at the country and firm level. The MFA phaseout led to increasing entry barriers at the country level as quotas no longer secure market access for LICs. At the firm level, global buyers' supply chain rationalization strategies have resulted in increased entry barriers as more capabilities and higher standards are expected from suppliers. Thus, firms are only able to enter supply chains of global buyers if they can offer high manufacturing capabilities, including low costs, high quality, short lead times, production flexibility, and labor compliance. In addition, buyers increasingly demand nonmanufacturing capabilities, including input sourcing on suppliers' accounts, product development and design understanding, inventory management, logistics, and communications. These capabilities require financial and human resources at the firm level as well as reliable and low-cost infrastructure and backbone services, education and training facilities, and access to finance at the country level. For LICs, these new developments are challenging as low labor costs and preferential market access are not enough to be competitive in the clothing sector today.

On the positive side, suppliers providing broader capabilities have developed strategic relationships with global buyers. Strategic relationships with core suppliers have become key in buyers' sourcing strategies. This trend has been accelerated in the context of the MFA phaseout and the global economic crisis as buyers have confined relationships to their most capable suppliers. These suppliers face further learning and upgrading opportunities—at least up to a certain level when upgrading does not encroach on buyers' core competencies. Some first-tier suppliers and intermediaries, in particular transnational producers and global trading houses, have captured high value-added activities and control far-flung manufacturing networks (Appelbaum 2008). Marginal and new suppliers are still able to enter global clothing value chains through intermediaries where entry barriers are lower. The persistence of intermediaries implies that despite of global buyers' supply chain rationalization strategies, there remains a role for second-tier suppliers integrated into global clothing value chains via intermediaries. In particular in triangular manufacturing networks of transnational producers, entry barriers are substantially lower and suppliers offering only basic manufacturing functions are able to enter. However, upgrading opportunities, in particular for functional upgrading, are also limited by the intermediaries' control over key decisions and functions. A main motivation for intermediaries to source from LICs has been preferential market access (and before 2005 also MFA quota hopping). The competitiveness of certain LICs, in particular in SSA, heavily depends on these preferences.

Related to and accelerated by the MFA phaseout, the global economic crisis, and supply chain rationalization strategies, there are two underlying structural challenges which further condition the role of the clothing sector in the industrial development process of LICs today: (i) changing global supply and demand structures, and (ii) asymmetric market and power structures within global clothing value chains. With regard to supply and demand structures, the second half of the twentieth century was characterized by rising demand in the global clothing sector (with slower growth since the 1970s, however) and replacement of production in developed countries by imports from developing countries. However, since the beginning of the 2000s, demand in major end markets has stagnated and import penetration levels in developed countries had already reached very high levels (Palpacuer et al. 2005). This trend recently has accelerated due to the global economic crisis. Kaplinsky (2005) points out that these developments have a decisive impact on developing countries with potentially severe implications for late clothing industrializers. The previous period of export growth by newly industrialized economies (NIEs) was primarily at the cost of domestic producers in developed countries and all NIEs could simultaneously increase their exports to the U.S. and the EU markets. Today, however, the growth of clothing exports from a few developing countries is largely at the cost of clothing producers in other developing countries (Morris 2006b). The heightened competition between developing countries has been reinforced by overcapacity in the global clothing industry due to the MFA phaseout and related to the entry of large developing countries such as China and India into clothing exporting (Kaplinsky/Morris 2008). The decline in unit prices of U.S. and EU-15 clothing imports underlines this heightened competition. In this context, it has become difficult for suppliers to capture margins and upgrade through participation in global clothing value chains (Palpacuare et al. 2005). With regard to asymmetric market and power structures, rents in the global clothing value chain do not derive from manufacturing but from design, branding, marketing, research and development (R&D), and retailing (Gereffi 1994), which are the core competencies of buyers and protected by high entry barriers. By controlling these high-rent activities buyers yield significant power over other actors in the chain. Power at the buyers' level has further increased due to consolidation among retailers resulting from mergers and acquisitions and the emergence of large discount chains and specialty clothing stores (Morris and Barnes 2009). These asymmetric market and power structures further impede the capture of gains and upgrading of suppliers to higher-value and higher-rent activities within global clothing value chains.

However, new global developments may signal a partial shift in competitive and power structures in global clothing value chains. First, some intermediaries and first-tier suppliers, in particular global trading houses and transnational producers, have captured high value-added activities and control far-flung manufacturing networks, which potentially signals a shift in the governance structure of global clothing value chains (Appelbaum 2008). Second, global demand structures may change as import demand for clothing in the United States, the EU, and Japan might stagnate while demand will increase in fast-growing emerging countries as well as in regional and domestic markets. This may also lead to changing governance structures as the role of traditional buyers may decline while developing countries' buyers may increase in importance. It will be central to understand sourcing policies and power structures within clothing value chains of these new buyers and associated entry and upgrading possibilities. Third, there is insecurity about China's future as a competitor to LIC clothing exporters. In the 2000s China at least partly upgraded its production to higher-value products, which was reversed, however, in the context of the global economic crisis. It is not clear how fast China will move into higher value-added products again in the post-crisis environment. Such a development would increase space for LIC clothing exporters, at least in the low-value basics market segment.

Country Differences: Type of Integration and Role of Ownership

Besides global trends with regard to entry and upgrading in global clothing value chains, country dynamics and the specific type of integration into these chains are crucial and can lead to very different outcomes. In chapters 3, 4, and 5 the experiences of the main SSA clothing exporter LICs, Cambodia and Bangladesh, were discussed. Notwithstanding different country-specific dynamics, the integration into global clothing value chains in SSA's main clothing exporting LICs is similar to Cambodia. These countries are broadly integrated into global clothing value chains via foreign direct investment (FDI) and triangular manufacturing networks of transnational producers based on MFA quota hopping, cut-make-trim (CMT) production, and, in particular in the case of SSA, preferential market access. In Kenya and Madagascar ownership and integration patterns are more diverse but the majority of firms are still integrated into triangular manufacturing networks. Furthermore, Cambodia and SSA LICs were integrated into global clothing value chains relatively late. In Cambodia the export clothing sector only started in the mid-1990s after almost three decades of political and social unrest; and although South Africa and Mauritius started clothing exporting earlier, the other important SSA clothing exporters only significantly increased their exports in the early 2000s with the African Growth and Opportunity Act (AGOA). This late and specific type of integration circumscribes upgrading possibilities.

Most foreign-owned firms in SSA LICs and Cambodia are local affiliates of transnational producers—located in Taiwan, China, Hong Kong SAR, China, and the Republic of Korea, but also Singapore, Malaysia, China, and India—and are integrated into their manufacturing networks. On the one hand this type of integration has promoted access to global sourcing and merchandising networks and, hence, facilitated entry into clothing exporting. On the other hand, it has limited upgrading possibilities as critical decision-making and certain higher-value functions are confined to the headquarters. Unlike locally owned factories, these foreign-owned firms have limited leverage and autonomy in terms of strategic decision making and in attracting orders as negotiations with buyers are located at the headquarters. Headquarters are generally in charge of input sourcing (often drawing on their own textile mills or sourcing networks based largely in East Asia), product development and design, logistics, merchandising, and marketing, and have direct relationships with buyers. Thus, transnational producers are able to leverage the capabilities of their headquarters and global sourcing networks for value-adding activities, which sets limits for capacity building, investment, and upgrading in lower-tier supplier firms. Which functions foreign owners decide to locate in SSA LICs and Cambodian plants is not only a question of local capabilities. Rather, it is determined by their strategic choice of what and how to produce in their global sourcing network (Natsuda et al. 2009). Thus, the upgrading challenge is not only one of developing skills and creating capabilities in SSA LICs and Cambodia, but also of changing their specific role and integration into global clothing value chains (Barnes/Morris 2010).

Production plants in SSA and Cambodia are generally only in charge of manufacturing (CMT). Few foreign-owned firms have invested in more capital-intensive finishing operations such as washing and embroidery and even fewer have integrated backwards into fabric and yarn production (Gibbon 2003; Natsuda et al. 2009). Transnational clothing producers generally own or source from production units in several countries and follow a global strategy. This can be seen in the set-up of firms (which is similar in different locations); the specialization in a limited number of long-run, low-value products; the widespread use of foreigners at the management and supervisory level; and the limited linkages to local or regional economies. These ownership structures and this specific business model have important impacts on the embeddedness of clothing firms, in particular on the location of critical decision-making processes (for example, sales and merchandising and input sourcing) and on local linkages and spillovers (for example, learning in management or supervisor positions, transfer of skills, and knowledge and technology). These conditions further limit the role the sector can play in promoting export diversification and industrial development. This specific integration into global clothing value chains has also led to increased vulnerability as evidenced by the decline of the sector in SSA LICs and Cambodia in the context of the global economic crisis, and challenges the sustainability of the industrialization process that was initiated by the clothing sector.

SSA LIC and Cambodian clothing exporters face challenges in how to use the presence of FDI and triangular manufacturing networks as a basis for upgrading and building locally embedded clothing industries. FDI has been central in the development of export clothing sectors in LICs. However, particularly the integration via triangular manufacturing networks has locked LIC suppliers into second-tier positions and has resulted in limited local linkages and spillovers. Building a locally embedded clothing sector is a precondition for sustainable upgrading (see Amsden 2003). Local involvement, however, is largely absent in SSA LICs and Cambodia. Nevertheless, other developing countries (for instance Bangladesh and Mauritius) have been successful in developing locally embedded industries. The timing of integration, local skills and entrepreneurship, the structure of local business systems, as well as government policies have played central roles in raising local involvement. When clothing exports started to take off in the 1970s and 1980s in Bangladesh and Mauritius, entry barriers in the industry were still relatively low and local firms were able to start exporting with 20 to 50 sewing machines and enter supply chains of global buyers. Furthermore, market access was guaranteed as those countries had excess quota, which was not only used by foreign investors motivated by quota hopping but also by local entrepreneurs. However, increased entry barriers have raised the bar for local firms in LICs such as Cambodia or SSA countries where the export clothing sector only started in the late 1990s and early 2000s.

Besides timing, institutional factors are central, in particular the existence of local skills and entrepreneurship and government support. In Mauritius, which has a long entrepreneurial tradition, in particular in the sugar industry, mostly sugar entrepreneurs, who wanted to diversify their business and saw the opportunities of quota access, invested in the clothing sector in the 1970s and 1980s. In Bangladesh there was no significant entrepreneurial tradition prior to the development of the clothing sector, but government support was crucial to raising local involvement. Moreover, Bangladesh had strict policies on FDI, which was limited to export processing zones (EPZs) and had to be linked to investments in vertical linkages into knitting, weaving, or spinning until 2005. In contrast, in Lesotho, Swaziland, Madagascar, Cambodia, and to a lesser extent in Kenya, there are only limited traditions in a local entrepreneurship. SSA business systems are further fragmented; the parastatal, the mostly foreign-dominated formal, and the indigenous informal sectors are poorly integrated (Pedersen and McCormick 1999). Furthermore, governments or industry associations have not supported local involvement in the clothing sector in SSA LICs and Cambodia. There are no explicit government poli-cies and programs to support local skills, linkages, and spillovers. Nor is there govern-ment support for locally owned firms that takes into account their specific challenges. These challenges include lack of finance through foreign headquarters; no established relationship with foreign buyers and input suppliers; and skill gaps in management, technology, and design/fashion capabilities.

Notwithstanding similarities with regard to integration into global clothing value chains via FDI and triangular manufacturing networks, there are also important dif-ferences between SSA LICs and Cambodia. For SSA LICs clothing exports, preferen-tial market access, in particular through AGOA and the Third Country Fabric (TCF) derogation, has been crucial to remain competitive (although only marginally). With-out preferential market access SSA LIC clothing exporters cannot compete with Asian producers such as China, Bangladesh, and also Cambodia. This strongly questions the potential developmental impact of a level playing field, free-trade environment as well as the belief that developing countries or LICs have a common interest in trade nego-tiations (Kaplinsky and Morris 2008). For instance, Cambodia, Bangladesh, and other Asian LICs have demanded duty-free access to the U.S. market for some time. However, this would have detrimental effects on SSA clothing exporters. Preference erosion due to more countries receiving preferences and generally declining tariff rates is a major challenge for SSA clothing exporters. For Cambodia preferential market access is also important but to a much lesser extent. Cambodia enjoys preferential market access to the EU but has difficulties in fulfilling the required double transformation rules of origin (ROO) (with the exception of sweaters). However, in its main export market—the United States—Cambodia competes without preferential market access. The main competitive advantages of Cambodia compared to SSA LICs are lower labor costs and comparatively higher productivity of firms, shorter lead times as main fabric suppliers from East Asia are closer to Cambodia than to SSA, and comparatively better infrastructure. Hence, SSA LICs and Cambodia face similar challenges due to their similar type of integration into global clothing value chains but, with regard to overall competitiveness, clearly play at different levels.

Bangladesh's situation is quite different from LICs in SSA and from Cambodia. With regard to the type of integration into global clothing value chains Bangladesh's export clothing industry also started with FDI motivated by MFA quota hopping and pref-erential market access. However, two important differences are that (i) Bangladesh's integration started in late 1970s and early 1980s, earlier than in SSA LICs and Cambodia; and (ii) local entrepreneurs have played an important role in the development of the clothing sector, which today is dominated by local ownership. Although there had been no relevant entrepreneurial tradition in Bangladesh prior to the growth of the clothing sector, the clothing sector came to be known as a sector where profits could be made eas-ily and without high risks as the investment to start a clothing factory was relatively low. This was related to markets guaranteed by quota and motivated by investments from and collaboration with in particular clothing manufacturers from Korea. Specific gov-ernment policies such as the bonded warehouse, back-to-back L/C, and cash incentive facilities were also central to facilitate local involvement. Two other key differences are (iii) very low labor costs (although the difference is more pronounced for SSA LICs since Cambodia accounts for the second-lowest labor costs among main clothing exporter countries after Bangladesh), and (iv) scale. The industry in Bangladesh is much larger than in Cambodia and SSA LICs: in Bangladesh there are around 5,500 exporting firms, in Cambodia around 250, and in SSA LICs between 30 and 120. This is particularly important for buyers demanding high volumes and 'one stop shopping' locations where they can source a variety of clothing products.

Common Challenges of and Policy Recommendations for LIC Clothing Exporters

Besides these important differences, there are common internal challenges that LIC clothing exporters face in the post-quota and post-crisis world. These challenges have to be addressed to increase the competitiveness of LIC clothing exporters, to sustain or accelerate their clothing exports, and to secure a sustainable impact of clothing exports on export diversification, industrial development, and economic growth. The main policy recommendations for LIC governments, industry associations, and clothing firms to better face challenges and harness opportunities in global clothing value chains include the following: (i) improve productivity, skills, and capabilities, and develop from CMT to free on board (FOB) and full-package suppliers; (ii) increase backward linkages and reduce lead times; (iii) improve physical and bureaucratic infrastructure, in particular with regard to transport and logistics, electricity, and access to finance; (iv) improve labor and environmental compliance; (v) diversify end markets to fast-growing emerging markets as well as regional and domestic markets; (vi) increase regional integration; and (vii) build locally embedded clothing industries.

First, increasing productivity by implementing more efficient industrial processes and upgrading production capabilities and skills is crucial for LIC clothing exporters in the context of supply chain rationalization strategies. In particular, in the case of SSA LIC clothing exporters, without a major productivity improvement and upgrading program, which assists clothing firms to remain (or become) internationally competitive, the industry will not be able to compete globally. Buyers increasingly demand high levels of manufacturing capabilities, including low costs, high quality, reliability, short lead times, production flexibility, and social compliance, as well as a broader range of capabilities and services such as input sourcing on suppliers' accounts, product development and design capabilities, inventory management, stock holding, logistics, communications, and merchandising skills. In this context suppliers have to move away from CMT and develop FOB and full-package capabilities. Firms will have a central role in this upgrading effort, but a government-supported 'upgrading fund' organized at the industry level could support productivity improvements and upgrading. These funds could offer low-cost funds for investments in new machinery, technology, and skills that enable more efficient and flexible production processes. In China and India such funds were used to scale up investments in T&C for upgrading technology. Education and training for production workers, but in particular for supervisors and managers, will be central to overcome skill deficits that hinder productivity improvements and upgrading. Maintaining or improving a country's position in the global clothing value chain requires a continuous process of workforce development and innovative capacities, which depend on human capital (Gereffi and Frederick 2010). Education should include the establishment of a consistent system of vocational training schools for sewing operators; training in technical skills such as production and technical management; and soft skills in areas such as general management, input sourcing, product development, design and fashion, and market research. Furthermore, research centers built on public-private partnerships could be established to gather and disseminate information to local manufacturers on the latest developments in products, inputs, and markets. Such initiatives would increase productivity of firms and improve skills and capabilities in the industry. They would also support involvement in more activities and value-adding steps, including input sourcing, sampling/pattern making, product development and design, the production of higher-value products, and the development of the industry from CMT to FOB or even full-package production.

Second, lead times have significantly increased in importance in buyers' sourcing decisions, which has been accelerated in the post-quota and post-crisis world. Fulfilling buyers' lead-time demands is a crucial challenge for LICs. The largest lead-time reduction would occur through backward linkages into textiles. In the LICs analyzed in chapters 3, 4, and 5, it would not make sense to produce all types of inputs locally, but certain basic fabrics and accessories that are broadly used could be produced locally in all countries discussed—in SSA ideally at a regional level. A favorable environment for textile investment should be ensured since a competitive local textile sector on the one hand contributes to the competitiveness of the clothing sector (for example, by reduced costs and lead times and increased flexibility) and on the other hand increases local value added, skills, and linkages. Policies could involve long-term loans at reduced interest rates for textile investments, the attraction of FDI or joint ventures specifically for the textile sector, greater emphasis on skill development in areas relevant for the textile sector, and the development of more efficient infrastructure with regard to electricity and water, which are crucial for a competitive textile sector. Increasing local supply of yarn and fabric to fill the large gap between demand and supply in LICs is challenging and is not attainable in the short run, in particular in Cambodia and in SSA LICs. However, there are complementary policy options to reduce lead times that are more promising in the short run, including (i) improvements in efficiency and productivity at the firm level, in particular with regard to decision-making processes, production structures, and supply chain management; (ii) improvements in trade facilitation, in particular in transport infrastructure, logistics, and customs facilities; (iii) increasing the capacity of the dyeing and finishing industry to be able to dye and finish fabric quickly and close to the production of clothing; (iv) establishing a central bonded warehouse (CBW) to be able to stock up T&C inputs that manufacturers can purchase directly as export orders are received; and most important (v) increasing regional sourcing, which can play a central role in reducing input costs and lead times and is still a largely unused potential in SSA LICs, Cambodia, and Bangladesh.

Third, productivity improvements and upgrading efforts at the firm level have to be complemented by improvements in physical and bureaucratic infrastructure. These improvements are crucial for competitiveness in the post-quota and post-crisis environment as exporters are faced with higher demands from buyers. Infrastructure and regulatory weaknesses that limit access to and raise the cost of backbone services have to be urgently addressed in LIC clothing exporters. Most LICs face huge challenges in these areas, which include transport, logistics, and customs facilities as well as energy, water, and waste treatment. In the context of the increasing importance of shorter lead times and flexibility, access to reliable, efficient, and cost-effective transport, logistics, and customs infrastructure and services is crucial to remain a competitive clothing exporter. In addition, access to a low-cost and reliable electricity supply is a major challenge, in particular in Bangladesh, which currently is experiencing a power crisis. If challenges related to transport and electricity are not addressed at the country and industry levels it will become increasingly difficult for LIC clothing exporters to compete in the global clothing value chain. EPZs have played a crucial role in clothing exporting LICs, in particular in SSA, by offering better access to infrastructure and backbone services. In addition, access to low-cost finance is central when firms develop from CMT to FOB and full-package suppliers as they have to be able to finance inputs and production and offer credit lines to buyers. This is particularly daunting for local firms that have no access to overseas headquarters for finance. Furthermore, a stable exchange rate constitutes a crucial macroeconomic requirement for export competitiveness and reliability. Governments play a central role in these areas. Given the changes in the post-quota and post-crisis world with regard to sourcing policies (short lead times, flexibility, and increased capabilities), the competitiveness of the private sector today is more than ever dependent on providing efficient physical and bureaucratic infrastructure and backbone services.

Fourth, compliance with labor and environmental standards has become central in sourcing policies of global buyers. Under pressure from compliance-conscious consumers and civil society organizations, buyers have taken labor compliance seriously and most have developed codes of conduct (CoC) since the second half of the 1990s, which generally include basic labor standards and often constitute a precondition for firms to enter sourcing networks. Labor compliance is an important concern in Bangladesh but less so in Cambodia and SSA LICs. Bangladesh has had a bad record with regard to labor compliance in the clothing sector; strikes and labor unrest have increased and culminated in large protests in summer 2010. There have been some improvements, but they are mostly limited to EPZs. The situation is better in Cambodia, which has a good reputation for labor compliance due to the Better Factories Cambodia monitoring program supported by the International Labour Organization (ILO). In SSA LICs labor standards are also generally higher, at least in the formal clothing sector and on paper, compared to LICs in Asia. LICs could approach labor compliance proactively and promote themselves as 'countries of choice' for global buyers. Departments of labor in LICs often have limited resources to implement and enforce labor compliance. However, as in Cambodia's Better Factories Program, government and industry associations in SSA LICs and Bangladesh could only provide export licenses to firms that are part of industry-wide compliance and monitoring programs. Governments could also work together with the ILO and the International Finance Corporation (IFC) in their newly established Better Works program, which extends Better Factories Cambodia to more countries. Buyers should also be involved in compliance programs. On the one hand many buyers in the clothing sector have developed their own CoC and demand the fulfillment of labor standards. On the other hand, suppliers are often not supported in fulfilling the CoC of buyers and, generally, there seems to be limited coordination between the sourcing and the CSR departments of buyers. Recently, pressures from buyers have also increased in the area of environmental compliance. Greener and more transparent supply chains will be mandatory to compete in the future (Gereffi/Frederick 2010). Thus, environmental compliance should be included in sector-wide compliance programs.

Fifth, diversification with regard to end-markets is crucial as LIC clothing exports are concentrated in few end markets in industrial countries and clothing import structures will change post-crisis. This dependency is strongest in SSA LICs, which nearly exclusively export to the United States (with the exception of Madagascar and also Mauritius). Nevertheless, exports of Cambodia and Bangladesh also are concentrated towards the U.S. and the EU-15 markets. Other markets offering duty-free access, including neglected EU countries, Norway, Canada, Australia, New Zealand, and Japan, could be targeted in a first step. Besides general problems and risks associated with export market concentration, three recent developments impact on export diversification patterns. First, demand in general and for clothing imports in particular may remain at a lower level post-crisis in the United States and the EU. Hence, it will become increasingly difficult to remain or increase export shares in these stagnating or even declining traditional markets. Second, there may be new opportunities in fast-growing emerging markets. Demand from emerging countries will increase in importance in global clothing trade—in particular from China, India, and other Asian countries, but also from the Middle East, in particular the United Arab Emirates, Turkey, the Russian Federation, Mexico, Brazil, and Argentina. The Economic Intelligence Unit estimates clothing retail demand for selected countries for the period 2008 to 2013. The fastest growth in this period is estimated for China, Eastern Europe (including Russia), India, Turkey, and Brazil (EIU 2008, cited in Textiles Intelligence 2009). Although the U.S. and EU markets will remain the major import markets at least for some time, there are increasing opportunities in these new markets. China has already diversified its export markets to emerging countries and important new markets include Russia and countries from the former Soviet bloc (for finished goods) and India, Brazil and Turkey (for intermediate goods such as textiles). Third, domestic and regional end markets have increased in importance for clothing sales from LICs in the context of the global economic crisis. For instance, in addition to new export markets, China has increased production for the domestic market. Estimates indicate that more than half of China's clothing production was for local consumers in 2007 (Clothesource 2008, cited in Gereffi/Frederick 2010). This mirrors efforts by T&C firms in India and Turkey (just-style 2010i).

Against the backdrop of these developments, it will be central for LIC clothing producers to diversify export markets and refocus on regional and emerging markets as well as on domestic markets if possible. These shifts in end markets may have significant impacts on the structure and governance of global clothing value chains as well as on entry and upgrading possibilities of suppliers. Buyers in China, India, Brazil, Turkey, or Russia as well as in regional and domestic markets may have different requirements and source differently than buyers in the United States or the EU. On the one hand these markets may be less demanding with regard to design, lead time, and fashion content than traditional export markets in the United States and the EU. They may also offer more opportunities to upgrade to higher value-adding functions such as design, marketing, and branding (Gereffi/Frederick 2010). On the other hand they may demand different capabilities such as smaller runs; different design and quality requirements; and different merchandising, marketing, and communication channels. Understanding these new markets and the sourcing policies of buyers selling in these markets will be key to entering and to upgrading within these clothing value chains. Negotiating favorable market access in the context of bilateral or regional trade agreements will support diversification to new end markets. More targeted policies at the industry level will also be necessary, including marketing, promotional, and networking initiatives.

Sixth, regional integration is crucial to improve the competitiveness of LIC clothing producers in the post-quota and post-crisis world. Regional integration could play a central role in reducing lead times and costs, capturing more value added in the region, and diversifying end markets. Buyers increasingly prefer one stop shopping locations where they can source a variety of T&C products, and lead times and flexibility have become key sourcing criteria. In this context, different complementary advantages in regions could be leveraged and economies of scale, vertical integration, and horizontal specialization could be promoted by regional coordination and integration. The most important challenge to increased intraregional trade and investment are intraregional trade barriers, which remain high in most developing countries. Despite regional integration efforts in SSA, Southeast and South Asia, tariff and nontariff barriers on T&C products are still comparatively high and T&C products are often found on sensitive lists. Improvements in intraregional transport, logistics, and customs facilities are also central to reduce costs and lead times of regional trade. Intraregional trade must also be actively promoted. A regional program that supports intraregional trade by facilitating partnerships between textile mills, clothing factories, and regional buyers to increase regional sourcing and production networks would be very useful. The ASEAN Competitiveness Enhancement Project (ACE) is a promising example in this regard.

Seventh, building locally embedded clothing industries is crucial for upgrading and for using the sector as a basis for export diversification and industrial development. FDI has been central in the development of export clothing sectors in most late-industrializing countries, but eventually local involvement, skills, linkages, and spillovers have increased. Such developments are largely absent in many LICs today (for instance in SSA or Cambodia), which limits upgrading possibilities and challenges the sustainability of the sector. Increasing local involvement, both at the owners and management level, is crucial for extending the impact of the clothing industry beyond its immediate employment-creation effect and using it to foster industrial development via local linkages and technology and knowledge spillovers. Other developing countries (for instance Bangladesh and Mauritius) have been successful in developing locally embedded industries. Besides the time of integration, local skills and entrepreneurship, the structure of local business systems, and government support policies are central to explain different developments in LICs. There are no straightforward policy recommendations for developing local entrepreneurship. However, certain internal conditions and policies are at least preconditions for local entrepreneurial activities: (i) access to low-cost and long-term finance as well as to insurance facilities to leverage certain risks; (ii) access to education and specific skill training in areas such as management, merchandising and sales, and technical and design/fashion capabilities; (iii) support in establishing relationships with foreign investors, buyers, and input suppliers; (vi) access to at least the same (or higher) incentives for local and foreign investment with regard to duty-free imports, infrastructure, fees for public services, access to land and factory shells, and tax holidays; and (v) incentives to hire locals at the management level.

These policy recommendations are challenging but crucial to sustain and increase competitiveness of LIC clothing producers and to secure a sustainable impact of clothing exports on export diversification, industrial development, and economic growth. In the case of SSA LICs, preferential market access remains essential in sustaining a position in global clothing value chains, at least in the short run. Preferences even have to be combined with single transformation ROOs (which are now in place for the United States and the EU) for SSA LIC producers to be able to take advantage of preferential market access and significantly higher effective preference rates as shown by nominal tariffs. However, as more countries receive preferences and as tariff rates are generally declining, preferences will erode in the future. In the case of AGOA and its rules (such as TCF derogation), there is also limited security and predictability. Thus, SSA clothing producers need to prepare themselves to be able to compete without preferences in the medium term. The policy recommendations identified above will be crucial in this regard.

Conclusions

The clothing sector still provides opportunities for export diversification and industrial development in LICs today. However, the global clothing value chain and associated entry and upgrading possibilities look different in the post-quota and post-crisis world. Entry barriers for first-tier suppliers have increased and low labor costs and preferential market access are not enough to compete in the clothing sector today. This provides opportunities for suppliers that can provide broader capabilities but challenges marginal and potential new suppliers. The latter group may still be able to enter global clothing value chains but only through intermediaries. In this case, entry barriers are lower but at the same time upgrading opportunities are limited. Two related underlying structural challenges have further limited possibilities to capture gains at the supplier level: (i) changing global supply and demand structures and (ii) asymmetric market and power relations within global clothing value chains, both of which have led to heightened competition between LICs. However, new global developments, including the emergence of powerful intermediaries and first-tier suppliers, shifting end markets, and the increasing importance of developing countries' buyers, as well as China's move to higher value exports, at least potentially change traditional competitive and power structures in global clothing value chains. These global developments could lead to new opportunities—but also new challenges—for LIC clothing exporters.

Besides these global trends, country-specific dynamics related to the specific type of integration into global clothing value chains are crucial and can lead to very different outcomes. Important factors in these country differences are the time of integration, ownership structures, scale, institutional structures, and government support. Notwithstanding these important differences, there are common internal challenges that LIC clothing exporters face in the post-quota and post-crisis world. These internal challenges have to be addressed to increase the competitiveness of LIC clothing exporters; sustain or accelerate their clothing exports; and secure a sustainable impact of clothing exports on export diversification, industrial development, and economic growth. Although entry and upgrading in global clothing value chains have become more difficult for LICs in the post-quota and post-crisis world, the clothing sector still offers a pathway to export diversification and industrial development—granted that proactive policies to increase the competitiveness and local embeddedness of LIC clothing exporters are adopted.

References

Abernathy, Frederick H., Volpe, Anthony, Weil, David (2006). "The Future of the Apparel and Textile Industries: Prospects and Choices for Public and Private Actors." *Environment and Planning* A38(12): 2207-2232.

Ahmed, Nazneen (2005). "Impact of the MFA Expiry on Bangladesh." In Kelegama, Saman (2005, ed.), *South Asia After the Quota System: Impact of the MFA Phaseout.*

Ahmed, Nazneen (2009a). "Sustaining Ready-made Garment Exports from Bangladesh." *Journal of Contemporary Asia* 39(4): 597-618.

Ahmed, Nazneen (2009b). "The Role of Economic Zones in Tackling Labor Compliance." *The Daily Star*, November 10.

Ahmed, Nazneen (2009c). "Elected Workers' Association in EPZs." *The Daily Star*, December 11.

Ahmed, Nazneen, Peerlings, Jack H.M. (2009). "Addressing Workers' Rights in the Textile and Apparel Industries: Consequences for the Bangladesh Economy." *World Development* 37(3): 661-675.

Amsden, Alice H. (2003). *The Rise of 'The Rest'. Challenges to the West from Late-Industrializing Economies.* Oxford University Press.

Appelbaum, Richard P. (2005). "TNCs and the Removal of Textiles and Clothing Quotas." Center for Global Studies, University of California, Santa Barbara, Paper 3, UNCTAD.

Appelbaum, Richard P. (2008). Giant Transnational Contractors in East Asia: Emergent Trends in Global Supply Chains. In: Competition & Change 12(1), 69–87.

Appelbaum, Richard P., Gereffi, Gary (1994). "Power and Profits in the Apparel Commodity Chain." In Edna Bonacich et al. (eds.), *Global Production: the Apparel Industry in the Pacific Rim*. Philadelphia, PA: Temple University Press.

Altenburg, Tilman (2006). "Governance Patterns in Value Chains and their Development Impact." *The European Journal of Development Research* 18: 4.

Arnold, John (2010). "Effects of Trade Logistics on the Strategy of the Garments Industry for Product and Market Diversification." Background Paper prepared for the Bangladesh Trade Note, Dhaka, World Bank.

Asian Development Bank (2004). "Cambodia's Garment Industry: Meeting the Challenges of the Post-Quota Environment." Manila, ADB.

Bair, Jennifer (2005). "Global Capitalism and Commodity Chains: Looking Back, Going Forward." *Competition & Change* 9(2): 153-180.

Bair, Jennifer (2006). "Regional Trade and Production Blocs in A Global Industry: Towards a Comparative Framework for Research." *Environment and Planning* A38(12): 2233-2252.

Bair, Jennifer (2008). "Surveying the Post-MFA Landscape: What Prospects for the Global South Post-Quota?" *Competition & Change* 12(1).

Bair, Jennifer, Gereffi, Gary (2003). "Upgrading, Uneven Development, and Jobs in the North American Apparel Industry." *Global Networks* 3(2): 143-169.

Bakht, Z., Yunus, M., Salimullah, M. (2002). "Machinery Industry in Bangladesh." Tokyo Institute of Development Economies Advanced School, IDEAS Machinery Industry Study Report 4.

Barnes, Justin, Morris, Mike (2010). "Innovation Challenges Facing the Lesotho Clothing Industry: An Analysis of 10 Firm-Level Case Studies." World Bank study, compiled for the Finance and Private Sector Development Unit in the Africa Region. World Bank, Washington, DC.

Begg, Robert, Pickles, John, Smith, Adrian (2003). "Cutting It: European Integration, Trade Regimes, and the Reconfiguration of Eastern and Central European Apparel Production." *Environment and Planning* A35(12): 2191-2207.

Better Factories Cambodia (2010). Website: www.betterfactories.org. ILO

Birnbaum, David (2009). "Recession Brings Chance for Suppliers to Change. In *The Clothing Industry and the Economic Crisis—A just-style Review*. Management Briefing, 20-25. just-style.

Brenton, Paul, Oezden, Caglar (2009). "Trade Preferences for Apparel and the Role of Rules of Origin: The Case of Africa." In Hoekman, Bernard, Martin, Will, Braga, Carlos A. Primo, *Trade Preference Erosion: Measurement and Policy Response*. Palgrave MacMillan.

Brenton, Paul, Hoppe, Mombert (2007). "Clothing and Export Diversification: Still a Route to Growth for Low-Income Countries?" Policy Research Working Paper 4343. World Bank, Washington DC.

Cattaneo, Olivier, Gereffi, Gary, Staritz, Cornelia (2010). "Global Value Chains in a Post-Crisis World: Resilience, Consolidation, and Shifting End Markets." In Cattaneo, Olivier, Gereffi, Gary, Staritz, Cornelia (eds.), *Global Value Chains in a Postcrisis World*. A Development Perspective, Trade and Development Series. Washington, DC: World Bank.

Coughlin, P., Rubin, M., Darga L. Amedee (2001). "The SADC Textile and Garment Industries: Constraints and Opportunities." Study commissioned by the South African Development Community.

Dickerson, Kitty G. (1999). *Textiles and Apparel in the Global Economy*. Upper Saddle River, NJ: Merrill.

Elmer, Diepak (2010). "The RMG Skills Formation Regime in Bangladesh: A Background Paper." Background Paper prepared for the Bangladesh Trade Note, Dhaka, World Bank.

Farole, Thomas (2010). "Special Economic Zones: Performance, Policy and Practice— with a Focus on Sub-Saharan Africa." Draft. World Bank, Washington, DC.

Feidieker, Thomas (2010). "Transport and Logistics Facilitation as an Effective Means Promoting Trade and Regional Integration within SADC." World Bank, Pretoria, February.

FIAS (Foreign Investment Advisory Service) (2004). "Cambodia—Corporate Social Responsibility and the Apparel Sector Buyer Survey Results." Foreign Investor Advisory Service, IFC and World Bank, Washington, DC.

FIAS (2006). "Lesotho—The Competitiveness of Regional and Vertical Integration of Lesotho's Garment Industry." Discussion draft, April. Foreign Investor Advisory Service, IFC and World Bank, Washington, DC.

Flanagan, Mike (2009). "Is Fast Fashion Starting to Fad?" In *The Clothing Industry and the Economic Crisis—A just-style Review*. Management Briefing, 7-11. just-style.

Flanagan, Mike (2010a). "The Flanarant: China Prices to Rise as Labour Shortages Grow." April 13. www.just-style.com.

Flanagan, Mike (2010b). "The Flanarant: Indian Cotton Ban Masks Higher Input Costs." May 4, 2010. www.just-style.com.

Fontaine, Thomson (2008). "Responding to the Challenges in the Global Trading Regimes for Swaziland's Textiles and Sugar Sectors." African Department, International Monetary Fund, Washington, DC.

Gereffi, Gary (1994). "The Organization of Buyer Driven Global Commodity Chains: How U.S. Retailers Shape Overseas Production Networks." In: Gereffi, Gary, Korzeniewicz, Miguel (eds.), *Commodity Chains and Global Capitalism*. Westport, CT: Praeger, 95-122.

Gereffi, Gary (1999). "International Trade and Industrial Upgrading in the Apparel Commodity Chain." *Journal of International Economics* 48(1).

Gereffi, Gary (2005). "The Global Economy: Organization, Governance, and Development." In Smelser, Neil J., Swedberg, Richard (eds.), *The Handbook of Economic Sociology*. Princeton: Princeton University Press, 160-182.

Gereffi, Gary, Humphrey, John, Kaplinsky, Raphael, Sturgeon, Timothy J. (2001). "Introduction: Globalisation, Value Chains and Development." *IDS Bulletin* 32(3): 1-8.

Gereffi, Gary, Memodovic, Olga (2003). "The Global Apparel Value Chain: What Prospects for Upgrading by Developing Countries?" United Nations Industrial Development Organization (UNIDO), Sectoral Studies Series. Vienna: UNIDO.

Gereffi, Gary, Humphrey, John, Sturgeon, Timothy J. (2005). "The Governance of Global Value Chains." *Review of International Political Economy* 12(1): 78-104.

Gereffi, Garry, Frederick, Stacey (2010). "The Global Apparel Value Chain, Trade and the Crisis—Challenges and Opportunities for Developing Countries." Policy Research Working Paper 5281. World Bank, Washington, DC.

Gibbon, Peter (2002a). "At the Cutting Edge? Financialization and U.K. Clothing Retailers' Sourcing Patterns and Practices." *Competition & Change* 6(3): 289-308.

Gibbon, Peter (2002b). "South Africa and the Global Commodity Chain for Clothing: Export Performance and Constraints." CDR Working Paper 02.7, Center for Development Research, Copenhagen.

Gibbon, Peter (2003a). "The African Growth and Opportunity Act and the Global Commodity Chain for Clothing." *World Development* 31(11).

Gibbon, Peter (2003b). "AGOA, Lesotho 'Clothing Miracle' & the Politics of Sweatshops." *Review of African Political Economy* 30: 96.

Gibbon, Peter (2008). "Governance, Entry Barriers, Upgrading: A Re-interpretation of Some GVC Concepts from the Experience of African Clothing Exports." *Competition & Change* 12(1): 29-48.

Gibbon, Peter, Ponte, Stefano (2005). *Trading Down: Africa, Value Chains, and the Global Economy*. Philadelphia, PA: Temple University Press.

Haider, Mohammed Ziaul (2007). "Competitiveness of the Bangladesh Ready-Made Garment Industry in Major International Markets." *Asia Pacific Trade and Investment Review* 3(1): 3-27.

Hatsukano, Naomi (2005). "The Current Situation of Cambodian Industry." In Ishida, M. (ed.), *Regional Development in Mekong, Chiba*. The Institute of Developing Economies, JETRO.

Humphrey, J., Schmitz, H. (2002). "How Does Insertion in Global Value Chains Affect Upgrading in Industrial Clusters?" *Regional Studies* 36(9): 1017-1027.

IFC (International Finance Corporation) (2009). *Second Investment Climate Assessment—A Better Investment Climate to Sustain Growth in Cambodia*. Washington, DC: World Bank. April.

ILO (International Labour Organization) (1998). Declaration on Fundamental Principles and Rights at Work. ILO, Geneva. Available at www.ilo.org.

ILO (2009). "Rapid Assessment of the Impact of the Financial Crisis in Cambodia." ILO Asia-Pacific Working Paper Series, Geneva, March.

IMF (International Monetary Fund) (2008). "The Ready-Made Garment Industry in Bangladesh: An Update." Prepared by Jonathan Dunn, IMF, Washington, DC.

ITC MacMap (2010). International Trade Center, Geneva. http:\\www.macmap.org.

Jassin-O'Rourke Group, L. (2008). "Global Apparel Manufacturing Labor Cost Analysis 2008, Textile and Apparel Manufacturers & Merchants." Available at http:\\www.tammonline.com\ researchpapers.htm.

Jones, Richard M. (2006). *The Apparel Industry*. Oxford: Blackwell.

Just-style (2009a). "The Clothing Industry and the Economic Crisis—A just-style Review." Management Briefing, Bromsgrove, United Kingdom: Aroq Limited.

Just-style (2009b). "Industry Insights: Super Suppliers Tipped as Sourcing Winners." July 27. www.just-style.com.

Just-style (2010a). "Sourcing: New Strategy to Help Africa Make its Mark in Fashion." April 14. Leonie Barrie, www.just-style.com.

Just-style (2010b). "Sourcing: U.S. Clothing Import Prices Hit a 20-year Low." April 26. www.just-style.com.

Just-style (2010c). "Update: Bangladesh Garment Wages to Rise 80 Percent." July 29. www.just-style.com.

Just-style (2010d). "Bangladesh in Brief: Apparel Industry Snapshot." August 2. www.just-style.com.

Just-style (2010e). "Analysis: Economic Crisis Accelerates Apparel Industry Change." March 30. www.just-style.com.

Just-style (2010f). "Continuing Protests Blight Bangladesh Pay Deal." August 2. www.just-style.com.

Just-style (2010g). "Bangladesh: Garment Factories Resume Operations." August 3. www.just-style.com

Just-style (2010h). "South Africa: Sourcing Event Targets Apparel and Textile." March 18. www.just-style.com.

Just-style (2010i). "August 2010 Management Brief: Part I—The Role of Location in Global Sourcing." March 26. www.just-style.com.

Kaplinsky, Raphael (2005). *Globalization, Poverty and Inequality. Between a Rock and a Hard Place*. Cambridge: Polity Press.

Kaplinsky, Raphael, Messner, Dirk (2008). "Introduction: The Impact of Asian Drivers on the Developing World." *World Development* 36(2): 197-209.

Kaplinsky, Raphael, Morris, Mike (2006). "Dangling by a Thread: How Sharp are the Chinese Scissors?" DfID report, IDS.

Kaplinsky, Raphael, Morris, Mike (2008). "Do the Asian Drivers Undermine Export-oriented Industrialization in SSA?" *World Development* 36(2): 254-273.

Lall, Sanjaya (2005). "FDI, AGOA and Manufactured Exports by a Landlocked Least Developed African Economy: Lesotho." *Journal of Development Studies* 41(6): 998-1022.

Malouche, Mariem (2009). "Trade and Trade Finance Developments in 14 Developing Countries Post-September 2008: A World Bank Survey." World Bank Policy Research Working Paper 5138. World Bank, Washington, DC.

Martin, Will (2009). "China's Textile and Clothing Trade and Global Adjustment." In Garnaut, R., Ligang, Song (eds.), *China's New Place in a World in Crisis*. ANU E Press, Brookings Institution Press and Social Sciences Academic Press, Canberra, Washington, DC and Beijing.

Mayer, J., Butkevicius, A., Kadri, A. (2002). "Dynamic Products in World Exports." UNCTAD Discussion Paper No. 159. Geneva, United Nations.

McCormick, Dorothy, Kamau, Paul, Ligulu, Peter (2006). "Post-Multifibre Arrangement Analysis of the Textile and Garment Sectors in Kenya." *IDS Bulletin* 37(1).

MFA Forum (2009). "Global Apparel Trade Trends Briefing." MFA Forum Secretariat, AccountAblity, London.

Milberg, William (2004). "The Changing Structure of Trade Linked to Global Production Systems: What are the Policy Implications?" *International Labour Review* 143(1-2): 45-90.

Milberg, William, Winkler, Deborah (2010). "Trade, the Crisis and Recovery: Restructuring of Global Value Chains." In Cattaneo, Olivier, Gereffi, Gary, Staritz, Cornelia (eds.), *Global Value Chains in a Postcrisis World: A Development Perspective*. Washington, DC: World Bank.

Miller, Doug, Nuon, Veasna, Aprill, Charlene, Certeza, Ramon (2008). "'Business—as usual?' Governing the Supply Chain in Clothing—Post MFA Phase Out. The Case of Cambodia." Global Union Research Network (GURN), copyright ILO 2007.

Morris, Mike (2006a). "Globalisation, China, and Clothing Industrialisation Strategies in Sub-Saharan Africa." In Jauch, Herbert, Traub-Merz, Rudolf (eds.), *The Future of the Textile and Clothing Industry in Sub-Saharan Africa*. Bonn: Friedrich-Ebert-Stiftung.

Morris, Mike (2006b). "China's Dominance of Global Clothing and Textiles: Is Preferential Trade Access an Answer for Sub-Saharan Africa?" *IDS Bulletin* 37.

Morris, Mike, Sedowski, Leanne (2006a). "Report on Government Responses to New Post-MFA Realities in Lesotho." Report for the Institute for Global Dialogue.

Morris, Mike, Sedowski, Leanne (2006b). "The Competitive Dynamics of the Clothing Industry in Madagascar in the Post-MFA Environment." African Clothing and Footwear Research Network.

Morris, Mike, Einhorn, Gill (2008). "Globalization, Welfare and Competitiveness: The Impacts of Chinese Imports on the South African Clothing and Textile Industry." *Competition & Change* 12(4).

Morris, Mike, Barnes, Justin (2009). "Globalization, the Changed Global Dynamics of the Clothing and Textile Value Chains and the Impact on Sub-Saharan Africa." UNIDO Working Paper 10, 2008.

Nathan Associates (2006). "Integration of the ASEAN Textile and Apparel Industries in the Post-quota Era." USAID, Washington, DC.

Nathan Associates (2007). "Factory-level Value Chain Analysis of Cambodia's Apparel Industry." USAID, Washington, DC.

Natsuda, Kaoru, Goto, Kenta, Thoburn, John (2009). "Challenges to the Cambodian Garment Industry in the Global Garment Value Chain." RCAPS Working Paper No. 09-3, July.

Ozawa, Terutomo, Bellak, Christian (2010). "Will China Relocate Its Labor-Intensive Factories to Africa, Flying-Geese Style?" *Columbia FDI Perspectives* 28, August 17.

Palpacuer, Florence (2004). "The Global Sourcing Patterns of French Clothing Retailers: Determinants and Implications for Suppliers' Industrial Upgrading." Presented at the workshop "Clothing Europe: Comparative Perspectives on Trade Liberalization and Production Networks in the New European Clothing Industry", University of North Carolina.

Palpacuer, Florence, Gibbon, Peter, Thomsen, Lotte (2005). "New Challenges for Developing Country Suppliers in Global Clothing Chains: A Comparative European Perspective." *World Development* 33(3): 409-430.

Pedersen, Poul Ove, McCormick, Dorothy (1999). "African Business Systems in a Globalizing World." *The Journal of Modern African Studies* 37(1): 109-135.

Phelps, Nicholas A., Stillwell, John C.H., Wanjiru, Roseline (2009). "Broken Chain? AGOA and Foreign Direct Investment in the Kenyan Clothing Industry." *World Development* 37(2): 314-325.

Polaski, Sandra (2009). "Harnessing Global Forces to Create Decent Work in Cambodia." ILO, IFC, Washington, DC.

Quddus, Munir, Rashid, Salim (2000). *Entrepreneurs and Economic Development: The Remarkable Story of Garment Exports from Bangladesh*. Dhaka: The University Press Limited.

Rahman, Mustafizur, Bhattacharya, Debapriya, Moazzem, Khondaker Golam (2008). "Dynamics of Ongoing Changes in Bangladesh's Export Oriented RGM Enterprises: Findings from an Enterprise Level Survey." Unpublished manuscript.

Rasiah, Rajah (2009). "Can Garment Exports from Cambodia, Laos and Burma be Sustained?" *Journal of Contemporary Asia* 39(4): 619-637.

Salm, A., Grant, W.J., Green, T.J., Haycook, J.R., Raimondo, J. (2002). "Lesotho Garment Industry Subsector Study for Government of Lesotho." DfID, London.

Seiha, Neou (2010). "Situation of Cambodia Garment Industry in 2010." PowerPoint presentation, Economic Institute of Cambodia, August 2010.

Tewari, Meenu (2006). "Is Price and Cost Competitiveness Enough for Apparel Firms to Gain Market Share in the World after Quotas? A Review." *Global Economy Journal* 6(4), Article 5.

Tewari, Meenu (2008). "Deepening Intraregional Trade and Investment in South Asia—The Case of the Textile and Clothing Industry." Working Paper No. 213, India Council for Research on International Economic Relations.

Tewari, Meenu (2010). "Easing the Burden of History in South Asia." *Business Standard* online, August 15.

Textiles Intelligence (2009). "World Trade in Textiles and Clothing." Presentation by Sam Anson at the World Free Zones Conference in Hyderabad, India, December 2009.

Traub-Merz, Rudolf (2006). "The African Textile and Clothing Industry: From Import Substitution to Export Orientation." In Jauch, Herbert, Traub-Herz, Rudolf (eds.), *The Future of the Textile and Clothing Industry in Sub-Saharan Africa.*

UNDP Regional Centre in Colombo (2006). "Sewing Thoughts: How to Realise Human Development Gains in the Post-Quota World." Tracking report, written by Adhikari, Ratnakar, Yamamoto, Yumiko. UNDP.

USITC (United States International Trade Commission) (2004). "The Economic Effects of Significant U.S. Import Restraints: Fourth Update." United States International Trade Commission Publication 3701. Washington, DC.

USITC (2005). "Export Opportunities and Barriers in African Growth and Opportunity Act-Eligible Countries." United States International Trade Commission Publication 3785. Washington, DC.

USITC (2009). "Sub-Saharan African Textile and Apparel Inputs: Potential for Competitive Production." United States International Trade Commission Investigation No. 332-502. Washington, DC.

World Bank (2004). "Cambodia Seizing the Global Opportunity: Investment Climate Investment and Reform Strategy for Cambodia." Report Nr. 27925. World Bank, Washington, DC.

World Bank (2005a). "Bangladesh Growth and Export Competiveness." Report No. 31394-BD, Poverty Reduction and Economic Management Sector Unit, South Asia Region. World Bank, Washington, DC.

World Bank (2005b). End of MFA Quotas – Key issues and strategic options for Bangladesh readymade garment industry, Bangladesh Development Series – paper no 2, PREM Unit, The World Bank Office Dhaka.

World Bank (2007). "Vertical and Regional Integration to Promote African Textile and Clothing Exports a Close Knit Family?" Report No. 39994—AFR, PREM 1, Southern Africa, Africa Region. World Bank, Washington, DC.

World Bank (2007). World Development Indicators. World Bank, Washington, DC.

World Bank (2010). "Export Bulletin." Bangladesh Country Office, World Bank.

Yamagata, Tatsufumi (2006). "The Garment Industry in Cambodia: Its Role in Poverty Reduction through Export-Oriented Development." Institute of Developing Economies Discussion Paper Nr. 62, The Institute of Developing Economies, JETRO.

ECO-AUDIT
Environmental Benefits Statement

The World Bank is committed to preserving endangered forests and natural resources. The Office of the Publisher has chosen to print World Bank Studies and Working Papers on recycled paper with 30 percent postconsumer fiber in accordance with the recommended standards for paper usage set by the Green Press Initiative, a non-profit program supporting publishers in using fiber that is not sourced from endangered forests. For more information, visit www.greenpressinitiative.org.

In 2009, the printing of these books on recycled paper saved the following:
- 289 trees*
- 92 million Btu of total energy
- 27,396 lb. of net greenhouse gases
- 131,944 gal. of waste water
- 8,011 lb. of solid waste

* 40 feet in height and 6–8 inches in diameter

green press
INITIATIVE

www.ingramcontent.com/pod-product-compliance
Lightning Source LLC
Chambersburg PA
CBHW081645280326
41928CB00069B/3021